Nietzsche as Stylist

NIETZSCHE *as* STYLIST

Aesthetics and Philosophy

Martine Béland

McGill-Queen's University Press
Montreal & Kingston • London • Chicago

ISBN 978-0-2280-2110-0 (cloth)
ISBN 978-0-2280-2111-7 (paper)
ISBN 978-0-2280-2165-0 (ePDF)
ISBN 978-0-2280-2166-7 (ePUB)

Legal deposit second quarter 2024
Bibliothèque nationale du Québec

Printed in Canada on acid-free paper that is 100% ancient forest free (100% post-consumer recycled), processed chlorine free

This book has been published with the help of a grant from the Canadian Federation for the Humanities and Social Sciences, through the Awards to Scholarly Publications Program, using funds provided by the Social Sciences and Humanities Research Council of Canada.

Funded by the Government of Canada | Financé par le gouvernement du Canada | Canada
Canada Council for the Arts | Conseil des arts du Canada

We acknowledge the support of the Canada Council for the Arts.

Nous remercions le Conseil des arts du Canada de son soutien.

McGill-Queen's University Press in Montreal is on land which long served as a site of meeting and exchange amongst Indigenous Peoples, including the Haudenosaunee and Anishinabeg nations. In Kingston it is situated on the territory of the Haudenosaunee and Anishinaabek. We acknowledge and thank the diverse Indigenous Peoples whose footsteps have marked these territories on which peoples of the world now gather.

Library and Archives Canada Cataloguing in Publication

Title: Nietzsche as stylist : aesthetics and philosophy / Martine Béland.
Names: Béland, Martine, author.
Description: Includes bibliographical references and index.
Identifiers: Canadiana (print) 20230586708 | Canadiana (ebook) 20230586775 | ISBN 9780228021100 (cloth) | ISBN 9780228021117 (paper) | ISBN 9780228021650 (ePDF) | ISBN 9780228021667 (EPUB)
Subjects: LCSH: Nietzsche, Friedrich Wilhelm, 1844-1900—Literary style.
Classification: LCC PT2440.N72 Z56 2024 | DDC 193—dc23

Set in 11.5/14 Fleischman BT Pro
Book design & typesetting by Garet Markvoort, zijn digital

Contents

Tables

Prologue

When in Weimar

In early June 2009 I was in Weimar, Germany, for a short research stay as postdoctoral fellow at the Kolleg Friedrich Nietzsche, a scholarly institute housed in the villa Silberblick — or "silver view." The 1890 house is now part of the Klassik Stiftung Weimar, the foundation that oversees and conserves the numerous buildings, archives, and monuments of German classicism and modernism in the UNESCO World Heritage town of Weimar.

The villa sits on a hill about a fifteen minutes' walk from the city centre, on a calm, tree-lined street. Its site transmits an atmosphere that I find common to Weimar landmarks: pure peace, most suitable for slow walks and contemplation. One can relax on a chair on the villa's lawn and read or simply gaze at the tall surrounding trees and hedges, where birds chirp and go about their business. One can also stroll the grounds to peek at the tranquil neighbouring houses. While thus enjoying a quiet afternoon, it is easy to forget that the villa "Silver View" has had a tumultuous history.

In 1897, Friedrich Nietzsche's sister, Elisabeth Förster-Nietzsche, transferred her newly founded *Nietzsche Archiv* to this grand house that was bought thanks to financial help from a friend of Nietzsche's, the Swiss historian and feminist Meta von Salis.[1] Elisabeth was aware of the aura of Weimar — the city of eighteenth-century duchess Anna Amalia, who amassed a unique collection of hundreds of thousands of books and who invited or attracted to Weimar the poet Christoph Martin Wieland, the philosopher Herder, and the writers Goethe and Schiller. At the time when Friedrich's sister settled in Weimar, the city was also the capital of a burgeoning modernist movement, "New Weimar," which encouraged artistic and social aspirations exemplified in *art nouveau*, arts and crafts, and eventually the Bauhaus school that Walter Gropius founded in Weimar in 1919.[2]

Elisabeth moved into the villa Silberblick with her sick and inactive but soon-to-be famous brother Friedrich. She presided over an editorial team and started a vast publication enterprise by using her sibling's notes and manuscripts as she saw fit. Nietzsche himself spent but three years in Weimar, before passing away in August of 1900, just as a wave of Nietzsche-craze was taking hold of Germany.[3] Fully committed to establishing an institution that would be both a memorial and a centrepiece for the Nietzsche *Kultus*, Elisabeth Förster-Nietzsche had the villa's ground floor entirely redesigned in 1903 by the famous Belgian art nouveau artist Henry van de Velde. The revamping was total: sweeping room design, new furniture and lamps, modern artwork, and even a monogram logo for the philosopher — a stylized capital N in a circle.[4]

The result was imposing. Fortunately, van de Velde's unique interior has been preserved: visitors can admire it by touring the small but magnificent art nouveau museum dedicated to the philosopher, on the ground floor of the villa Silberblick. Fellows and guests of the Kolleg Friedrich Nietzsche, meanwhile, stay in the different rooms on the upper floors of the villa.

Upon arriving in Weimar I learned, much to my surprise, that I was to be lodged ... in Nietzsche's own bedroom. Van de Velde had not redesigned the upper floors, and today they retain almost nothing of the typical turn-of-the-century look they had during the last decade of Nietzsche's life and the first decades of the twentieth century. Indeed, the villa Silberblick's upper floors are an unexpected tribute to a quite different style: communist functionalism.

With the partition of Germany in two distinct countries after the Second World War, Thuringia, where Weimar is situated, became the westernmost state of East Germany. The fate of Nietzsche's manuscripts and the villa Silberblick was now tied to East German cultural and political imperatives. It is complicated to discern how it came to be that Nietzsche's manuscripts were kept in Weimar and not sent abroad or lost or destroyed. But even if the archives remained, research on Nietzschean philosophy was not encouraged under the communist regime of the German Democratic Republic. Although his thought and even the Nietzsche Archiv had quickly attracted socialist and communist thinkers in the 1910s and 1920s (most notably the French scholar Charles Andler and the writer and supporter of non-violence Romain Rolland), his sister, surfing on the Nietzsche cult and eager for recognition and prestige, had found dubious supporters just before her death, in 1935: Nazis and fascists.[5]

A Hitler-approved construction of a memorial on the grounds neighbouring the villa was started in 1938. It was never finished (the ruins are still visible, covered in weeds), but the abandoned building, as well as the photos of Hitler's visit to the villa in 1934, are a testimony to the fraught relationship that Nietzsche's name and heritage have had with history.

During the communist regime some scholars nevertheless did secure access to the manuscripts and the numerous editorial documents that Förster-Nietzsche had kept. Most notably, two scholars from Italy, philologist Giorgio Colli and German literature scholar Mazzino Montinari, started a comprehensive chronological publication in the 1960s. Their philological endeavour led to the critical edition that was immediately translated into Italian and French from 1967 onwards and that is still in use today.

Political regimes may fall, and cultural trends may change, but the layers of interpretation remain. They are slowly and often imperceptibly deposited around us, as so many translucent skins on the objects of our world. When we look upon a building or a statue, when we pick up a book or a score, we do not always see them — and we certainly do not see them all.

When I stayed at the villa Silberblick in 2009, Nietzsche's bedroom and even the director's office and the other upper-floor bedrooms still had a functional look and technologically out-of-date apparatus. The villa had dial-up Internet access only and GDR-era electrical sockets and light plugs. There was no charm whatsoever to my bedroom — but fortunately, my living quarters had a very large windowed and covered balcony that looked onto the tall pines that line the back of the villa. I had seen pictures of Nietzsche in his last years, sitting in an armchair on this very balcony under layers of blankets, his eyes blank in a stupor that even in a late nineteenth-century black and white photograph effectively transmitted the image of a mind lost.

I had placed my laptop computer and my research material on a long wooden table that was on the covered balcony — certainly one of the most enjoyable writing settings that I have had the chance to experience. I was there to research the archives and library and to write, but also to gain inspiration from the simple fact of taking in sensations and experiencing feelings in that place. And so it was that when sitting on the balcony, I would very often abandon myself to contemplation and appreciate the view that the hillside villa afforded.

To the right, my eyes could see to the trees that marked the start of the park in which Goethe had a cottage by the river Ilm, his first residence in Weimar, as of 1776. Straight ahead, I could peer onto the hill beyond which was the Nazi concentration camp Buchenwald, which opened in 1937 and where more than 56,000 prisoners died.[6] And under my feet in the downstairs museum lay a turn-of-the-century tribute to artistic expression and social renewal, while the walls around me told of ideological wars and power struggles. From eighteenth-century classicism and humanism to twentieth-century terrorism and dehumanization in one turn of the head, one glance, one *silber Blick*.

The layers of interpretation were laid bare on that hill in Weimar, much like some landscapes offer an open window onto the layers of geological time. There was certainly a message to be drawn from this experience. On the very day that I installed my workspace on the balcony table and took in the view for the first time, US president Barack Obama was presenting a speech at Buchenwald, accompanied by the author and ex-prisoner Elie Wiesel.[7] The event seemed to magnify the thickness of the time and place.

What was it about a town like Weimar that turned it into such a crossroad? That was surely too vast a question. But what was it about Nietzsche that made him a window onto our propensity for interpretation and appropriation? Why were his works the locus of reading and disputes and creation from so many differing angles?

Why the craze, the praise, the "cult"? Designers and musicians, philosophers and psychologists, sociologists and utopians, feminists and socialists and politicians from the left to the right had all avidly read this self-professed philosopher and made something out of his philosophy while also making him into something: an icon, for better or for worse.

Surely something in Friedrich Nietzsche's writing permitted such a wide reception.

Acknowledgments

I have conducted most of the research for this book at the *Centre canadien d'études allemandes et européennes* (CCEAE), at Université de Montréal, between 2015 and 2021. I thereafter had a wonderful occasion to write the manuscript in a beautiful setting: the coastal city of Halifax, Nova Scotia, during year two of the pandemic, while I was Guest Scholar at the department of philosophy at St Mary's University. I wish to thank professors Mark Mercer, Scott Edgar, and Sophie Beaulé, as well as Associate Vice-President for Research Adam Sarty for making this fantastic stay at SMU possible.

The very last parts of the manuscript were written in my new office at Université Sainte-Anne, in Halifax and in Church Point, on Nova Scotia's Acadian Shore. I wish to warmly thank President Allister Surette, as well as Souhaël Bouallagui and Amédée Aucoin at the Halifax campus, for welcoming me in a most friendly manner. It was an honour and a great joy to be writing the last words of this book amongst them all.

Parts of this book are expanded versions of papers that I have published in French. Chapter 2 is adapted from "Anéantir l'opéra pour guérir la musique? Critique et thérapeutique dans l'esthétique musicale de Nietzsche," in *Die Frage der Medizin in Nietzsches Philosophie*, edited by I. Wienand, 111–26 (Basel: Schwabe, 2020). Parts of chapter 3 have appeared in "Le type du savant, pivot de la critique culturelle: une étude des *Inactuelles* de Nietzsche," in *Logiques du discours philosophique en Allemagne*, edited by A. Fillon et al., 297–316 (Reims: Éditions et presses de l'Université de Reims, 2019). Chapter 6 is adapted from my article "Les préfaces de Nietzsche, invitation à la philosophie comme expérience," *Revue philosophique de la France et de l'étranger* 139, no. 4 (2014): 495–512.

Chapters 1 and 7 are expanded versions of papers that I have published in English in "Vocation as Therapy: Nietzsche in Academia," in *Nietzsche's Therapeutic Teaching*, edited by E. Friedland and H. Hutter, 13–30 (London: Bloomsbury, 2013), and "Style & Synaesthesia: Nietzsche's Philosophical Use of the Em-Dash," in *Nietzsche on Making Sense of Nietzsche*, edited by M. Béland, C. Denat, C. Piazzesi, and P. Wotling, 147–63 (Reims: Éditions et presses de l'Université de Reims, 2021).

I presented some of the research essential to this book at the annual conferences of the Canadian Society for Continental Philosophy, German Studies Association, International Nietzsche Research Group, and Society for Existentialist and Phenomenological Theory and Culture, as well as international conferences hosted by Université catholique de Louvain, CCEAE, Université de Namur, Université de Reims, Klassik Stiftung Weimar, and Canadian Cultural Centre in Paris.

Between 2015 and 2021 I also received wonderful invitations to present my research on Nietzsche, reception studies, and aesthetics at Dalhousie University, in Halifax; the 2021 Montréal *Philopolis* event; the North America office of the German Academic Exchange Service (DAAD) during its 2019 meeting in Portland, Oregon; the Université du Québec à Montréal's Department of Art History; the Department of Philosophy at Université de Reims; the Université Laval's Department of Philosophy; and Bishop's University. For their invitations and for their comments on my work I wish to thank professors Philippe Despoix, Don Dombowsky, Ghyslaine Guertin, Marie-Andrée Ricard, Itay Sapir, Patrick Wotling, and all their students who energetically engaged in many discussions during my talks, as well as Michael Thomanek and Benedikt Brisch at the DAAD, and Letitia Meynell at Dalhousie. I also wish to extend my heartfelt gratitude to Patrick Wotling, Helmut Heit, Mike Rottman, Clément Bertot, and Jean Leclercq for their generosity and hospitality in Reims, Weimar, Louvain, and Namur.

Special thanks are sent to those who I was extremely lucky to have as students for two short, but rich and intense periods: my winter 2019 course on Nietzsche at the Department of Philosophy and Arts at Université du Québec à Trois-Rivières, and my fall 2020 informal grad seminar on "How to Read Nietzsche," held remotely at the CCEAE during the pandemic. To you all who were there, thank you for your keen eye when studying Nietzsche's texts, your precise questions, and your constant curiosity and enthusiasm.

I wish to extend my gratitude to those with who it was a pleasure to discuss and share ideas on the many paths taken by the reception of Nietzsche's ideas, and whose energy, impressive scholarship, intellectual curiosity, and friendship are dear to me — most notably Patrick Wotling, Mélissa Thériault, and Chiara Piazzesi. I also thank the anonymous readers who took the time to read the manuscript and offer comments and suggestions for revisions, which were most useful in preparing a final version and turning a draft into a book.

As all researchers know, the possibility for research depends not only on the person conducting it, but for a very large part on the many persons helping the researcher. In this respect, I must thank first and foremost my assistant at the CCEAE between 2018 and 2022, Flora Roussel, for her diligence, hard work, sharp eye, and, simply put, her literary intelligence. Special thanks to the staff at McGill-Queen's University Press, most notably Khadija Coxon, for her encouragement, suggestions, and patience with me throughout the many stages of getting this manuscript out of my computer and onto bookshelves, and Kathryn Simpson for her sharp eye and passion in reading and editing the manuscript. Many thanks, also, to Marie-Michèle Blondin for sharing some of her extraordinary knowledge on Schopenhauer, to Philip-Emmanuel Aubry who worked on technical aspects of some of this book's chapters, and to Valérie Damourette, at the Research Office of Cégep Édouard-Montpetit. I express my gratitude as well to the librarians at the Anna Amalia Bibliothek in Weimar, who were of precious help in many ways, and to Rüdiger Schmidt-Grépaly, who hosted my very first stay in Weimar, at the Nietzsche Haus, in the summer of 2009.

Finally, I wish to acknowledge the generous support of Université Sainte-Anne and the CCEAE, as well as Cégep Édouard-Montpetit, the DAAD, Université de Montréal, the Social Sciences and Humanities Research Council of Canada, the International Research Training Group Diversity, and the ministère de l'Éducation du Québec.

One last and important word of heartfelt thanks to two persons: Augustin Simard, who has been my ever-present discussion and travel partner, and who with me went through it all, and more; and Jules Simard, who brings constant light and joy to my everyday life, who already loves words and puns, and who knows that style never takes a day off.

Martine Béland
Church Point, November 2023

Abbreviations

Unless otherwise stated, emphasis in all quotations is in the original.

Abbreviations to Nietzsche's Texts in German

EKP	*Encyclopædie der klassische Philologie*
HKP	*Homer und die klassische Philologie*
KGB	*Briefwechsel. Kritische Gesamtausgabe*
KGW	*Werke. Kritische Gesamtausgabe*
KSA	*Kritische Studienausgabe*
KSB	*Sämtliche Briefe. Kritische Studienausgabe*
NF	*Nachlaß* (unpublished fragments)
PTZ	*Die Philosophie im tragischen Zeitalter der Griechen*

Abbreviations to Nietzsche's Texts in English

STANFORD UNIVERSITY PRESS

AC	*The Antichrist*
BGE	*Beyond Good and Evil*
BT	*The Birth of Tragedy*
CW	*The Case of Wagner*
CWN	*The Complete Works of Friedrich Nietzsche*
D	*Dawn*
EH	*Ecce Homo*
GM	*On the Genealogy of Morality*
HAH I	*Human, All Too Human*, part 1
TI	*Twilight of the Idols*
UO	*Unfashionable Observations*
	UO 1 (*DS*) *David Strauss the Confessor and the Writer*
	UO 2 (*UL*) *On the Utility and Liability of History for Life*

	UO 3 (*SE*)	*Schopenhauer as Educator*
	UO 4 (*RWB*)	*Richard Wagner in Bayreuth*
WS	*The Wanderer and His Shadow* (*HAH*, part 2 [*HAH* II])	
Z	*Thus Spoke Zarathustra*	

OTHER PRESSES

GS	*The Gay Science*, trans. J. Nauckhoff, poems trans. by A. Del Caro (Cambridge: Cambridge University Press, 2001)

Nietzsche as Stylist

Introduction

Elements of Style

NIETZSCHE'S AESTHETIC LEGACY

We *are* different from scholars.
Nietzsche, *GS*, §381

In 1882, Friedrich Nietzsche was enjoying a very early retirement from his academic position as professor of classical philology at the University of Basel, Switzerland. He was spending the summer in the small town of Tautenburg, in the eastern part of Germany's Thuringia. Once a young and promising scholar of ancient Greek, by the early 1880s Nietzsche was a largely unknown thirty-eight-year-old self-proclaimed philosopher.

He was not vacationing on his own: his sister Elisabeth was with him — but more importantly, so was the young freethinker Lou von Salomé. While in the same town, Friedrich and Lou wrote letters to each other regularly, much as friends or lovers of today would text many times during the day: they made plans and appointments, they exchanged thoughts and poems.

Their intimate context was one of shared creativity. One letter that Nietzsche wrote to von Salomé at that time reads like the summary of a lecture on aesthetics more than a missive to a woman he hoped to marry. The letter — to which he even gave a title: "On the Doctrine of Style" — has ten short paragraphs that delineate ten elements of written style. The first is perhaps the most general, and Nietzsche underlines that it is certainly the most important: "Style must live."

In his letter he develops ideas that go back and forth between the perspective of the writer and that of the reader. For instance, he mentions that style must be suitable to the person who will read the text, but also that it must be an imitation of what one wishes to say. Through style the author must show a belief in the thoughts that are transmitted, but also appeal to the senses so as to have an effect on readers. Surely style must be "expressive": the reader must feel writing as a "gesture." Yet some gestures are ill-suited to modern languages: Nietzsche stresses that one must beware of writing in "periods" — the long phrases that were common in Greek and Latin rhetoric — a stylistic device, he warns, that most modern writers do not master and should not even try to imitate.

Nietzsche finishes his "Doctrine" by pointing out that style should border on poetry without actually being poetic, and that one should not write everything on one's mind: "It is very good and very wise to leave it to your reader to pronounce the last quintessence of your wisdom." The letter ends on a personal, affectionate note: "A good morning to you, my dear Lou!"[1]

Nietzsche wrote these thoughts on style in August of 1882, just as he was publishing his ninth book, *The Gay Science*. His earliest works had been categorized as critical pamphlets by the German press, while the following ones elicited interrogations and even uneasiness for the way in which they blurred the lines separating literary quality and philosophical expectations. What exactly was, for instance, this strange 1878 book entitled *Human, All Too Human*? Or the two works that Nietzsche published the following year, *Mixed Opinions and Maxims* and the presumably esoteric *The Wanderer and His Shadow*? These books proposed maxims, aphorisms, and poems. They developed critiques of the history of philosophy and showed a profound interest in science. They deployed humour alongside a tone of grandeur. And they were evidently well-written: witty, provocative, inspiring, but also rebuking, all at once.

Were they personal essays? Freestyle philosophical treatises? With such an arsenal of knowledge and literary devices, for whom were these works intended and what was their author's purpose? The German journalist Hans Herrig, who wrote the first — and only contemporary — review of these three 1878–79 books that Nietzsche would come to regroup under the title *Human, All Too Human, Parts I and II*, found them "wholly inspiring and worthy of reading." But he also suggested that with such a "transformation" of his style, Friedrich Nietzsche would have trouble finding readers.[2]

Nietzsche is now well-known for the style to which Herrig alluded, although it is not totally unique in the sphere of philosophical works: aphorisms and short essays, in which a treasure trove of literary devices is used in the service of transmitting ideas, hypotheses, critiques, or thought experiments. This style would put him squarely outside academia, and firmly in the centre of cultural creation, debates, and appropriations.

This book focuses on Nietzsche as a writer. It examines how he came to write in such varied voices, how style served the transmission of his ideas, and how this participates in a wider discussion on the nature of reading and understanding.

Crossroads

It should come as no surprise that Nietzsche had a precise idea of style when he wrote his August 1882 letter to Lou von Salomé. Indeed, in the early 1880s, he was at a crossroads. Evidently, he took pleasure in composing works: he published seventeen books in as many years.[3] But after five books written in a polemical, essayistic tone between 1872 and 1876 — *The Birth of Tragedy* and the four *Unfashionable Observations* — he adopted a different authorial voice as of the four 1878–81 books *Human, All Too Human* and *Dawn*: this was the period during which he developed his now-famous aphoristic style.

An aphorism is a short and compact self-standing literary form for a complete thought-development, whether assertive or hypothetical, humorous or sententious. This form was not new in Nietzsche's time: there were instances of it in antiquity, and it was brought to a high degree of completion in the seventeenth and eighteenth centuries by French moralistic writers such as La Rochefoucauld or Vauvenargues — whom Nietzsche admired — and the German writer G.C. Lichtenberg. Nietzsche praised the philosophical brevity that the aphorism could supply: a minimum number of signs, as he put it in one of his last works, for a maximum energy of these signs. Faced with a topic, a problem, a question, a thinker writing in aphorisms could be "In quickly, out quickly."[4]

During the same period, Nietzsche also started using more metaphors. A metaphor is a process of word substitution: it illustrates that which is signified, thereby placing it under new light. In fact, writing metaphorically is to constantly shift from one context to another. As the French philosopher Sarah Kofman put it in her seminal but oft-overlooked 1972 book *Nietzsche and the Metaphor*, Nietzsche believed philosophers should not summarize and condense life through abstract and general concepts. Instead they must "use expressive and vivid metaphors to resurrect a personality in its most typical attributes."[5] Metaphors are not self-standing: by appealing to the senses, they convey something of the writer's experience and sensory imagination and ask that the reader make sense of these through feeling and imagination. While this makes for a more active communication between writer and reader, it also encourages reader response by inviting a subjective participation in the thought experiment at hand. By expressing a lived, embodied understanding, metaphors are a means of triggering one.

Metaphors are perhaps the most famous apparatus in Nietzsche's stylistic toolbox. By focusing on metaphors — what Barbara Neymeyr calls Nietzsche's "experimental forms of thought" — Nietzsche turned philosophical writing away not only from argumentative demonstration, but also very far away from German philosophy's trademark: metaphysics' reliance on conceptual abstraction.[6]

His next book, *Thus Spoke Zarathustra*, went very far in that direction. (First published in three separate volumes in 1883–84; a fourth, privately printed volume was circulated in a pressing of forty copies in 1885.) It formed a long, lyrical philosophical poem that heavily reverted to imagery, symbolism, rhyme, rhythm, and biblical parody. Nietzsche qualified this four-part book as a "symphony," thereby ascribing a metaphor to his own work.[7]

He thereafter published the books that are arguably his most known and studied works today: *The Gay Science* (1882, with a second, expanded version in 1887), *Beyond Good and Evil* (1886), and its complement, *On the Genealogy of Morality* (1887). They were composed mostly of what could be called "short essays": one-paragraph developments that generally range between a dozen of lines to a couple of pages. These short essays are often numbered and sometimes titled. In these works, Nietzsche makes heavy use of metaphor, rhyme, alliteration, exclamative or rhythmic punctuation, verse, dialogue, interjection, self-quotation, parody, pun, humour, and more. His final works, written (though not all published) in 1888 (*The Case of Wagner*, *Twilight of the Idols*, *The Antichrist*, *Ecce Homo*), again revert to the stylistic devices that he had mastered in the mid-1880s.

Even a rapid survey of Nietzsche's published corpus makes evident that stylistic techniques are everywhere. Style is more than the ideas' cloak: it is the shape, sound, and sheer presence of the philosopher walking onto a stage.

Elements of Style

In his book *The Wanderer and His Shadow*, Nietzsche noted how to write better is also to think better: one is thereby able to invent things worthy of being communicated to one's neighbours. He thus equated the capacity to write and think well with the capacity to be a free human being — one who strives, through communication and debate, to continue and even improve civilization. By contrast, one who ascribes little or no value to writing or reading well contributes to the closing of both minds and nations.[8]

Writing well, for Nietzsche, meant to know the many tools at a writer's disposition and, through an inner feel for the possibilities offered by a specific language, to use them to express oneself to another living person. Writing well, in other words, required *style*.

In his autobiography *Ecce Homo*, Nietzsche described style as serving "To communicate a state, an inward tension of pathos, by means of signs, including the tempo of these signs." He also stressed his own unique richness in this matter: "I have many stylistic possibilities — the most multifarious art of style that has ever been at the disposal of one man."[9] Style concerns different categories of discursive expression: syntax (clauses) and grammar (pronouns), but also lexicon (rhymes, metaphors) and rhythm (punctuation), as well as narrative flow and argumentative structure.

Many linguistic tools and techniques have been tallied, described, and used since antiquity.[10] As authors from Plato and Cicero to Montaigne and Kierkegaard knew — and as authors of our own time from Didion to Dillard still know — style is not reserved for writers of fiction: essays and scholarly discourse have styles of their own, which may vary across cultures. An author formulates ideas by choosing tools within the syntaxial, grammatical, and lexical parameters of the language in use, and builds one's own personal expression through repetitive use, experiment, and trial and error. The author articulates a voice, sometimes creatively, sometimes conventionally — but always in the hope of transmitting meaning by affecting readers.

Ecce Homo's claim may sound inflated, even wildly so, but actually Nietzsche was not exaggerating. To quote the two American scholars Babette Babich and Tracy Strong, Nietzsche "has the art of style 'down to a science,'" and "the rhetorical quality of what he says is prominent." Many other readers and scholars have also noted Nietzsche's mastery of multiple styles of writing. Echoing Nietzsche's self-assessment in *Ecce Homo*, the German scholar Werner Stegmaier went so far as to state that "none of the other great philosophers has used such varied forms nor shaped or created new ones for his philosophical writing." In fact, Nietzsche's style has fascinated readers from the start. In his famous 1919 book *Nietzsche: Attempt at a Mythology*, the poet and German literature professor Ernst Bertram presented Nietzsche as a unique *Sprachbildner* — one who forms or sculpts language, an image that the philosopher would surely have approved of.[11]

We may well accept Nietzsche's claim to stylistic fame: his elements of style are indeed multifarious. He writes in rhymes and alliterations, verses and allegories, puns and questions. He invents characters — the wanderer and the madman, the scholar and the philosopher — who make recurring appearances in his works, sometimes through scenes, sometimes through dialogues.[12] Nietzsche also confounds the reader by playing with pronouns (here a "we," there a singular or plural "you"). He does not shy from antinomies and he jokes; he wants us to laugh, or cringe — or do both. He uses multiple markers of hypothetical thought, which he frequently prefers to declarative statements. He often addresses himself directly to the reader and asks for reactions. He stages thought experiments in diverse settings: mountain tops, swamps, tightropes — no decor seems uncalled for, no animal is out of place, no colour is left untouched.[13]

Nietzsche also played with varied possibilities of expression that solicit faculties other than the purely argumentative. As Wojciech Simson wrote in a study of Nietzsche's punctuation, a heavy use of question marks, for instance, assures Nietzsche "of an agreement with his discussion partner that is more emotional than rational."[14] In a similar way, landscapes solicit one's visual imagination and forces one to consider ideas within a wider, not-so-abstract context that may at times be musical, or chromatic, or rhythmic.

Evidently, Nietzsche crafted his published works meticulously. While pondering style, he noted that "The art of writing requires above all *substitutes* for the modes of expression that only a speaker has available: hence for gestures, accents, tones, looks."[15] This statement in *The Wanderer and His Shadow* makes an obvious reference to ancient oratorical style; but it also shows how written language must translate physical ways of conveying meaning. Nietzsche's readers thus often stumble upon sound (through alliterations or characters' dialogues), rhythm (through punctuation or rhymes), or image (through descriptions of landscape or meteorological events). In fact, he so developed the embodied quality of his language that his style appears deliberately synesthetic, in that it is meant to trigger the experience of a simultaneous stimulation of more than one sense.[16]

By appealing to the senses, many stylistic traits reflect the author's lived experience of ideas. As Keith Ansell-Pearson noted, Nietzsche's works show how he believed that "the thinker needs to make himself vulnerable to all kinds of experience."[17] Yet his works also show how Nietzsche proposed all kinds of experiences to his readers. By appealing to the senses, his writing offers the reader an embodied experience of understanding. Indeed, style echoes the bodily dimension of thinking, writing, and reading. Style is meant to spark a similar experience in other persons, too, thereby offering creativity to the reader.

Nietzsche and Academia, Academia and Nietzsche

Nietzsche sometimes pondered the type of reception and even reputation he would have in the decades after his death. He often specified how his readers should read and hear him, and even enacted ways in which readers were likely to grasp his ideas: he acquiesced to some interpretations, rejected others, laughed at a few more.[18] In short, writing philosophy was inseparable from ensuring that philosophy be read. (He even went so far as to argue with his publisher about which font and cardboard his book covers should sport so that they might catch the eye of potential readers in bookstores.)[19] A variety of stylistic tools and techniques thus made for a larger collection of hooks and baits.

In this sense, the journalist Hans Herrig — who worried, in 1880, that Nietzsche's style would hinder his reception — was not shortsighted, he was simply oblivious to the effect of style. The best way to find readers — and that is, many readers with different backgrounds and professions and from distinct cultures, in short: a diverse multiplicity of individual readers — was precisely by writing philosophy with a rich assortment of literary and synesthetic tools. By explicitly writing from the self and to other singular selves and marrying argumentation with humour, poems, and staged characters and animals, Nietzsche could reach a greater audience than merely professional philosophers.

All the resources of style with which Nietzsche was experimenting opened a path to an enhanced attention and embodied reception on the part of the reader. This would also be the path to a wide cultural impact of his philosophy beyond the walls of the famed German academies devoted to knowledge. Nietzsche's conception and practice of philosophical enquiry was as foreign to academic production as Nietzsche himself was detached from the bourgeois model of a professional existence.

For a time, he was a scholar, a historian of ancient literature, and a professor of Greek. His music for a while was Richard Wagner's and his philosophy Arthur Schopenhauer's, but he remained a lifelong admirer of the American essayist Ralph Waldo Emerson (1803–1882) and the French writer Stendhal. He was a pianist and a poet, an essayist and a self-published author. He was a brother and a friend, a bachelor, and a perpetual traveller. Born a German citizen, Nietzsche remained simply a European after renouncing his Prussian passport.[20] He read many languages, cherished many projects, wrote many letters. As these and other markers of identity suggest, he had different voices. And as his writings show, he tried out different styles in a constant effort to express a plurality of voices and perspectives.

Since Nietzsche's elements of style are varied and rich, and since they are closely related to his philosophy, one would assume the issue would have been the focus of much scholarly attention. Stylistic commentary, however, is not a traditional path trodden by philosophers — most notably because to examine a philosopher's style implies that one is examining philosophical works as discourses. The linguist Dominique Maingueneau points out that "generally speaking philosophy dislikes to be studied as a discourse among other discourses, or even to be treated as a discourse."[21] Yet as French philosopher Jacques Derrida insisted, "to analyze a 'philosophical discourse' according to its form, composition, rhetoric, metaphors, language, and fictions does not mean that one is reducing it to literature ... To study these 'forms' is even a largely philosophical task (albeit not a purely philosophical one)."[22]

Recent studies, mostly in Germany, have taken up the task of showing "how an attention to the literary-poetic composition of Nietzsche's writing can bring us closer also to his philosophical-theoretical ideas." Today, "Readers of Nietzsche have reached a point in the ongoing interpretation and appropriation of his work at which the question of its literary form can no longer be separated from its content," as Hans Ruin noted a few years ago.[23] Scholarly and popular readership has unanimously recognized from an early point on that Nietzsche is a stylist. But the interest in analyses of his literary forms is still recent.

This situation could have several explanations, one of which concerns the fact that Nietzsche was an author in a time of turmoil. The fate of his works became tied to that of twentieth-century German culture. Post-war German academic philosophy was wary of associating with authors deemed to be anti-Enlightenment and anti-rationalist. Most notably through the Marxist impetus of Critical Theory's aim for social emancipation, at the Frankfurt School and beyond, this situation led to a rejection of Nietzsche as a philosophical candidate for reconstructing social thought in German universities. As a result, Nietzsche has not been the focus of as much philosophical attention in Germany as other leading figures of the philosophical canon such as Kant or Hegel.[24]

This wariness towards Nietzsche on the part of liberal or left-leaning social philosophy may nevertheless be counteracted specifically by looking at the history of the reception of Nietzsche's ideas. His ungendered notion of *Übermensch* and self-determination appealed to women of the early German and American feminist movements; interwar socialists turned to his ideas for a revaluation of the individual person within a community; and scholars in the German Democratic Republic and other communist contexts turned to Nietzsche as a field of study, while many artists searching for liberating and creative impulses read him in original ways.[25]

Another factor is that studying Nietzsche's style asks that one work on the original German texts — or at the very least, that one be able to trust that the available translations have respected his stylistic choices. However, as anyone who has ever engaged in a comparison of translations knows, this, unfortunately, has not always been the case. Some early and even mid-twentieth-century translators of Nietzsche in English or in French, for instance, have omitted some or many of his punctuation choices, italics, pronouns, or even verbal moods.[26] The ongoing retranslation of Nietzsche's complete works into English, undertaken by Stanford University Press, as well as the current retranslation of his works into French, for Garnier-Flammarion's popular pocketbook series "GF," seeks to ameliorate this situation. But to study Nietzsche's style, nothing replaces the capacity one may have to read and hear how he wrote in his own language.[27]

A third factor concerns the current state of the academic field of philosophy. For all his popular appeal, Nietzsche is not highly represented in philosophy departments today. In many North American universities, so-called "continental philosophy" has dwindled, as has the history of philosophy, which is often considered to be of marginal if not fully unphilosophical interest.[28] In the same way, academic philosophical circles are not often open to issues considered to rest outside their scope. An enquiry into the nature of evil, for instance, is considered a philosophical topic, whereas an enquiry into the use of literary devices or the authority-effect of certain claims are not: they are related to literary theory and to the sociology of ideas, respectively. Philosophy, in short, appears reluctant to turn to studies of its own practice that stem from other fields of the humanities or social sciences, whether, for example, the literary analysis of philosophical writing or the sociology of philosophy.

Perhaps an interest in style is seen as synonymous with the frivolity of aestheticism and taken as the sign of a lack of seriousness regarding the theses being discussed in the text at hand. As philosophers, we may tend to grow suspicious of an author who seeks to multiply reading reactions rather than assert a claim clearly and unanimously. Yet multiple reactions are precisely what Nietzsche's style deliberately causes. Perhaps we do in fact acquiesce here and chuckle there, but as philosophers attuned to the meaning and effect of ideas, if we are to understand and debate, we need to assess. We thus need to ask questions that concern both the author's intent and the reader's reaction, such as these: Why is there a pun here and why does the author want us to laugh now? Why does the author so often conclude a thought on an interrogation or dash rather than an assertion or end-period? Why are there sixteen markers of hypothesis in the famous *Beyond Good and Evil* paragraph where Nietzsche introduces the idea of the will to power?[29] What are the recurring metaphors, characters, or animals in his works and do they always convey the same message, even when their staged context changes?

Simply put, we need to focus on how Nietzsche wrote if we are to understand what he intended to convey to his readers in writing that way. Nietzsche's style is his work.

The Meaning of Stylistic Analysis

Some fifty years ago, the German studies scholar Richard Roos attempted to persuade a roomful of philosophers to see the relevance of style to philosophical issues, by asserting that "even though it is descriptive, stylistic commentary leads directly to philosophical explanation." He stressed the importance of analyzing the poetic landscape of Nietzsche's words, but noted that on the issue of his style, "almost all has yet to be done."[30]

The year was 1972. Roos was speaking at a now famous ten-days long French conference on Nietzsche at Cérisy-La-Salle. Seated in the room were the leading European philosophers who were deeply interested in Nietzsche's ideas: Karl Löwith, Jacques Derrida, and Sarah Kofman were among the many attendees. The critical edition of Nietzsche's complete works, which had been instigated, in the 1960s, by two Italian philologists, G. Colli and M. Montinari, was being translated into French under the editorial supervision of Gilles Deleuze and Michel Foucault.

Roos's remarks on style were not well received, as the question period, which was recorded and added to the conference proceedings, shows. The problem was not that his paper was too technical; it was that Roos was speaking as a scholar of German philology and literature to a public almost exclusively composed of philosophers. Surprisingly, the fact that they gathered to speak about a philologist, moreover during a period of frenzied editorial and translation enterprise, seems to have been ignored by most participants. In fact, given that context, by pondering the practice of writing, style, punctuation, and translation, Roos's was perhaps the timeliest talk of the 1972 conference. Nevertheless, the Cérisy philosophers saw him as an outsider.

Yet Roos's invitation was all the more promising in the case of a study of style, given that Nietzsche believed that in order for the new philosophy that he advocated to be emancipated from idealist prejudices or theological reflexes, it needed to be written in a "new language."[31] The mere fact that Nietzsche let style take up so much space within the philosophical exposition of his ideas is an immediate sign of his philosophical innovations. He thus transmitted his ideas not only through what he wrote about, but also and explicitly through how he wrote — and in both ways his philosophy parted with academic tradition.

Roos, though isolated, was not alone in seeing the importance of stylistic analysis. In her book published the same year as Roos's talk, Sarah Kofman stressed the relationship between Nietzsche's style and his ideas: "Just as he multiplies perspectives, so Nietzsche intentionally diversifies his styles in order to save the reader from misunderstanding a single style as a 'style in itself.'"[32] Style was thus a tool in Nietzsche's ongoing critique of the notion of absolute in philosophy. Indeed, Kofman clearly saw how for Nietzsche style echoes the important philosophical idea of perspectivism, that is the epistemological notion according to which our descriptions of the world are always interpretations and that there is no absolute, objective standpoint.[33] It follows, as Robert Norton wrote, that "What cannot be observed from a single vantage point ... must necessarily be seen from a variety of angles if one is to do justice to its scope and complexity."[34]

Two scholars are well known for having stressed the connection between perspectivism and style in Nietzsche's philosophy. One is the Princeton scholar Alexander Nehamas in his now classic 1985 *Nietzsche: Life as Literature*; the other is the Sorbonne professor Éric Blondel in his equally iconic 1986 *Nietzsche, the Body, and Culture*. Blondel opened his book by stating that what distinguishes Nietzsche as a philosopher "can only be his *text*."[35] From the onset he was agreeing with Nehamas who saw that Nietzsche's insistence on interpretation and reliance on philology motivated him "to create what we may well call a literary product" in accordance with "his conception of the world as text." Of course, Nietzsche's "variety of literary genres and styles" enabled him "to make his presence as an individual author unforgettable to his readers."[36] As Hans Ruin recently put it, Nietzsche is "a philosopher for whom aesthetic appearance is precisely a mode of appearing, and perhaps even a mode of seduction in the service of philosophy,"[37] because through style, Nietzsche could present his philosophical ideas in a performative manner. Nehamas, for instance, showed how Nietzsche's conception of the self also echoed his larger view on perspectivism: "Nietzsche's effort to create an artwork out of himself, a literary character who is a philosopher, is then also his effort to offer a positive view without falling back into the dogmatic tradition he so distrusted."[38]

Some readers of Nietzsche who evidently grasped the creative potential of Nietzsche's style were modernist artists. Many saw that

Nietzsche's practice of writing critiques the domination (in the dual sense of a preponderance and a belief in the superiority) of conceptual abstraction and the indicative mode in Western thought. It should come as no surprise that painters (Edvard Munch, Marianne von Werefkin), designers (Henry van de Velde), composers (Gustav Mahler, Richard Strauss), and novelists (D.H. Lawrence, Gabriele Reuter), often enthralled by Nietzsche's penmanship, have metabolized some of his ideas and traits in creative works of their own. They were perhaps the first to see how his style rejects certain ways of speaking about the world while promoting others — and how it invites readers to create new ones.[39]

Perhaps one aspect of Nietzsche's experiments with style that artists were particularly attuned to is the relation of style to values. Style both communicates and promotes experience and interpretation, and in so doing style reveals and transmits values. Nietzsche believed that philosophers (and non-philosophers alike) reveal values through their life-choices: in what environment they choose to live and in what context they choose to write — whether in a natural setting, on an academic campus, or on the road.[40] But was Nietzsche not also suggesting that philosophers reveal their values through the way in which they write? If style is an expression of value, the formulation of an idea is never neutral.[41] Through experience and interpretation, maximizing style to maximize reception and transmit values: style was how Nietzsche's ideas would find resonance in individual persons, but it was also how they would achieve cultural meaning.

Diving In by Opting Out

This book does not aim at an exhaustive study of Nietzsche's rhetoric. Nor does it seek to define "Nietzschean style" in a definitive or authoritative way. It also does not propose an overview of all of Nietzsche's works or stylistic traits: some are left to other readers' and scholars' passion and scrutiny and to future studies. This book rather wants to show the pervasiveness of style within Nietzsche's work and life by retracing the development of his focus on style, by contextualizing the development of his philosophical style, by looking at specific voices and devices, and by showing how a close attention to style makes for a better and precise understanding of philosophical ideas and praxis.

As the preceding discussions were meant to show, stylistic traits in Nietzsche's texts are not mere embellishments. Style and thought have an intimate relationship. In fact, we must not separate them if we are to make sense of Nietzsche's ideas. This means that to understand his philosophy, it is not sufficient to focus on the theses that he addresses: we must focus on how he formulates his points through lexicon, verb mood, pronouns, punctuation, but also form and textual context.

The following pages show that by opting out of academic philosophy and experimenting with style, Nietzsche dived into embodied experience. From his repudiation of university as the primary locus of philosophical action to his self-publication of idiosyncratic philosophical essays, he tried, through different voices and forms, to open philosophy onto a wider field of attention, thought, and experience. He maximized contexts for and types of reception, sometimes speaking to music lovers, other times to readers of German philosophy, other times still to young people seeking guidance before embarking on a career path. He focused on means for triggering in his readers a simultaneous stimulation of more than one sense, hoping to permit synesthesia and visualisation. Style was how his ideas could live — through time.

This book follows two methodological leads. The first is an approach to style that is informed by literary theory. While one would be hard-pressed to define style in a way that could satisfy theorists of all schools and allegiances, one can minimally say with Collège de France professor Antoine Compagnon that style concerns "the relation between text and language." Before him, the Austrian theorist Leo Spitzer defined style in relation to expression: style is the way in which an author uses linguistic material to express oneself and reach, affect, and convince readers.[42] Nietzsche's stylistic sources or inspirations were numerous. He was a connoisseur of Biblical allegories (his father was a Lutheran pastor), a lover of German alliteration, an avid reader of French authors and Roman orators, an admirer of Jonathan Swift and Laurence Sterne, a teacher of Greek rhetoric. From very early on Nietzsche understood that style is the author's means of expressing the self, and a way to meet the challenge of reaching and holding readers.

The second lead in this study is phenomenology's approach to reception. The field of phenomenological aesthetics, especially as it has been delineated by Romanian philosopher Roman Ingarden, considers reception as an aesthetic phenomenon: it is an embodied participation into the structure of the work that is read. As the German literary theorist Wolfgang Iser also put it, reception is the creative reconstruction of meaning through reading.[43] The author's ideas find new meaning and life through the reader's understanding, but more importantly, the work does not fully exist outside of this active reception. (This goes to say, in phenomenological language, that a work of art is an "intentional object.") Production and reception are thus entwined: writer and reader are two sides of a coin that consists of thought through both communication and subsequent interpretation. As we will see in the following pages, Nietzsche was acutely aware of this.

Far from a passive position towards the work, readers are immersed in a process of understanding through their own context and embodied experience. As an expression and transmission of experience, style concerns experimenting with written language, but also with different lifestyles: schedules and rhythms, contexts and socialization, activities and obligations, to name but a few aspects. To maintain a distinction between writing philosophy and living as a philosopher would therefore be artificial: Nietzsche's philosophy is transmitted through style in a way that connects to different experiences in his life. This book is thus also immersed in Nietzsche's many contexts.

This study contextually retraces four steps in Nietzsche's self-development as a stylist. The first was his initial attraction to but rapid repudiation of professional philosophical style (chapter 1). This was followed by his larger critique of scholarly life and his giving a central role to criticism as a stylistic device and investigative tool (chapters 2 and 3). A third step was his interest in creative free thinkers: his early reading of Schopenhauer's, Emerson's, and Wagner's essays inspired him to use artistic means for developing a philosophical style and language (chapters 4 and 5). The last step was his endeavour to trigger readers' embodied experience by performatively pointing to the multiplicity of experience and interpretation (chapters 6 and 7).

The first chapters of this book follow Nietzsche's repudiation of scholarly life, endeavours, and style, and his concomitant adoption of cultural criticism. Chapter 1 examines Nietzsche's experience with and abandonment of academic style — by which I mean academic writing and scholarly life — and shows how his early career led him to confront the insurmountable conflict between profession and vocation. Nietzsche's first stage as an author was academic: after his studies in Leipzig, he started his professorship at the University of Basel, in Switzerland, in 1869. Although he arrived there as the rising star of classical philology, he immediately envisioned his contribution to knowledge in the field of philosophy. He made no effort to conceal this. On the contrary, he (unsuccessfully) applied to be transferred to the vacant chair of philosophy at Basel. In the following years, while he stayed a philologist professionally speaking, he proceeded to present himself in his writings as a philosopher within a certain tradition: that of the non-writing Greek philosophers, that of Schopenhauer the essayist, and that of Emersonian individualism.

Accordingly, his first five published books adopt an essayistic and polemic style aimed at disparaging a way of life that he knew first-hand and sought to move away from: the life of the scholar. This was manifestly a self-critique: as an academic he was expected to become an eminent specialist and remain a lifelong professor. But he did quite the opposite: Nietzsche opted out. Chapters 2 and 3 thus turn to his participation in aesthetic debates and culture wars. By calling to "destroy the opera"[44] and critiquing the extremely popular German author David Friedrich Strauss, he took a stance against the culture that German musical and historical scholars embodied. Criticizing opera and rejecting scholarly life were part of the same enterprise: as a self-appointed and unconventional philosopher, Nietzsche aimed at curing culture by appealing to the creative individual outlook and drives that the singular person embodies.

Nietzsche's preoccupation with fostering a creative individuality is the object of chapters 4 and 5. His experiment with another model than the scholar is examined through his reading of — but also his partly emulating — Schopenhauer, Emerson, and Wagner. Interestingly, in the case of Schopenhauer, for instance, it was Schopenhauer the person and author (and not so much the philosopher per se) who offered a model of the independent, free thinker that Nietzsche strived for. It was through his reading of such non strictly philosophical essays — and perhaps most notably those of Richard Wagner, rarely read today — that Nietzsche first expressed the need for a new language that would be something other than abstract and conceptual.

The last two chapters may be read as case-studies in philosophical stylistics. Chapter 6 examines the role of prefaces within Nietzsche's philosophy. During his active years Nietzsche wrote more prefaces than books (twenty-six of the former, compared to seventeen of the latter). He came to believe that the five prefaces he completed in 1886 for the reissue of his five most important books were his best prose to date.[45] Chapter 7 turns to Nietzsche's heavy use of em-dashes to illustrate the phenomenon of synesthesia. He admittedly preferred his dashes to his "communicated thoughts," and prized their effect so much that he often used em-dashes to open aphorisms or to play the role of end periods.[46]

These chapters open onto a discussion of Nietzsche's understanding of embodied reception as an active participation in the work being read, heard, or contemplated. Drawing on ongoing discussions on the nature of a written work and the meaning of interpretation, the epilogue examines the diverse practices of curating Nietzsche and relates them to our cultural issues and values, thereby shedding light on the diversification of the reception of his works. In this way, the methodological lead on reception circles back to the philological lead on style: by diversifying his style, Nietzsche sought to maximize the effect of his works on readers, and thus to maximize embodied reception. Through the specific case of Nietzsche's style, this book is thus concerned with philosophical aesthetics and reception theory. By contributing to these discussions, it hopes to show how a close attention to style makes for a precise understanding of an author's philosophical ideas, but also to a better understanding of the aesthetic processes at work in the reading and interpretation of essays and works of philosophy.

In the fifth section that he added to his book *The Gay Science* for its 1887 reissue, Nietzsche wrote: "We *are* different from scholars."[47] While the italics emphasize the assertion, it is striking that Nietzsche conjugates it in the first-person plural, thereby including his reader in his declaration. What is that if not a stylistic device in the service of philosophy? By doing so, Nietzsche is saying something as to the effect of his work. Having read the book up to that point, the reader should indeed understand what it means to be "something other" than a scholar. His book prepares an experience to foster thinking, writing, and creating in non-scholarly ways.

Just as a pronoun may be revealing, the images in Nietzsche's texts must not be shunned: they are his philosophical "objects." The formulation of his ideas is not a cloak: it is the way in which Nietzsche decided to present them. It is useful to remember that Nietzsche did not write for conventional philosophers. In other words, he did not write for readers who look for theses and assertions concerning abstract, universal truths or concepts. He wrote for readers who would aesthetically receive his writings and subjectively feel them to have meaning, much as an artist creates, so that this experience may transform the reader. He did not write for seekers of the absolute: he wrote for those curious to experiment.

Given the vast reception of his works in numerous domains (many schools of philosophy and social sciences; modern art, music, and literature; or the early German feminist movement — to name but a few), it is obvious that Nietzsche's experimental philosophical style has had a huge cultural impact. If we are to decide up to where we can or even want to follow his thoughts, we need to see how his style works: how it invites us to try out his experiments and how it helps us understand what philosophy may do and be. Tracking his style (and our reactions to it) therefore tells us a lot about ourselves as readers and philosophers. It tells us about our prejudices and reflexes, our weaknesses and strengths, our drives and hopes. In other words, it tells us much about our culture and our values.

By circumscribing the embodied understanding that Nietzsche advocated, this book hopes to trigger a philosophical interest in stylistic commentary. As Richard Roos said more than fifty years ago, much has yet to be done. This book also makes a case for a renewed philosophical interest in an interpretation of Nietzsche's texts stemming from fields outside academic philosophy, and most notably from the visual and musical arts. From Mahler and Strauss to Münter and Munsch, the creative reception of Nietzsche's language and ideas has certainly had its heyday. These artists' creations show us exactly what the effect of a work of philosophy may be. They show us how style may transmit ideas and trigger new experience and thus insight. It is perhaps again time that we let artists and creators show us the meaning of understanding.

Chapter 1

A Shooting Star

NIETZSCHE, PROFESSION, AND VOCATION

Our destined vocation disposes of us, even when we do not yet know it.
Nietzsche, *HAH* I, preface, §7[1]

In many ways, Friedrich Nietzsche's professional conditions as an academic at the University of Basel, Switzerland, were no different than those of today's scholars. As professor of philology, he was expected to remain up to date regarding the latest research in his field, to publish original work as well as review essays, and to represent his institution during congresses abroad. He was also expected to train future specialists through lecture-based courses and research seminars.

But Nietzsche found no pleasure in most of these endeavours. He hated to bear the "face of a university-representative," as he wrote while travelling to the University of Munich's jubilee in July 1872. He stopped publishing book reviews very early in his career. And instead of training his students as specialized philologists, he exhorted them to widen their horizon by taking up the study of philosophy. More importantly, rather than seeking to build his reputation as a specialized scholar, he wrote his first book, *The Birth of Tragedy*, which came out in January 1872. As a philosophical essay it ignored established stylistic rules of scholarship: his book has no footnotes, no quotations from Greek sources in the original, and no references to specialized literature.[2]

It is certainly telling that at the outset of his career, Nietzsche was already criticizing the narrowness of his academic specialization and pondering what it meant for knowledge to be divided into separate disciplines. Reflecting upon his own experience through studies and teaching, he rapidly became conscious of the ever-widening gap between the demands of his profession in classical philology and the necessities of what he deemed his "natural" inclination towards philosophy.

He spoke of a personal crisis as early as January 1871: not even two years into his professorship, he wrote in a letter to his dean that his profession was contradicting his "task" and keeping him away from his "path." A "conflict" "wore him down," he believed, even "physically."[3] The conflict to which he alluded was one between profession and vocation. Its repercussions were deeply felt; Nietzsche interpreted his illnesses — both moral and physical — as the result of his having not followed his calling from an early point on.

And yet, it was as a rising star that Nietzsche had first arrived at a professorship in Basel, at the precocious age of twenty-four.

Academia: Philology as a Profession

His letters show that the young professor Nietzsche arrived in Basel, in the spring of 1869, with enthusiasm but also with apprehensions regarding his decision to devote himself entirely to philology. He was undertaking a heavy workload. Teaching amounted to fourteen hours weekly: eight hours of university lectures, plus six hours of secondary school courses at the Basel Pädagogium. Not surprisingly, he found his task most tiresome, although he was content that the appointment had transformed him from a "shooting star" into a "fixed star." After but five months in Basel, he wrote to his friend, Carl von Gersdorff: "I am quite satisfied with my academic activity, of which I have now happily finished the first semester. I notice that my students participate avidly and have a real sympathy for me, in that they often and gladly seek advice from me."[4]

Nietzsche was simultaneously satisfied with his recent philological research (his papers and reviews published since 1867),[5] worried by the fatigue caused by his professional activities, and convinced of his pedagogical mission. In fact, he knew what it meant to be a rising star, that of the Leipzig school of German classical philology. Expectations were high.

During the second half of the nineteenth century, in the midst of a rationalization and bureaucratization of the German universities and academies, classical philology was among the first disciplines to become specialized and professionalized. "Specialization" can be defined as "the degree to which scientific work is concentrated narrowly in one or a few areas, rather than broadly diffused over many," whereas "professionalization" "refers to the possibility of making a career out of scientific work, both in the sense of earning a livelihood and achieving a collective identity with other practitioners in the field."[6] In this context, classical philology rapidly rose to the forefront of scientific disciplines, thanks to a series of innovations that took place precisely in this field: professional associations (the first was formed in Leipzig, in 1837), scientific journals (of which there existed already four in 1846), and uniform professional training for future professors (through the seminar, which was developed in 1810 by the German philologist August Boeckh). As the historian of science Lorraine Daston puts it, philology, which "had been the ancillary sciences of the eighteenth-century universities, became the certification of the serious scholar in the nineteenth-century university seminar."[7]

One must not conclude from these innovations that academia as a whole was enthusiastically embracing this new stance. Many criticisms of specialization emerged, and they mostly came from the Berlin Academy of Sciences, whose members — in the spirit of German classicism and Idealism — strived to maintain the fundamentally "organic" unity of knowledge, as the German Idealist philosopher F.W.J. von Schelling put it in his 1802–03 *Lectures on the Method of Academic Studies*. The historian Theodor Mommsen, in an 1895 lecture to the Berlin Academy, provides a telling example of this attitude: "We do not accuse nor complain; the flower withers and the fruit must ripen. But the best amongst us sense that we have become specialists." In the 1880s, the German Hellenist J.G. Droysen lamented much in the same way: "The humanities' privilege is shaken, philology's era has passed; philologists are no more than monograph writers of classical Antiquity."[8]

In fact, during the last quarter of the nineteenth century, precisely at the moment when classical philology was defining new criteria for modern academic research and training, German historical sciences were going through an important crisis that lasted at least through half of the twentieth century. In a 1941 talk, the classicist Karl Reinhardt described what he considered as the tragic dilemma of German classical philology: while the late eighteenth and early nineteenth centuries held high hopes for a rebirth of antiquity within the German spirit, the rapid subsequent development of the historical sciences revealed the profound dilemma that lay at the heart of philology. "The 'classical' ... must be recognized at the same time as a historical value bound to a specific epoch and as an eternal value."[9] In fact, once that "historical truth" became the guiding criteria for philological research, it was not possible to maintain that the principal value of classical studies rested upon aesthetic grounds — as had been the case for Goethe or Schiller, for instance. Philology, as Reinhardt put it, was facing "the dilemma between its classical ideal and the historical reality of its undertaking." To quote the philologist and Nietzsche scholar James Porter: "In this new uncertainty was encapsulated the whole of modernity's relationship to the classical past, and so too its own historical self-image."[10]

Such were the times during which Nietzsche took the chair of classical philology in Basel. He was the rising star of a field that took pride in being at the forefront of modern higher education. But at the same time, he was heir to a view that saw the value of classical studies in the fact that they were — well — *classic*. While Nietzsche was representative of the issues facing German historical sciences in the time of their modernization and professionalization, his originality lay in that he readily reflected upon philology's theoretical issues and faced head-on the question of the value of history and of historical studies. In most of his early essays he addressed the crisis of classical studies: its sociological causes (the transformation of the learned class as a consequence of increasingly technical disciplines in the context of industrialization); its pedagogical consequences (the transformation and perhaps disappearance of the classical education, or *Bildung*); and its political context (that of nation-building in the aftermath of the Franco-Prussian war).[11]

Nietzsche's Classical Philology

At the outset of a career, after long research studies, it is habitual, as philosopher Wilhelm Wundt noted in an 1876 article, to consider the task at hand and the means with which one hopes to accomplish it.[12] That is what Nietzsche's inaugural lecture intended to do. His entry in professional philology, as Porter noted, is a reflection on "the entire attitude of modernity to the study of the 'so-called "classical" antiquity.'"[13] Nietzsche was conscious of the importance and difficulty of founding and defending the absolute value of the classical. As an admirer of Goethe and Schiller, he argued for a classical vision of antiquity: philology's pedagogical mission is "to uncover a buried, ideal world and to show the present the mirror of the classical as an eternal model."[14] This task required that philology open itself to other areas of knowledge.

In this respect, Nietzsche's perspective recalls that of Schelling's *Lectures on the Method of Academic Studies*. Schelling stressed that the philologist must work with artists and philosophers: "His task is the historical construction of the works of art and science; he must understand their history and expound it vividly." In Greek antiquity, "festivals, public monuments, dramatic performances, and other communal activities together made up a single, universal, objective, and living work of art."[15] That was precisely Nietzsche's thesis in 1869: to guarantee the status of the classical, philology must define itself as a "scientific-artistic movement."[16] Nietzsche would go on to develop his thoughts on the relationship between historical knowledge and culture in his famous second *Unfashionable Observation*, titled *On the Utility and Liability of History for Life* (1874). There he wrote that rather than achieving a "complete" knowledge of the past, history must strive to be recognized as an artistic or symbolic force.[17]

Perhaps in today's terminology, Nietzsche's perspective on his profession would be viewed as "interdisciplinary," though in this regard it was not particularly original in its time. In Germany classical philology has always been conscious of integrating different disciplines such as history, linguistics, literary studies, archeology, and the arts. As Reinhardt has said in words that could well have been Nietzsche's or Schelling's, "the classical — one cannot research it as a scientific object without it starting to crumble or to evaporate. For it to make sense, it must be depicted, felt, embraced, it must become spirit and body — but that was and remains a task for other spirits than philologists."[18]

Nietzsche's distinctiveness is that he gave all the importance to *philosophy's* contribution to classical studies. As he told his first-year students, one must emphasize the intimacy between philology and philosophy so that the claim "to the classicality of Antiquity against the modern world does not sound like a laughable pretention."[19] A broader philosophical perspective would enable philology to overcome its internal crisis, and for this to be achieved the classicist's personal attitude was of utmost importance. Nietzsche thus defended ideas that were also held by academicians such as Mommsen and by pioneers of classical philology. Indeed, Boeckh, founder of the philological seminar, insisted that the "philologist give unity to his material by reliving it in his own mind."[20]

Following this both classical and "interdisciplinary" conception of philology, Nietzsche's courses directed classical studies towards philosophy. He enthusiastically traced philosophical issues in the Greek texts that his students read, as he explained in a letter to his former professor Friedrich Ritschl in May 1869: "By making them read Plato's *Phaedo*, I can inoculate my pupils with philosophy." He explained that it would be profitable "if all future expert first studied *philosophy* for one year, so that he would not resemble the factory worker who screws his bolts day in day out."[21] There again, Nietzsche voiced worries that were common in German academia. Physiologist Emil Du Bois-Reymond described similar concerns in his 1882 lecture to the Berlin Academy: "Relinquishing their claims to fame, a thousand diligent, scientific workers daily put forth innumerable details, unconcerned with internal and external completeness, only eager to attract instant publicity and gain the best price for their commodities."[22]

Nietzsche's harsh appraisal of professional research, which he shared with many German scholars, is rooted in his thoughts regarding the disciplinary constitution of knowledge. At the start of his career, he noticed an inner contradiction in all knowledge-oriented professions. This contradiction can be summarized by two parallel assertions: "Life is worth living," and "Life is worth knowing." The 1869 lecture accordingly opposed two impulses: an impulse that leads the professional classicist's scientific work, and an impulse that leads the instinctive pleasure that enticed one to precisely research the Greeks rather than another field of knowledge. Nietzsche showed that sadly, as scholars excel in their scientific work they overlook — and perhaps even lose — the initial pleasure that they first took in Greek works, ideas, or objects: "When we consider

Antiquity scientifically, when we try to take hold of its becoming with the eye of the historian, or when, like the naturalist, we try to categorize and compare the linguistic forms of ancient masterpieces to relate them to morphological laws, then we always loose the wonderful form, the particular atmosphere of Antiquity, we forget the nostalgic impulse that brought us towards the Greeks with the power of our instinct, this sublime guide of ours."[23]

Nietzsche thus pointed to an incompatibility between the instinctive impulse — the passion — that had initially determined the choice of his career, and the scientific impulse that guided his professional research work. While both impulses feed on the same ideal, one expression of this ideal tends to silence and even extinguish the other.

The inner contradiction of philology as a profession is thus double. On the one hand, the philologist's professional activity rests upon a classicist ideal that is slowly obliterated by the "historicist" perspective resulting from scientific historical data. This disciplinary contradiction entails the general problem of the historical conscience in nineteenth-century Germany, as mid-twentieth-century philologists such as Reinhardt have remarked.

On the other hand, the scientific impulse towards knowledge that motivates the scholar tends to deaden the passionate drive that brings one to a particular field of knowledge. This personal contradiction causes a malaise within the scholar, whatever one's discipline. Nietzsche suggests that this second contradiction characterizes the disciplinary constitution of knowledge as such. It is thus impossible for a scholar to escape it and the problems, the difficulties, and — eventually — the crises that it causes. One who has chosen a scholarly career will necessarily be confronted to the contradiction between passion and knowledge. Nietzsche's Basel writings indeed show that he did not escape this existential difficulty: he rapidly felt the contradiction between his profession and his "instinctive passion" and "inclination" towards the Greeks.[24]

Three Attempts at Reconciling Profession and Vocation

Although his inaugural lecture showed that a scholar could not escape the contradiction between passion and science, it seems that

Nietzsche did not immediately grasp the practical — and radical — implications of his position. Indeed, in the first half of the 1870s he made three attempts at reconciling his profession with his vocation. These turned out to be three failed efforts at healing what he interpreted as an existential illness.

The first happened in January 1871. Not even two years into his professorship, Nietzsche applied to the chair of philosophy at the University of Basel. His long and inauspicious letter to the president of the University, philologist Wilhelm Vischer-Bilfinger, illustrates the conflict between his profession and what he deemed to be his proper task — his "*eigentliche Aufgabe*" and "natural" calling:

> I live here in a most peculiar conflict that has exhausted and physically worn me down. Naturally I am strongly inclined to philosophically unify my reflections and to dwell undisturbed and with sustained reflection on one problem. I feel myself always thrown hither and thither, and driven off my course, by my daily variegated professional work and by the way it is disposed. This juxtaposition of Pädagogium and university I cannot in the long run tolerate, because I feel that my real task, to which I *must* necessarily *sacrifice any profession*, my *philosophical* task, is being made to suffer by it, and is even being reduced to an activity on the side.[25]

Nietzsche cherished many hopes regarding this new position. His project even included proposing his close friend and spiritual ally Erwin Rohde as successor to his chair of philology. Perhaps unsurprisingly, no aspect of this unusual project materialized. To fill the philosophy position, the University of Basel hired yet another Aristotelian, Rudolf Eucken.

Nevertheless, Nietzsche's attempt at becoming a professional philosopher is revealing. First, it shows that his initiative was an attempt to unify profession and task — in other words, to fulfill his vocation within a profession. This project thus ignored the final implications of the contradiction between scientific drive towards knowledge and passionate attraction towards the Greek world. Second, it is worth noting that Nietzsche singled out his Schopenhauerian philosophy as the cause of his application's rejection. He wrote to Rohde on 29 March 1871: "Think how much one has me, when one refers to my never withheld Schopenhauerianism!"[26] Curiously, Nietzsche said nothing of his unusual attempt to change departments and to be recognized as a scholar of a discipline that he had not specialized in. He simply concluded that to maintain the possibility for him to eventually become a professional philosopher *he must prove and legitimize his identity as one*. He announced to Rohde that his next step in this direction was his upcoming book on tragedy. Let us now turn to this second attempt.

While his first attempt sought to engage in a profession that would respect his vocation, Nietzsche's second attempt rather sought to unify profession and vocation within his philological career. He told Rohde in March 1871 that his upcoming publication was his main strategy. *The Birth of Tragedy*, Nietzsche's first book, was an effort to renovate the field of philology: in the spirit of his inaugural lecture, he guided scientific philological endeavours towards philosophy and art as curative forces, in order to develop a newly self-conscious practice of philology.[27]

The book's reception, though, reveals that Nietzsche was wrong about the impact his book would have. *The Birth of Tragedy* was indeed echoed mostly by silence. During its first year, it gave way to only two responses in the press: Rohde's celebratory review in the 26 May 1872 *Norddeutsche allgemeine Zeitung*, and young doctor of philology Ulrich von Wilamowitz-Möllendorff's two-part critical pamphlet (spring 1872 and winter 1873). In both pamphlets, Wilamowitz made "out as if Nietzsche was arguing from philological fact, or that he was at the very least arguing on the basis of philological knowledge," when in fact he was not. In *The Birth of Tragedy* Nietzsche did not defend theses on the grounds of scholarship, "but on some other level, which we might variously call rhetorical, aesthetic, or cultural grounds, with a heavy dose of imaginative invention besides."[28] Yet some classicists did recognize the usefulness of Nietzsche's intuitions. For instance, amid the criticisms that he addressed to Nietzsche, philologist Ernst Leutsch of the University of Göttingen nevertheless wrote that here was a "scholar who does not lack spirit, as several insights in the book show." But most scholars in the field deemed that with *The Birth of Tragedy* Nietzsche "was indeed risking academic notoriety."[29]

In a broader perspective, one can see that Wilamowitz was criticizing Nietzsche's philosophical stance inasmuch as he was arguing against the possibility of doing classical philology in any other way than a purely scholarly one. From the outset, Wilamowitz considered philology as a science that had a solid, critical method that yielded definite results and enabled scholars to make precise, substantial progress in an exact knowledge of the past. His second pamphlet against Nietzsche ended with these words:

> "If he [Nietzsche] now were to reply to me that he simply did not want to know anything of 'so-called world history,' nor of 'history and criticism,' that he merely wished to create a Dionysian-Apollonian work of art, a 'metaphysical consolation' ... then I revoke my critique and lower its import ... then I will gladly permit his gospel, for my weapons are unable to touch it ... but one thing I would then demand: that Mr Nietzsche keep his word and take the thyrsus and move from India to Greece and climb down from his pulpit on which he is meant to teach scientifically."[30]

Wilamowitz's conclusion was clear: as his first book — an unscientific essay written by a sloppy scholar — showed, Nietzsche was not worthy of his academic position.

Interestingly, while "the immediate response of the profession" to Nietzsche's book was silence, Nietzsche's answer was the same. The 1872–73 quarrel around *The Birth of Tragedy* was mostly between Rohde and Wilamowitz (with a stint by Richard Wagner). Indeed, Nietzsche did not answer directly to Wilamowitz. In fact, the event even prompted Nietzsche to decide to keep away from future disputes. After reading Wilamowitz's first pamphlet, he wrote to Gersdorff that he would never again get involved in a polemic.

However, his first book did have an important consequence on Nietzsche's disciplinary status: as of this publication, he was considered mostly as a philosopher (and more often than not, as a Wagnerian philosopher). A short column in the *Philosophische Monatshefte* even named Nietzsche among the philosophy professors of Basel.[31] Ironically, he was listed between two holders of the Basel chair of philosophy, one of which was the recently appointed Eucken. Nietzsche wrote on 30 April 1872 that he was most happy to be "included among the 'professors of philosophy.'"[32] This, however, shows that he still ignored the final consequences of the contradiction between profession and vocation. It is certain that this attempt at realizing his task within his profession failed because the highly specialized philological profession was not open to outside methodological, philosophical, and cultural perspectives.

Nietzsche's third attempt at reconciling profession and vocation pondered precisely on that question. While he faced two public failures early in his career, it is telling that his third attempt remained private. During the winter of 1875, Nietzsche took notes for an essay on philology entitled *We Philologists*. He never published nor even finished this project that he considered as a potential fourth (at the time) *Unfashionable Observation*.[33] In his partial draft, Nietzsche reflected upon his profession in a more personal manner than he had in his 1869 inaugural lecture. He noticed that like marriages, successful careers are extremely rare because "one *chooses* a profession when one is not yet able to do so: one does not know the different professions, one does not know oneself." He thereby identified a cause to the failure of a career: not knowing oneself can lead one to the wrong profession.[34]

While he was speaking on his own behalf, Nietzsche was also considering that most scholars do not have the right job for them: they sit in their chair because they wrongly interpreted their passion. They mistook their drive towards a particular type of knowledge (or their drive towards a particular type of life: professional, salaried, public, etc.) for their true vocation. In other words: most academics' careers reveal that they ignore (possibly in the two senses of the word) their vocation. Nietzsche was sour as to the outcome of such a personal mistake: a scholar "spends his most active years in a profession, uses all of his capacity to reflect upon it, then he becomes more experienced; but should he reach the height of his professional insight then it is usually too late to begin anything new." While writing this Nietzsche was thirty-one years old, and more than five years into a career he had been turning away almost from the start. And as previously mentioned, he was also convinced that this situation was contributing to his moral and physical illness.[35]

The Conflict between Profession and Vocation

Nietzsche's attempts at reconciling his philological profession and his philosophical vocation failed not only because of an increasing specialization of philological research and training. They also failed, on the one hand, because of the structural contradictions between passion (vocation) and science (scholarly profession), and, on the other, because of the inner tensions of a philosophical vocation. To better understand Nietzsche's position on this matter, it is useful to turn to the Lutheran tradition in which Nietzsche was raised and which infuses the concepts that he used. And to do this, we can turn to a thinker who was Nietzsche's junior by twenty years and who later proposed an exemplary definition of profession: the German sociologist Max Weber.

While speaking of the Lutheran usage that recognizes the vocational meaning of a professional activity, Weber explains that the German word *Beruf* names a particular area of work, but also a position that one holds for life.[36] This concept has both an external and an internal signification: a Beruf is a profession and at the same time a vocation or calling. As Weber stressed in his famous 1917 conference *Science as a Vocation*, the scholar's Beruf as a profession (in its external sense) follows the demands of disciplinary specialization and method. As for its internal sense, the scholar's Beruf is necessarily linked to a passion for knowledge per se. Passion and work, "both *together*," are the prerequisite for the scholar's inspiration — which Weber assimilates to an "intoxication" (*Rausch*) — and thus for a scholar's ideas.[37] Without an inspiring passion and without conscientious work guided by method, one cannot make a profession out of knowledge as science.

As work and passion, a profession has exterior and interior effects. Through profession, scholars participate in the progress of knowledge in their field, but they also make considerable progress as to the knowledge of themselves as individual persons. That is why

Weber's conference ends on his saying that science as a vocation entices the individual in such a way that "We must go about our work and meet the 'challenges of the day' — both in our human relations and our vocation."[38] Beruf is a "profession-calling": in this Lutheran-Weberian sense, a scholar's task or vocation is the scholar's profession.

Rather than following on this "existential" understanding of profession as a calling (or *Berufung*), Nietzsche dissociates Beruf and *Aufgabe* (task). He considers "profession" in its external sense as a concept that has to do only with professional work. To quote Weber again, one can say that for Nietzsche profession is the "activity under the division of labor, which is thus (normally) his source of income and in the long run the economic basis of his existence."[39] Weber adds that this meaning of Beruf characterizes Latin languages that lack a word for the German concept, which encompasses both ideas of "profession" and "calling." Nietzsche, therefore, precisely distances himself from the Lutheran concept: the "organic" unity of profession is impossible for one who recognizes one's vocation as a philosophical calling.

Based on a Greek definition of philosophy and on his reading of Schopenhauer Nietzsche proposed that philosophy cannot be an academic endeavour.[40] In other words, inner philosophical passion and the calling that it ignites cannot be exteriorized in a career, socially and economically speaking. In other words, the conflict between profession and vocation, when it concerns a philosophical vocation, is bound to be insurmountable because it is structural. Let us look now at three aspects of Nietzsche's important position.

First, it is clear that to change careers would not be a solution to the conflict. Indeed, the problem does not reside in the passion — be it understood as an "instinct" (*Trieb*), an "enigma" or a Weberian "intoxication"[41] — that prompts one to apprehend a particular field of knowledge. Rather, *the problem lies in the disciplinary constitution of this passion*. Nietzsche suggests that if it engages with the demands of a scholarly discipline, one's drive towards knowledge will unavoidably become inclined to seeking its own accomplishment above all else, as is the case with philology: "classical philology pursues only the final end of its own being, which is the fusing together of the initially hostile and violent impulses that have only forcibly been brought together. Let us talk as we will about the inaccessibility of this goal, and even designate the goal itself as an illogical pursuit — the pursuit for it is very real."[42]

This goes to say that disciplinary endeavours do not primarily function to quench the scholar's passion, but rather to define, circumscribe, limit, and preserve the academic discipline itself.

This observation precisely refers to the activities of the bustling scientific labourer whom Nietzsche criticized as dangerously resembling more and more a factory worker.[43] The scientific labourers shun their passion for the "enigma" as they turn to more practical objectives. Some of these objectives contribute to maintain the discipline (such as finding data that confirm the disciplinary constitution of knowledge), while others contribute to maintain the researcher's own status (such as building one's reputation and negotiating a salary). In fact, these practical objectives accomplish the specialization and professionalization of the discipline. One can understand Nietzsche's words in his 1875 notes accordingly: "When we observe how few philologists there actually are, except those that have taken up philology as a means of livelihood, we can easily decide for ourselves what is the matter with this impulse for antiquity, it *hardly* exists at all; for there are no disinterested philologists."[44]

Second, it appears that while a profession entails many public actions (lectures, conferences, publication of research, professional representations, social mingling, etc.), a vocation as Nietzsche understands it — that is, a philosophical vocation — rather commands some degree of private expression. Indeed, because "particularly sad facts lie in the essence of things," philosophy expresses disturbing ideas that are not for all ears to hear.[45]

In the early 1870s Nietzsche cherished the idea of a gathering of philosophical kindred spirits. He used the expression *Bildungs-Sekte* — something like a "cultural-educational sect," akin to the philosophical communities of antiquity, "a new *Greek* academy," as he wrote to his close friend Erwin Rohde.[46] Even in these dreams of private communion did Nietzsche's intellectual desires echo those of Mommsen and other academicians who felt part of a group of initiates at the Berlin Academy of Sciences. Indeed, through this multidisciplinary quasi "religious confraternity," the unity of knowledge could survive despite the increasing specialization of academic disciplines.[47] Yet Nietzsche did not think of the universities or scholarly academies as places where the philosophical spirit could flourish. He saw how the amount of administrative work and the detail of minutiae took up most of the scholar's precious stamina and time.

Third, it follows from his three failed attempts and his definition of profession that Nietzsche considered the conflict between profession and vocation to be irreconcilable. This observation became concrete reality when he completely retired from academic life in 1879. Erwin Rohde had insisted in a letter to Nietzsche that an academic career "is in all circumstances the safest and most reliable one for confronting all dangers." But Nietzsche disagreed. Because he considered that philosophy could not be a profession, he opted for a non-professionalized vocation. He abandoned his profession to lead a philosophical life and in effect became what Rohde dreaded: a "wandering doctor."[48]

Commentators do not hesitate to say that Nietzsche at this point was "liberated" by his physical illness. And Nietzsche indeed acknowledged this fact in 1888 when he wrote about his 1876–78 years: "Sickness *slowly released me*."[49] His bad health no doubt intervened in his decision to quit academia. Yet one must not conclude that this was the only or even the major reason for his retirement. Nietzsche's 1870s crisis was fundamentally philosophical: it pertained to a deeply reflected upon conflict between profession and vocation. It was Nietzsche's task, perhaps more so than his body, that led him towards a "philosophical life" independent from a profession.

Philosophical Life

Nietzsche's understanding of this conflict and his parallel project to resign his chair of philology progressed throughout the 1870s. His letters reveal that he considered the possibility of quitting academia from an early point on. In 1872 he talked of long trips away from Basel, and he wrote to Rohde on 11 April: "For the purposes of this endeavor I now define my position so that you may be my successor in *every* respect."[50] Yet Rohde did not support his friend's anti-professional stance. He constantly reminded Nietzsche that "at no price" should he abandon the position that secured the financial, intellectual, and social means "to build his life in a grand style without fear."[51] Though he did believe that in an ideal world, philosophical spirits could shut themselves off from everyday life, Rohde held academia to be "without doubt the noblest among all professional duties."[52] He invariably tried to convince Nietzsche to keep his chair: as he wrote on 14 November 1872, in their common war against the new German culture "to give up *material* chances would be the greatest folly."[53] Rohde dearly hoped that Nietzsche would abandon his "wandering doctor plans" rather than his career, and he himself in no case wished to become a literary vagabond.[54]

Clearly Nietzsche and Rohde defended two opposite visions not of the task at hand, but rather of the site from which this task could be fulfilled. Rohde wanted to pursue their cultural movement in the academic world, supported by professional titles, grants, and networks, whereas Nietzsche talked of "running away" from academia to "travel," of "abandoning" his career for new "philosophical sects," and of finding "radical truths" that would define a "philosophical life."

In fact, as a classical philologist who was not trained in philosophy, Nietzsche had a vision of philosophical life that was inspired by the philosophers that he did know well, the ones he had read either out of professional interest (the Greek philosophers of the fifth century BC and Hellenistic period) or sheer luck (Schopenhauer and Emerson). Nietzsche found a work by Schopenhauer in a second-hand bookshop in 1865. He thereafter read Schopenhauer every year between 1865 and 1878.[55] His 15 December 1870 letter to Rohde shows how important Schopenhauer's 1851 essay *On Academic Philosophy* was for him: "in the long run, I also realize what Schopenhauer's doctrine of university wisdom is all about. A completely radical institution for *truth* is not *possible* here."[56]

Schopenhauer believed that "if profit is being derived from it, intention at once gains an ascendancy over insight and from self-styled philosophers we get mere parasites of philosophy." According to him, the demands of a profession paralyze the mind in such a way that ideas simply cannot bloom: "hardly anything is so obstructive to the actual attainment of a thorough or very deep insight and thus of true wisdom, as the constant obligation to appear wise, the showing off of so-called knowledge in the presence of pupils eager to learn and the readiness to answer every conceivable question." Schopenhauer indeed stressed that philosophy as a profession cannot be truly independent because it must answer to the authority that supports it: "a government will not pay people to contradict directly, or even only indirectly, what it has had promulgated from all the pulpits by thousands of its appointed priests or religious teachers, for in so far as such a proceeding were effective, it would inevitably render ineffective the former organization."[57]

Schelling had already raised this issue in his lectures on academic studies: "The usual view of the universities is that they should produce servants of the state, perfect instruments for its purposes." And Wolf, the founder of classical philology, held the same conclusion about universities in 1787: "the state has little use for the mere humanist."[58] But Schopenhauer further suggested that philosophy simply cannot exist if a superior instance imposes a dogma upon it, whether it be the Christian religion, Hegelianism, the omnipotence of the Prussian state, or the disciplinary definition of knowledge. Schopenhauer stressed that "the atmosphere of freedom is indispensable to truth,"[59] and accordingly he urged that philosophy should stop being a profession. Evidently, Nietzsche heard him.

Nietzsche was a lifelong follower of Schopenhauer at least on this issue. He noticed that scholarly work unfortunately does not serve the goal of defining one's own existence: "Just take a look at the activities with which a scientific person spends and thus kills his life: what does the Greek view of particles have to do with the meaning of life?" Because a philosopher "is meant to seek the truth for himself and not so as to write books," Nietzsche repeatedly returned to one of the first philosophical principles: "Know thyself."[60]

This phrase naturally calls to mind Ancient philosophy. It goes without saying that Nietzsche as a philologist knew the Greeks very well. He gave lectures on Plato's dialogues, Aristotle's metaphysics and rhetoric, Diogenes Laërtius, Democritus, and the Pre-Socratics. In his lectures Nietzsche reiterated Socrates' definition of the origins of philosophy: he stated that philosophical insights originate from "astonishment at everything that lies before one."[61] In fact, it is this fundamental wonder, this "enigma" of the unknown that ignites passion and determines the choice of a career.

In philosophy this impulse should take a practical form: Nietzsche believed that philosophers must give an example by their life more than by their writings: "I attach importance to a philosopher only to the extent that he is capable of setting an example ... the philosopher must supply this example in his visible life, and not merely in his books; that is, it must be presented in the way the philosophers of Greece taught, through facial expressions, demeanor, clothing, food, and custom, more than through what they said, let alone what they wrote."[62] He further believed that "in a refuted system, the only thing of interest is the personal element," that is, the efforts towards philosophizing.[63]

And indeed, for Nietzsche philosophy is better understood as a verb than as a noun. This reflexive activity encompasses the individual's entire existence, so much so that it defines a particular type of life — a philosophical life. As Nietzsche stressed, "The only possible criticism of any philosophy, and the only one that proves anything, is trying to see if one can live by this philosophy, and this has never been taught at any university."[64] That is to say that the most important philosophical attitude does not take place within academia.

As early as March 1871, Nietzsche wrote to Rohde: "I am gradually habituating myself to being a philosopher, and already I believe in myself."[65] As a philosopher he wished to realize what he called a type, a "heretofore undiscovered, supreme *possibility of the philosophical life*."[66] This life must be guided by a precept that defines philosophy since Socrates: "At the very beginning of your journey to that goal the God of Delphi will call out to you his imperative, 'Know thyself.' It is a difficult imperative."[67] The Delphic precept invites a person to return to the first site of philosophical investigation, because the knowledge of oneself opens onto a knowledge of the world. Nietzsche also tied his reflection to Heraclitus' motto: "I sought and consulted myself."[68] Because he followed the Delphic precept, Heraclitus showed that one must first turn towards oneself in order to learn what it means to be a human being. And as we have seen, Nietzsche believed that it was precisely this knowledge, this first stage of philosophical investigation that philologists lack. As most scholars in all fields, they chose their career out of a lack of self-knowledge. Philologists failed to notice, as Dale Wilkerson rightly points out, that "All examinations of the past are explorations of oneself."[69]

Nietzsche did not stay a rising or even a fixed star of classical philology for long. With his early retirement from academia, he found a wandering star status: he lived the philosophical life of a "literary vagabond" that his former kindred spirit, Erwin Rohde, dreaded. Perhaps "The loss was philology's," as some scholars today consider that Nietzsche must be remembered "as one of the more promising and least realized classicists of all time."[70]

Nietzsche was physically ill in the 1870s, but his decision to resign from his academic chair was essentially philosophical. It stemmed from his having identified the cause of his mental and physical illnesses as an irreconcilable existential conflict between his profession and his natural calling to philosophy — a conflict that he felt since starting his career. Turning away from academia and favouring a non-professional philosophical activity was a therapeutic process: the only possibility of healing was to quit the profession for the vocation. Nietzsche's understanding of both conflict and therapy rested upon his "material" definition of profession and his Schopenhauerian and Delphic conception of a philosophical calling and life.

Nietzsche's decision to leave academia was no doubt radical. In fact, it appears unique when one considers that the reflections behind it — regarding the limits of the disciplinary constitution of knowledge, the problems facing specialization in the humanities and social sciences, the structural paradoxes of knowledge-oriented professions, and the limits to philosophy as a profession — were actually shared by many nineteenth-century scholars. Schelling,

Schopenhauer, or Mommsen, though, did not turn away from their university chairs or their prestigious positions at the Berlin Academy.[71]

On this backdrop, the issues raised by Nietzsche resound even more clearly. Can science be reconciled with passion within a knowledge-oriented profession, in a more Weberian than Nietzschean sense? Can one practice philosophy in its existential definition from within academia? And perhaps more pressingly, does the disciplinary definition of knowledge impose limits to a scholar's "inspiring passion"?[72] Indeed, these are fundamental and pressing interrogations in an academic age dominated by the obligation for scholarly research to fit into predefined disciplinary categories asking for quantifiable and operational data, and this in all fields of inquiry — even philosophy.

A contextual appraisal of Nietzsche's ideas thus enables one to grasp his true originality. It does not lie in his young age when he started his professorship, nor in his defense of artistic vocation in classical philology, nor in his longing for a global philosophical perspective to historical studies.[73] Nietzsche's originality lies in the radical decision in favour of a philosophical life, following his assessment of the crisis in philological studies. Nietzsche's originality was rooted in issues concerning life, voice, and style. He radically moved away from academic life and writing — but not without trying his hand at another style: cultural criticism.

Chapter 2

Against Opera

A WAR ON ENTERTAINMENT

The human being, believe me, is only an instrument,
our fibers echo the strings of the instruments.
Chabanon[1]

While he was pondering the limits of scholarly life and seeking to pursue his philosophical vocation within academia, Friedrich Nietzsche was immersed in music. *The Birth of Tragedy*, his first book, published some two and half years after he started his professorship, was a work on Greek tragedy that mixed references to ancient tragedians (Aeschylus, Euripides) and philosophers (Socrates, Schopenhauer) with praises for German music (most notably Beethoven) and critiques of lyrical innovations from the Renaissance.

The Birth of Tragedy also voiced Nietzsche's rejection of scholarly life. As we saw in the previous chapter, the book took part in many debates in an unscholarly fashion: no notes or references to scholarship, a dash of what we today call interdisciplinarity, and a certain disregard for historical chronology make for a style that was as surprising then as it may be difficult now. In just one section, for instance, Nietzsche praises Beethoven and lambasts Italian Renaissance composers while also stating that his nineteenth-century culture was Alexandrian, Socratic, optimistic, and decadent. In fact, the core of Nietzsche's first book critiques a form of culture that values the pursuit of knowledge above all else. This critique stresses that there are models for a culture other than that which Germany was then furiously pursuing: extremely specialized higher education, professionalized research, technical education in the service of industry, and, at the end of the day, art as entertainment for exhausted workers.

Nietzsche's first work, in short, makes a plea for an artistic culture. Nietzsche makes his point by defending a position in aesthetics that was at odds with most musical trends in his time, but in unison with the views of a pariah of the musical establishment, the Bavarian court, and German bourgeois life in general: Richard Wagner, composer, and cultural activist in exile.

From the moment Nietzsche first met Wagner, in 1868, the composer made major or minor appearances in the philosopher's endeavours until the 1876 publication of the fourth *Unfashionable Observation*. In fact, in the first half of the 1870s arguably all of Nietzsche's writing and projects were engaged with Wagnerian culture, as I will discuss at length in chapter 5.

But beyond — or rather, before — his early infatuation with (and later disapproval of) Wagner, Nietzsche was a musician himself. He excelled at piano, and it seems he was gifted above all for interpretation. His composition skills paled in comparison to his improvisation ones: scholars tend to note that his music "suffered from formal imperfections." Perhaps his imagination "exceeded his compositional abilities," as one commentator generously puts it. But it was clear to those who were close to him that he was "a great improviser."[2] In truth, Nietzsche was always immersed in interpretation, whether he was perusing texts or deciphering scores.

While music was an integral part of his life, it is perhaps especially as a philosopher that Nietzsche embraced music. As the essayist Georges Liébert remarks, "there is no work by Nietzsche in which music is not more or less present."[3] Surprisingly, despite his training as a philologist Nietzsche made few pronouncements on theories of music from the Greek antiquity, including those of Plato and Aristotle. In the early 1870s, Nietzsche's work on music followed three paths: thoughts on the Greek music drama, on Schopenhauer's philosophy of music in his magnum opus *The World as Will and as Representation*, and on Wagner's essays, operas, and artistic endeavours.

These three paths connect in *The Birth of Tragedy*. Written in 1871, the book relied on and expanded talks that Nietzsche had presented at the University of Basel the year before: *The Greek Music*

Drama, *Socrates and Tragedy*, and *The Dionysian Worldview*.[4] It also incorporated material from his lectures,[5] thoughts from his reading of Schopenhauer, and reflections — often quite lyrical — on Wagner's music.

In these ways, music, in Nietzsche's first book, was at the forefront of cultural criticism. It was in fact the ground onto which a war was to be waged, the war on Germany's model for culture. On this battlefield, music was everywhere: it was in the target, the weapons, the warriors, and even the objectives. Under the guise of a book "on tragedy," Nietzsche in fact published a work of cultural criticism that took part in timely debates surrounding a most fashionable form of musical art: opera.

One of the last sections of *The Birth of Tragedy*, §19, calls for nothing short of the destruction of opera: "He who would destroy the opera must take up the struggle against Alexandrian cheerfulness, which expresses itself so naïvely in opera concerning its favorite idea."[6] By singling out opera in this way and encouraging an outright war against it, Nietzsche in fact participated in disputes that had been shaking the world of music since the beginning of the nineteenth century: composers, conductors, and music theorists debated whether music should serve words and texts or the opposite, whether it was necessarily national or could be universal, whether it imitated the natural world or opened a door onto other realms and experiences.

Not only do such debates echo in *The Birth of Tragedy*, Nietzsche also firmly states his own position and arguments. These controversies and their stakes still ring loud provided one reads *The Birth of Tragedy* contextually — and perhaps more specifically its §19. Nietzsche's attack on opera emerges on the backdrop of different influences: Wagnerianism, of course, but also larger disputes in music aesthetics through which Nietzsche expresses his opinion on the legacy of Renaissance music, the specificity of music in the face of the other arts, and the active role of the listener.

When we delineate this context, Nietzsche's specificity emerges in his defense of participatory aesthetics. And on that terrain, he belatedly found unexpected allies.

Against Alexandrian Culture

Before we turn to Nietzsche's war on opera, it will be useful to consider his thoughts on culture. Indeed, his critique of both Renaissance and modern lyrical music is largely a cultural critique. This is because opera, for Nietzsche, is more than a musical genre: it is a shorthand or a symbol for the form of culture that he was combatting as an educator, writer, Wagnerian, and self-proclaimed philosopher. As an art form, opera is a cultural form: it is the artistic symptom of the weakness affecting Germany and Western culture generally.

The Birth of Tragedy asserts that every art form is the manifestation of a certain "form of existence."[7] To criticize opera is therefore to criticize the form of existence that corresponds to it. The notion of "forms of existence" and the idea that these embody "impulses" are two early insights that may well have had the most lasting effect on Nietzsche's philosophy. By "form of existence" is meant a way to live one's life that is valued, encouraged, and thereby culturally transmitted through education, institutions, practices, and various subtle or explicit prompts and rewards. In these ways, a culture fosters certain "forms of existence" more than others — that is, certain ways of leading one's life, such as the scholarly. These recurring forms are *types* — that is, equilibriums of inner impulses, or drives.[8]

Nietzsche extensively worked with the notion of drive in the 1880s, but he already used it in his 1870s works. From the outset, *The Birth of Tragedy* describes the phenomena of artistic creation by looking at two impulses. Indeed, the ancient Greek gods Apollo and Dionysus are names for two different involuntary thrusts, impelling, internal urges that push towards their exteriorization. The gods are thus metaphors for different drives leading to different forms of artistic creation. There can be a more Apollonian form of existence, creation, and action, and a more Dionysian one. Nietzsche described ancient Greek tragedy as a healthy and productive marriage or "fraternal union" of Apollonian and Dionysian drives.[9]

As a bodily event, a drive precedes the conscious acts for which we as individual persons usually prize ourselves. Drives are prior to one's rational decisions or to the internal discourse that serves to justify these decisions. Drives "do not have moral character": they are preconscious, bodily impulses, and as such they manifest themselves whether we like it or not — even whether we notice them or not.[10] As Nietzsche writes in *Beyond Good and Evil*, "every drive is tyrannical," all drives have competing demands and seek to impose themselves, thereby achieving a hierarchical balance.[11] In that sense, Nietzsche interprets them as a synonym and sign (or symptom) of energy and vitality.

A type, then, is an embodied set of values expressing impulses, or drives, whose hierarchically organized equilibrium forms a way of life that is culturally valued and transmitted. Different cultures value, and strive to inculcate, different types. A type can be temporary because it is alterable, susceptible as it is to exterior influence — that is, to a reinforcement or weakening (through education, institutions, etc.) of the drives that a culture values or depreciates.[12]

Nietzsche thus studies culture by looking at the forms of existence that it values above all else: his is a typology of culture as drive-analysis. As such, his study of culture is not historical in the chronological sense. As drive-equilibrium or embodiment of values, a similar type may surface at different times in history and in contexts that may seem quite different on a technological or social level. This explains why Nietzsche's war on opera makes constant leaps from ancient Greece (time and place of Socratic and Hellenistic culture) to the Italian Renaissance (birthplace of opera) to nineteenth-century Germany (terrain of aesthetic debates on the nature of music).

To better criticize opera, then, Nietzsche turns to the form of existence that the culture that produced opera valorized. He shows the form of existence corresponding to opera to be the "theoretical type": that of the person who values knowledge above all else and who thus embodies a serene optimism as to knowledge's benefits.

In the first *Unfashionable Observation*, as the next chapter will discuss, Nietzsche casts the theoretical type in the guise of the scholar, which he lambasts. But in *The Birth of Tragedy* the theoretical type is impersonated by the recurring figure of Socrates, the philosopher *par excellence*. In the first sentence to §19 Nietzsche connects opera to what he identifies as "Socratic culture": "We cannot indicate the innermost modern content of this Socratic culture more distinctly than by calling it *the culture of the opera*." He goes on to state, more precisely, that "Opera is the birth of the theoretical man, the critical layman, not of the artist."[13]

While at first glance one could take this coupling of Socrates and opera as a Nietzschean idiosyncrasy, it is in fact a Wagnerian commonplace. Richard Wagner believed opera to be a symptom of an artistic decadence whose roots were the decline of Greek tragedy and the concomitant expansion and soon-to-be reign of abstract, theoretical thought. Wagner wrote that "The twenty centuries that have elapsed since the decline of Greek tragedy to the present day belong to philosophy, and not to art."[14] In other words, opera and rational thought go hand in hand. In his 1849 essay *Art and Revolution* Wagner announced that an art form inspired by Greek art was finally emerging despite two millennia of rationalist philosophy. The new, modern (Wagnerian) art form, which appealed to other faculties than the rational, was to be an antidote to modern decadence.

Because that was also the basso continuo of Nietzsche's critique in *The Birth of Tragedy*, the book played a familiar tune to Wagner devotees (and critics, for that matter). A Wagner enthusiast who read in the composer's 1851 essay *Opera and Drama*, for instance, that "no pact is possible with modern society" could find in Nietzsche's first book the arguments supporting Wagner's point. This clear and distinct dialogue between Nietzsche and Wagner was read as an alliance. The art critic Bruno Meyer wrote in the November 1873 issue of the monthly literary magazine *Deutsche Warte* that Nietzsche's first book was the "Wagnerians' new gospel."[15]

Meyer was right. Twenty years apart, Wagner's *Opera and Drama* and Nietzsche's *Birth of Tragedy* described their time in identical terms: they believed they were living in a selfish, utilitarian *Unkultur*, a "non-culture" that was guided by a *Geldtendenz*, a selfish tendency to seek gains that benefit but a few.[16]

On the one hand, they believed this culture was led by a fierce desire and need for knowledge. This desire has two symbols: the philosopher Socrates and the ancient city of Alexandria. The quest for knowledge is symbolized in philosophy's pronouncement of love for truth: this is, as Nietzsche puts it, "the knowledge-craving Socratism."[17] But it is also encapsulated in what he calls "Alexandrian culture." With its library, many scholars, and museums, Alexandria, capital of the Hellenistic world, is a symbol for a culture that favours a theoretical impulse, one that derives pleasure from knowledge. This culture "proposes as its ideal the theoretical man equipped with the greatest forces of knowledge, and laboring in the service of science, whose archetype and progenitor is Socrates."[18] The Alexandrian is thus at home in the modern world of universities and science academies. (This goes to show how Nietzsche's study of culture is not "historical." The Alexandrian type is not limited to ancient Hellenistic culture: it also haunts the Berlin university library.)

On the other hand, Wagner and Nietzsche saw that this quest for knowledge was engaged upon for economic reasons. Indeed, knowledge is profitable: "As much knowledge and education as possible — from there as much production and demand as possible — consequently as much happiness as possible: — thus and thereabouts runs the formula. Here we have utility as the goal and purpose of education, still more exactly acquisition: the highest possible winning of great amounts of money."[19] In this equation, the theoretical drive and the desire for happiness are subservient to the desire to reap financial gain from whatever may be produced. Greed dominates the contest of drives. It is the cunning tyrant in this new hierarchy.

However, as Nietzsche seeks to show in all his 1870s works, a frantic race towards knowledge can lead to quite the opposite of culture. Indeed, it can lead to barbarism, that is, to a simple disregard or even contempt for goals other than knowledge, action, or profit — such as experiment, contemplation, or creation. This risk appeared ever greater in the context of rapid industrialization and academic modernization that Germany was experiencing in the second half of the nineteenth century, as we saw in the previous chapter. Nietzsche therefore deemed it urgent to reveal the desires for knowledge and profit wherever they lurked, sometimes working under the guise of other desires, needs, or objectives.

One needed to combat these tendencies so that they would not remain hegemonic. The worry that underlies Nietzsche's stance in *The Birth of Tragedy* is that modern culture only favours forms of art capable of reaping profit through mere entertainment. This is where his will to "destroy the opera" comes in — and in this manner Nietzsche is once more an ally of Wagner. In *Art and Revolution*, the composer turned essayist wrote that the "true nature" of opera was in fact "industry; its moral purpose, the acquisition of money; its aesthetic pretext, the entertainment of the bored."[20] Modern opera was a lucrative entertainment industry: it needed to be exposed as such, and fiercely combatted, as I will explain in more detail in chapter 5.

Nietzsche's position towards opera therefore echoes Wagner's socialism from the late 1840s, which linked a rejection of the domination of greed with a concern for the happiness and cultural elevation of the German people.[21] At the same time Nietzsche adopted the tone and themes of 1870s *Kulturkritik*: a critique of journalism and the media industry and a rejection of mass culture and specialized, technical education.

Nietzsche was a man of his time. And perhaps nothing shows this best as his position on music aesthetics.

Against Renaissance Representative Music

Since the end of the eighteenth century, composers and theorists alike had been striving to establish the autonomy of music to better defend its pre-eminence in the face of the visual arts. Some did not believe music to be but one among other forms of representative art, while others believed lyrical music needed to serve the text being sung. Some parties in these debates referred to Plato's oratorical music aesthetic (taken up in the Italian Renaissance) and some to the Aristotelian imitative aesthetic (taken up during the Enlightenment), while others in Nietzsche's time and culture devised a new, formal music aesthetic.

In §19 of *The Birth of Tragedy* Nietzsche summoned the terms of these quarrels only to better reject them all. Indeed, by hoping to "destroy opera" he was in effect arguing against almost all parties. His place, rather, was alongside Schopenhauer and Wagner. But let us first go back a century to better understand the stakes and debates — and Nietzsche's position.

In the middle of the eighteenth century the consensus in aesthetics was that music, much like all fine arts, served imitation. Swiss writer Jean-Jacques Rousseau's *Dictionnaire de musique* (written between 1749 and 1767) is emblematic. Rousseau's entry on "Imitation" specifies that "Dramatic and theatrical music concurs to imitation, as well as poetry or painting; 'tis to this principle that all the fine arts are connected." But as music can neither tell nor paint, its imitative function is to excite the passions: "the art of the musician consists in substituting, in the place of the insensible image of the object, that of the movements which its presence excites in the heart of the contemplator."[22]

From rationalist philosopher René Descartes to Rousseau and the composer and theoretician Jean-Philippe Rameau, the French tradition defined music as the expressive art par excellence. This tradition continued well into the nineteenth century when opera remained associated with the expression of pathos. Nietzsche, then, had much to summon if he was to argue against the idea that music's function is to express individual passions through voice and arouse "pathological-moral" emotions within listeners.[23] For Nietzsche, rejecting imitative aesthetics implied showing how it was linked with discursive aesthetics. It thus implied critiquing its model: Plato.

In book III of the *Republic*, Plato states that music is composed of words, harmony, and rhythm. He names the parts of music precisely in that order: words come first. When discussing the musical education of the guardians of the republic, Plato announces that "the harmonic mode and the rhythm must follow the speech," "and not speech them."[24] This Greek primacy of word over harmony was taken up by the composers who invented a new style in Renaissance Italy: the *stile rappresentativo*. This "representative style" which gave much space to recitatives — long semi-spoken, semi-sung passages in which characters express their emotions — was the ancestor of operatic music. It is against this trend that Nietzsche rages in *The Birth of Tragedy*.

Nietzsche judges recitative music as superficial and incapable of recollection, a "half-musical mode of speech." It is striking that even while he discusses a point that goes back three hundred years in music history, he uses the vocabulary of his time's *Kulturkritik* when he lambasts the singers' "vanity" and the composers' yearning for entertainment. Nietzsche was a child of his time as a critic — but also as a musicologist. Indeed, when he opposes the music created for poetry in Renaissance Florentine circles to the "vaulted structure of Palestrina's harmonies" and their "ineffably sublime and sacred music," he builds upon a polarity that was common in his time.[25] It is precisely in the opposition between Palestrina and madrigals — or, in other words, between structural harmonies and poetic pathos — that Renaissance music was represented during the nineteenth century. The terms of opposition that Nietzsche uses, therefore, are typical of the historiography of Renaissance music — a historiography that was first (and, it seems, rather permanently) established in the nineteenth century.[26]

But let us return to the stile rappresentativo. In sixteenth-century Italy, while Palestrina and others perfected counterpoint and polyphony, a new "representative" music proposed madrigals and recitatives. That was the target of Nietzsche's critique. He condemns the semi-musical elocution typical of recitatives, whose evolution (which gave shape to the first operas at the turn of the seventeenth century) Nietzsche understands "only by a co-operating, *extra-artistic tendency* in the essence of the recitative." This non-artistic tendency lies in the importance that it gives to *text*: music thereby appeals to "thoroughly unmusical hearers."[27]

That claim, in fact, was explicitly made by Italian madrigalists — with pride and authority. One of the most active members of the Florentine scene, Giulio Caccini (1551–1618), published his *Nuove Musiche*, or *New Music*, in 1601. The scores were preceded by a short treatise, in which Caccini invoked Plato:

> these most knowledgeable gentlemen kept encouraging me, and with the most lucid reasoning convinced me, not to esteem that sort of music which, preventing any clear understanding of the words, shatters both their form and content, now lengthening and now shortening syllables to accommodate the counterpoint (a laceration of the poetry!), but rather to conform to that manner so lauded by Plato and other philosophers (who declared that music is naught but speech, with rhythm and tone coming after; not vice versa) with the

> aim that it enter into the minds of men and have those wonderful effects admired by the great writers. But this has not been possible because of the counterpoint of modern music ... wherein not a single word has been understood for the multitude of passaggi on both short and long syllables.[28]

This excerpt shows how Caccini represents everything that Nietzsche criticizes in representative music: he rationally justifies his practice of recitative composition; quotes Plato; criticizes counterpoint; and affirms that music must act on the mind and speak its language. In short, music is thus subordinated to words in both its composition and reception.

Rousseau's *Dictionnaire* shows that this practice of recitative composition had a lasting effect. He makes the following remarks in his entry on "Recitative": "The Greeks could sing in speaking; but amongst us we must either sing or speak ... 'Tis this very distinction which has rendered the recitative necessary for us. The music predominates too much in our arias; the poetry is almost forgotten ... An opera which would be only a collection of airs, would tire almost as much as a whole single air of the same length. We must divide and separate the airs by words."[29] A purely musical creation would bore the mind, according to Rousseau, because sounds, intervals, melodies, and harmonies alone cannot create an effect in the listener's soul. According to imitative aesthetics, these purely musical means need to be supported — more: they need to be led — by words and the message conveyed through them.

Nietzsche addresses several criticisms to this oratorical style. On the one hand, he believes that the representative and oratorial forms were aimed at an audience that was not musically literate. By putting so much emphasis on language, these compositions made for a confused artistic genre, "an entirely superficial mosaic conglutination" of dramatic, textual, and purely musical elements.[30] The objective of representativeness needed to be kept out of music aesthetics. That is why he rejected the three main types of imitation: descriptive, expressive, and oratorical, which respectively correspond to the imitation of phenomena, emotions, and words.

However, in his will to detach music aesthetics from these objects of representation Nietzsche, yet again, was a man of his time, as a look at the debates in music aesthetics in his time will show.

Against Imitation: German Music Theory in Nietzsche's Century

Musicological debates in the nineteenth century were kindled by a variety of factors, including cultural transfers by expatriate composers, the differently perceived musicality of European languages, the development of philosophical aesthetics in Germany, the all-encompassing effect of Beethoven's music and persona, and instrumental music's emancipation from text. It was in this rich context that theories on "absolute" or "pure" music were developed in Germany. With *The Birth of Tragedy from the Spirit of Music* — to quote the complete title of the book's first edition — Nietzsche explicitly subscribed to one current in these discussions on the autonomy of music while he criticized the other.

Let us first look at his critique. Nietzsche rejected the thesis of the Austrian theorist Eduard Hanslick (1825–1904). Hanslick had published a treatise entitled *On the Musically Beautiful*, in 1854, which became immensely popular. (It went through ten printings during the author's lifetime.)[31] Hanslick argues that feeling is neither the content nor the goal of music: he instead defines music as form. Since "the content of music is *sonically moved forms*," music must be considered in its purity by separating it from drama and words.[32]

In the penultimate paragraph of *The Birth of Tragedy*'s section 19, Nietzsche makes four critical references to Hanslick's thesis. (He does not explicitly name him, but he mimics Hanslick's vocabulary: most notably, the words "*forms*" and "arabesques.") He deplores that Hanslick assesses music in reference to two criteria typical of the representative arts: beauty and pleasure. Hanslick seeks to define music in its purity, but in fact he retains the original presuppositions "of the Socratic world view" when he asserts that a rational activity directs creation towards the pleasure that may be derived from contemplating beautiful forms. Because he continuously refers to beauty and pleasure, Hanslick is unable to think of music in non-representational terms. He cannot explain the autonomy of music, and does not grasp what the evolution of German music from Bach to Beethoven to Wagner means. In Nietzsche's words, Hanslick does not see "*the gradual awakening of the Dionysian spirit* in our modern world!"[33]

Within these debates on the autonomy of music, Nietzsche relates to the position of philosopher Arthur Schopenhauer. In the last section of *The World as Will and as Representation*, book III, Schopenhauer stresses from the outset that music "stands completely apart from all [other arts]. What we recognize in it is not an imitation or repetition of some Idea of the essence of the world."[34] Schopenhauer firmly exits the realm of imitative aesthetics by giving preeminence to music as the "universal language," which "never expresses appearance but only the inner essence, the in-itself of all appearance, the will itself." In short, music is "the expression of the world," not its representation.[35]

While the impact of Schopenhauer's thesis on Wagner and Nietzsche is well known, it should be noted that Schopenhauer himself was metabolizing theses that circulated in his time.[36] When he strives to demonstrate the autonomy of music as compared to the other arts, Schopenhauer echoes the Romantic movement. Take the composer E.T.A. Hoffmann, for instance: in an 1810 article on Beethoven's Fifth Symphony, Hoffmann asserted that music was an autonomous genre: it "opens up to man an unknown realm totally foreign to the sensitive world that surrounds him, and where he strips himself of all the feelings that can be named in order to plunge into the unspeakable."[37] Another filiation, however, deserves attention. It is less well-known that Schopenhauer had a precursor in French Enlightenment in the person of composer and theorist Michel-Paul-Guy de Chabanon (1730–1792).

In a 1779 treatise entitled *Observations sur la musique et principalement sur la métaphysique de l'art* (*Observations on Music, and especially on the Metaphysics of Art*) Chabanon stressed that music speaks to the ear, not the mind.[38] He thereby rejected the aesthetics of imitation and asserted that music, the art of sound, had intrinsic meaning. Would Schopenhauer, however, have read this French treatise? Perhaps not — but he may well have known its German counterpart.

In 1781, the Leipzig composer and conductor Johann Adam Hiller (1728–1804) translated Chabanon's treatise into German. In fact, the book was published under Hiller's own name and circulated in German countries under its Germanized title: *Über die Musik und deren Wirkungen*.[39] In its pages Chabanon (through Hiller's voice) defends positions that are later found in Hoffmann, Schopenhauer, and Nietzsche, most notably a critique of the reign of fine arts in music aesthetics.

Chabanon insisted on the physical effect of music and its embodied experience. As musicologist Ghyslaine Guertin notes, his thesis was that music is a universal language: it "makes sense in itself thanks to the intrinsic elements that constitute it ... This discourse is perfectly autonomous and does not require any other language ... to be translated or understood." This is so because music does not solicit the mind: it acts on the body and makes "an impression as prompt and communicative as an electric shock."[40]

In short, Chabanon believed music is felt more than it is reasoned. His thesis had important consequences. First, it implied that the language of music was not that of a nation. Musical language is mixed and fluid, it is cosmopolitan: "it is one for all the peoples of the earth." Accordingly, Chabanon rejected Rousseau's position: he judged recitatives to be "heavy and boring," "harmful to music's effects."[41] Finally, he stated a position that brings us closer still to Nietzsche. As Guertin asserts: "The need to look for a precise meaning to sounds is convenient for listeners who do not have the necessary training to refer to the object itself" — that is to say, to pure music in its embodied immediacy.[42]

Schopenhauer could certainly have found much to ponder in Chabanon's musicology. In fact, did he perhaps encounter Chabanon's ideas via Hiller's 1781 treatise? A filiation between Chabanon and German Romanticism, and moreover between Chabanon/Hiller and Schopenhauer, and then on to Wagner and Nietzsche is likely.[43] Whether these questions may one day be resolved or not, they nevertheless show how Nietzsche's 1872 critique of imitation took part in lively debates on the autonomy of music, its pre-eminence, and its relationship to language. In fact, it seems that everyone's goal was to break with classical aesthetics.

For Active Listeners

This contextualization of Nietzsche's call for the destruction of opera in *The Birth of Tragedy* opens many paths for reflection. The possible filiation between Chabanon/Hiller and Schopenhauer raises the issue of cultural transfers. It is generally accepted that the Romantic music aesthetic "of the unsayable, the ineffable, the inexpressible" emerged in Germany.[44] Despite their disagreements on some points, composers and theorists such as Hoffmann, Schopenhauer, Hanslick, and also Nietzsche are seen as participants to this diverse movement. But the case of Hiller shows that some aspects of German Romanticism find their roots in French Enlightenment. Hence the development of ideas was less national than we may be led to think. (That observation, in turn, would surely have pleased the supranationalism of Chabanon, who was Creole, and Nietzsche, who was an expatriate.)[45]

The contextualization of Nietzsche's call to arms also sheds light on his music aesthetics. Perhaps its most striking element is his rejection of beauty. According to Nietzsche one cannot "demand of music an effect similar to that produced by works of plastic art, namely, the arousing of *delight in beautiful forms*."[46] Taking pleasure in beautiful forms precisely summarizes Hanslick's position, which Nietzsche associates with "esthetic Socratism." In *Republic* III, Socrates states that "Surely musical matters should end in love matters that concern the fair."[47] Long before Hanslick's 1854 treatise *On the Musically Beautiful*, Euripides was, according to Nietzsche, the first artist in that realm whose "supreme law reads roughly as follows, 'To be beautiful everything must be intelligible,' as counterpart to the Socratic dictum, 'Knowledge is virtue.'"[48] Nietzsche thus rejects the equation between beauty, pleasure, and intelligibility: music does not speak to the mind's rational faculty. (Let us recall that Wagner praised Beethoven because he believed "there had never been an artist who thought less about his art than Beethoven").[49] But to reject the criterion of beauty also implies to reject the activity traditionally recognized as that of the receiver of a work of art, namely contemplation of beauty. For as Schopenhauer writes, "When we call something *beautiful*, we are expressing the fact that it is the object of our aesthetic contemplation."[50]

Hence, two very precise elements of Nietzsche's music aesthetics emerge from this contextualization: music is not for the mind, and the stance of the hearer is not one of passivity. Indeed, Nietzsche understands the reception of a work of art in terms not of contemplation but participation. Through art one can grasp one's "oneness with the inmost ground of the world."[51] Nietzsche thus follows in the path of Schopenhauer's description of art's "effect." The reception of a work of art leads to a specific state: rapture. It is "a state of ... absorption in intuition, losing oneself in the object, forgetting all individuality, abolishing the mode of cognition that follows the principle of sufficient reason."[52]

In *The Birth of Tragedy* Nietzsche described Dionysian ecstasy at lengths. And many years later, in an 1888 notebook he wrote that "the effect of the works of art is to cause *the state in which one creates art, intoxication*."[53] Insisting on rapture as he does, Nietzsche leaves two classic notions behind. For one, he blurs the lines that are traditionally maintained between creation and reception. Indeed, the last quote could not be clearer: the effect of art is to foster a creative state. Through art, then, the spectator experiences the work as an artist does. For two, Nietzsche correlatively abandons the contemplative, passive stance traditionally reserved to the receptor of a work of art. While music aesthetics have been dominated by criteria imported from visual arts (the listener is often thought of as a viewer), the rapture and ecstasy that Nietzsche describes are far removed from the traditional definition of reception.

In short, Nietzsche proposes that musical works must arouse "the experiences of the truly aesthetic listener." Reception, in other words, is an active process: the true listener is one who participates in the aesthetic process and therethrough embodies the powerful "art impulses" "which burst forth from nature herself," much as the composer did.[54] The human person — whether a composer or a listener — is "the intermediary" through which natural artistic impulses are discharged and expressed. The human being, then, is an artist in the same sense as nature is an artist. For Nietzsche, that is the only meaning that a reference to imitation may have in music aesthetics: "With reference to these immediate art-states of nature, every artist is an 'imitator'" of natural impulses.[55]

The music aesthetics which Nietzsche delineates could best be deemed "participative." One of its consequences is a disinterest in judgement. During an aesthetic experience thus understood, judgment is suspended precisely because the artist (whether the musician performing or the listener receiving the work) entirely participates in the work. The value of a work rests in its aesthetic effect and not in its respecting certain forms of composition or feats of execution, not in its beauty or imitative capacity.

On this terrain, Nietzsche found allies after his time, in the twentieth century. Perhaps the most famous one is the Canadian pianist Glenn Gould. Gould exposed his position on aesthetics in the many essays that he wrote for music magazines. He believed that participating in a work of art prohibits one from judging the qualities of that work. He stated, for example, that he could not make an aesthetic judgment about Sibelius's Fifth Symphony when he heard it conducted by Herbert von Karajan: "Although I was aware of being witness to an intensely moving experience, I had no idea as to whether it was or was not a 'good' performance. My aesthetic judgments were simply placed in cold storage — which is where I should like them to remain, at least when assessing the works of others."[56] Gould asserted that the artist (whether a creator or a listener) is not in a position of distance towards the work of art. Yet it is only distance and hindsight that allow for a critical view of a work.[57] When receiving a work one is rather in a state of ecstasy, of "internal combustion,"[58] as Gould said: an aesthetic experience is a most physical one.

There is a natural link, so to say, between participative aesthetics and the refusal of criticism. Indeed, both Gould and Nietzsche critiqued critics. The critics' work relies on the capacity to dissociate oneself from the work at hand to better judge it. Critics are thus still attached to the traditional passive posture of reception. Gould and Nietzsche's rejection of this posture also kindled a hope as to a rejuvenation of music as social institution — music as a "scene," as we would say today — so that music could be given more occasions to arouse aesthetic experiences. Both Gould and Nietzsche thus reflected upon a new meaning for the role of the "public." Near the end of *The Birth of Tragedy*, Nietzsche noted that "the aesthetic *listener* is also reborn with the rebirth of tragedy," whereas hitherto "the critic got the upper hand in the theatre and concert hall."[59] In a similar way, Gould hoped for the dawn of a new period in art, where a "creative audience" would signal a break from market demands and non-artistic hierarchies such as the ones encapsulated by the words *public* and *artist*.[60]

But Gould saw that for an active reception of musical works to be experienced, there was still much to destroy in the so-called "classical music" institution. He hoped, for instance, to "ban applause" so that the performance of works would no longer be confined to a place (the concert hall) that was inappropriate for aesthetic experiences. This was a struggle of the utmost importance, for Glenn Gould conceived the purpose of art as "the gradual, life-long construction of a state of wonder and serenity."[61]

This formula sums up the therapeutic effect of music on an individual level. It is in view of this effect that, according to Nietzsche, music aesthetics must be reformed. And the first step in this reform was to work toward the destruction of opera. This meant to refuse the posture of the listener-as-critic by turning away from a form of music-as-entertainment. Music must be liberated from text, emotions, the narcissism of the virtuoso, and market demands. To "destroy the opera," then, meant to destroy an institution that placed listeners in a position from which they could not be artists.

Destroying opera therefore means to think beyond binary categories such as author and work or composer and listener, for it may well be given to each person to feel in oneself the flow and power of creation.

Alexandrian culture, though, was not only symbolized in its artistic forms. It was also lived and developed through another form of existence that Nietzsche rejected: that of the scholar. So as not to be "so tumultuously carried away by the present time," Nietzsche believed one had to learn from the Greeks — not only from tragic art, but also from the way in which they might well have encouraged a larger flourishing of human life through many experiences, forms of life, and types. This is why as a professor Nietzsche encouraged his students to "seriously ask themselves in the end whether the increase of knowledge ... is ultimately a progress."[62]

Chapter 3

Nuts and Bolts

INSIDE THE FACTORY OF SCHOLARSHIP

All of us are familiar with that peculiar manner in which our age pursues scholarly inquiry; we are familiar with it because we live it, and this is precisely why almost no one asks himself about the possible benefit such a preoccupation with scholarship could ever have for culture.
Nietzsche, *UO* 1 (*DS*), §8

Immediately after the *Birth of Tragedy* polemic Nietzsche started working on a new book, *David Strauss the Confessor and the Writer*, which came out in August of 1873. Conceived as the first volume in what was to be a series of short *Unfashionable Observations*, the book vilifies an essayist who was widely held as emblematic of Germany's high culture and powerful language, and famous for his historical approach to matters of faith.

In 1873 the Protestant theologian David Friedrich Strauss was sixty-five. His life and works had been successful yet tumultuous. In the book that had made his reputation, *The Life of Jesus*, published almost forty years earlier, Strauss adopted a critical approach to his subject to demonstrate the mythical nature of many biblical events. In some milieux scathing critiques and controversy arose, while to many — including young Nietzsche — the book was an eye-opener.[1]

But Nietzsche's 1873 *Observation* was not concerned with Strauss's contribution to the historical study of Christianism. It rather took aim at a more recent book of Strauss's, *The Old and the New Faith*, which had come out in October of 1872. This was a more personal work, in which Strauss explained that he had laid aside the "old" faith and turned resolutely to Darwinian science while remaining a Christian.

Seldom read today, Nietzsche's second book was actually his biggest success in terms of sales and reviews during his active years.

David Strauss the Confessor and the Writer was the second-most reviewed of his published books in his time, after *The Birth of Tragedy*: twenty-four reviews — most of them very critical — appeared during Nietzsche's active years, thirteen of which in the year of the essay's publication. Late into his career he insisted on the importance of his polemic against Strauss. The reputation of the *Observation*'s subject matter and Nietzsche's ironic, disparaging, and at times aggressive style certainly elicited response. In the months following its publication the Strauss essay had "a fantastically hostile press reception," as Nietzsche lamented in a September 1873 letter to Richard Wagner, adding "but everyone has read it."[2]

Nietzsche was never again to witness such an important reception for one of his works. As for Strauss, it would be the last of the polemics surrounding his name and work: the theologian died in February 1874. At first glance, the Strauss essay appears so closely related to its period — so timely — that it could seem irrelevant to readers of another time and place. Although this judgment may explain why the essay is the least read of Nietzsche's books today, it is certainly mistaken. His book does much more than denigrate the theologian. As a learned man and as a famous author Strauss was for Nietzsche a window into a form of life. He was a specimen typical of the culture that values scholarly endeavours. As such Strauss enabled Nietzsche to closely study that culture through one of its live exemplars. This was to be the overarching theme of all *Unfashionable Observations*. Indeed, the title of the series condenses a sizeable project aimed at observing, criticizing, and eventually replacing a type of life to which Nietzsche himself could testify firsthand: that of the scholar.

An Imposing Project

From the outset Nietzsche entitled his series in the plural form: *Unzeitgemäße Betrachtungen, erstes Stück*. The series has known different titles in English — from *Thoughts out of Season*, in 1909, to *Unfashionable Observations*, in 1995. The German adjective *unzeitgemäß* qualifies the author's observations as untimely: they are not of their time in at least two ways. First, as a philologist Nietzsche speaks from the standpoint of one who dwells in other eras than his: "it is only to the extent that I am a student of more ancient times — above all, of ancient Greece — that I, as a child of our time, have had such unfashionable experiences." Second, thanks to this historical awareness and cultural experience Nietzsche's thoughts mean to be unconventional or nonconformist: they go against their time. Simply put, Nietzsche's *Unzeitgemäßigkeit* is a critical stance towards his culture, as he makes clear in the short preface to his second *Observation*: "The observations offered here are also unfashionable because I attempt to understand something in which our age justifiably takes pride ... as a detriment."[3]

Upon its publication, in the summer of 1873, the first book's complete title thus conveyed two messages: the author — still unknown outside German philological circles — was proposing a critique of his time, of which this was but the first act ("*erstes Stück*"). Indeed, Nietzsche intended to publish twelve polemical essays in but six years!

Needless to say, the actual output did not follow up on this ambitious initial projection. After the first *Observation*, Nietzsche published the second in February 1874, *On the Utility and Liability of History for Life*. While it received close to no attention in its time, this essay is today one of Nietzsche's most famous works, and assuredly the best known of his *Unfashionable Observations*. A third one came out eight months later: *Schopenhauer as Educator*. As we will see in the next chapter, this essay has an important reception in the United States since the 1990s, although it continues to be little read elsewhere.[4]

Nietzsche's pace slowed after the essay on education. Nevertheless, a note from the winter/spring seasons of 1875 shows that he still envisioned to write nine new *Observations*. He planned for the series to end in 1880, for which year he wrote down in his publication plan: "*Weg der Befreiung*," "The Path to Freedom." Was this to be a concluding *Unfashionable Observation* or was it the horizon that Nietzsche hoped would greet him after finishing twelve pamphlets of cultural criticism? As we saw in chapter 1, in March 1875 he started working on a fourth *Observation*, which he tentatively entitled *We Philologists*. Yet he just as quickly laid it aside, never to come back to it. (The unfinished notes were published posthumously in the 1970s in the *Nachlaß*, Nietzsche's notebooks and commonplace books.) At that point, Nietzsche seemed to relinquish his project.[5]

Nevertheless, during the fall of 1875 he wrote eight sections of a new essay, this time on the composer Richard Wagner, in whom he had found inspiration while writing *The Birth of Tragedy*, whose music and aesthetics he had greatly admired, and with whom he had been in close contact and intellectual discussion since their chance meeting in 1868, as we will see in chapter 5. Yet Nietzsche was once more reluctant to finish this book and he laid his notes aside.

In fact, he was no longer inspired by his subject matter, as his letters of the time make clear.[6] But prompted by the upcoming inauguration of Wagner's theatre and festival in Bayreuth, where the complete operatic cycle of the *Ring of the Nibelung* would be staged for the very first time, Nietzsche took up his draft again in the spring of 1876. He was finally able to publish his fourth *Unfashionable Observation* in time for the opening of the *Festspiel*, with an augmented print run of 1500 copies. His essay was entitled, appropriately but soberly, *Richard Wagner in Bayreuth*. It would be the last installment in the *Unfashionable Observations* series.

Contrary to his anticipation, the *Observations* sold badly. This would be the case during much of his active life: between 1874 and 1889, Nietzsche published and often even self-published seventeen books to the general indifference of the forty-two million citizens of the German empire. Consequently, all but the first *Observation* received close to no reviews, either in the general press or in specialized journals and magazines. The numbers are there: only about five hundred copies of the first essay and two hundred of the second were sold — this is roughly equivalent to selling between thirty-eight and ninety-five copies of a book in present-day Quebec province (population eight million), indeed a very small readership for any type of book. Between 1874 and 1876, the second and third essays received only three and four German-language reviews respectively (there was also one review on the first three *Observations*), and the Wagner essay elicited only three responses in the German-language press during the years 1876 and 1877.[7]

Nietzsche's disenchantment with what was initially a sizeable project had several causes. Surely the negative polemic surrounding his first two books had an impact, as did his disgust with polemics itself — already in the summer of 1872 he had written to his friend Carl von Gersdorff: "I will never again let myself be carried into a polemic!"[8] But the silence with which the next *Observations* were met was also a cause of Nietzsche's discontent. In the short preface to his *Observation* on history he wrote of daring "to go public with the natural description of my feeling" in the hope of inspiring a public discussion about the "orientation of our age."[9] But no such discussion arose. Indeed, the essay on history and the one on education fell into oblivion as soon as they hit the bookshops. Perhaps Nietzsche had not yet found the proper form, style, and tempo to voice his ideas on culture.

Possibilities of Life

The discrepancy between an initially large (albeit negative) reception and the disregard that followed was hard to swallow given Nietzsche's hopes as to his series' success and impact. These hopes and expectations were evident in the series' title and the essays' tone, but also in the project's scope. His notebooks from 1872–75 contain many plans for *Unfashionable Observations*. These often appear as lists of cultural targets "to attack."[10]

Targets include universities: that of Strasburg, which was inaugurated in the spring of 1872 in a context of nation-building following the Franco-Prussian war, and Leipzig, Nietzsche's alma mater where he had been the star graduate student in philology. They include German painters, writers (such as Berthold Auerbach or the novelist Gustav Freytag), and composers (such as Wilhelm Heinrich Riehl and his popular *Hausmusik*). They also include newspapers such as the literary journal *Literarisches Centralblatt* and the illustrated family-oriented newspaper *Die Gartenlaube*. And they of course include scholars such as musicologist Eduard Hanslick, historian Georg Gottfried Gervinus, or theologian David Friedrich Strauss.[11]

Popular novelists, dinner music, well-known newspapers, prominent universities ... A present-day reader perusing these lists cannot fail to notice how timely these targets were to the contemporary readership. As a consequence, most of these targets may be close to unknown to us now. Today, perhaps only historians of German theology or music may be interested in Strauss and Riehl ... Where does the untimeliness of Nietzsche's *Unfashionable Observations* project lay? And concurrently, how can the series appeal to readers of another time than his?

It is useful to stress here that Nietzsche considered these targets as cultural specimens. Each is akin to a slide under a microscope: the biologist looks at a cell, but it is the larger organism that is under scrutiny. Nietzsche's slides contain examples of makers and products of the culture that he is studying. He aims to better criticize this culture by examining how specific examples embody its values and strive to reproduce them.

Nietzsche was immersed in the study of cultural life forms since the start of his career. As a philologist, though, he was not interested only in past cultural configurations, but first and foremost by his own culture seen through the lens of history. Already in his 1870–71 notebooks he summed up modern Western culture as the "new form of existence" brought about by "the birth of scholarship and science."[12] While this culture of scholarship was present in his book on tragedy — most notably in its critique of "Socratism" and Alexandrian culture, as we saw in the previous chapter — it was brought to the forefront in his subsequent publications. Indeed, the basso continuo of the *Unfashionable Observations* is the anatomy of a specific form of life: that of the scholar.

A scholar embodies fundamental decisions as to what is deemed important to life. For instance, claims as to why truth, knowledge, or honesty are important, or claims as to why one should pursue an academic career. These claims are not value neutral: on the contrary, they reflect answers to perennial questions concerning the good life. In other words, they reflect cultural values. The scholar thereby represents a certain way of living one's life that is culturally encouraged, sustained, and transmitted through educational institutions, cultural manifestations such as works of art or science, and the rewards given to the professionalization of scholarship (salary, social recognition, etc.). In other words, a scholar embodies values. As such, the scholar, in Nietzsche's vocabulary, is an example of a *type*. As we saw in chapter 2, a type is an embodied set of values expressing drives whose hierarchically organized equilibrium forms a way of life.

While Nietzsche used the notion of drive (Trieb) extensively in his writings of the 1880s, it is present in all *Unfashionable Observations*, just as it was present already in *The Birth of Tragedy*. In the second *Observation*, for instance, Nietzsche describes life as a "dark, driving, insatiable power that lusts after itself." He describes the historian's scholarly work as a "blind mania" led by a "significant impulse" or an "all-encompassing desire for what is old."[13] In the fourth essay, the term Trieb appears seven times while Nietzsche proposes a drive-analysis of the artist. Nietzsche's message is clear: it would be utterly naïve to consider that scholarly work is pushed forward by a pure and simple love of knowledge, or that artistic creation is driven only by a love of newness. Indeed, these phenomena are the outer manifestation of inner drives that Nietzsche hopes to pinpoint.[14]

When they attain equilibrium drives form an embodied possibility of life that can recur with regularity, especially if it is encouraged and transmitted through cultural practices, mechanisms, and institutions. A "possibility of life": that is the sense in which Nietzsche uses the term "type" as of his 1878 book *Human, All Too Human*, most notably in sections that he wrote while using his summer of 1875 notebooks.[15] As a possibility of human life, a type is not necessarily confined to a specific culture or historical time, just as during one's lifetime one is not necessarily confined to a unique type. There are many ways in which our drives' competing demands can find equilibrium and form the shifting self that we are. Throughout one's life one can thus experience different values and embody different types — just as Nietzsche himself started out as a scholar but experimented with the possibility of being a "wandering philosopher," as we saw in chapter 1.

To study types thus means to study different possibilities of life as value-sets. It is also to study the processes through which values are internalized, embodied, and replicated: that, in turn, is culture. Nietzsche's most famous study in this respect is his 1887 *Genealogy of Morality*. Again, this mode of genealogical enquiry on culture is already at work in the *Unfashionable Observations*' drive-analysis.[16]

Examining values through types that embody them is a major endeavour in Nietzsche's philosophy of culture. Indeed, in his last *Observation* he defines his philosophical task towards culture as the "*improvement of that aspect of the world recognized as being alterable*."[17] To do so the philosopher must see what is valued and act on this valuation. Now, in order to study drives so as to eventually modify values, what better path than to examine values through a lived experience, a live example? When disparaging his cultural targets, Nietzsche is in fact criticizing a certain drive-organization, that is, *a certain way of being human* that may occur at different historical times. That is why he is not only interested in the type *per se*, but also in the way in which a culture may strive to foster some types more than others. Philosophy, in other words, uses drive-analysis to focus better on drive-reconfiguration.

In his *Observations* Nietzsche examines several different types: the educator, the philosopher, the scholar, the artist, even the saint. Strauss, Schopenhauer, or Wagner are exemplars, they are names for types which one could see walking on a street in another country than Germany and a different time than the late nineteenth century. Strauss, in fact, is the name for an embodied set of values that reflect a certain drive organization: the drives and values of the scholar as a type. And this scholar is a mainstay of bourgeois culture.

Biedermeier Aesthetic and "Cultural Philistinisim"

By targeting works of literature, music, visual arts, as well as academic institutions or newspapers intended for the educated public of his time, Nietzsche indicates that he wants to scrutinize the way in which the *Bildungsbürgertum* — the educated bourgeoisie — represents and reproduces itself. For Nietzsche, who was a pure product of Germany's learned class, this was also a form of self-criticism. This is manifest in all *Unfashionable Observations*: as a scholar, a historian and philologist, as an educator, and as a Wagner enthusiast, Nietzsche was himself comprised in his choice of topics. In a way, while gazing at the learned class's self-portrait, Nietzsche is his own target. He believes that the artists and authors of the learned class produce "a picture book of reality": "A few people with a gift for painting were at hand, and with graceful strokes they portrayed the bliss, the coziness, the triviality, the peasant-like healthfulness and all that contentedness that the rooms of children, scholars, and peasants exude."[18]

This passage from the first *Observation* evokes a specific cultural trend: the Biedermeier, for which the German period between 1815 and 1860 remains famous to this day. The Biedermeier aesthetic sprung from a rapid industrialization and urbanization, but also from the demand that culture be non-political. It appealed to bourgeois values by representing middle-class aspirations to wealth and culture and focusing on domesticity. Biedermeier painters depict scenes of comfortable family life, with cultural objects such as musical instruments, and symbols of wealth such as modern furniture and tailored gowns.[19] While gazing at Biedermeier paintings, one can imagine that the family gathered around the piano is playing Riehl's *Hausmusik* or reading Freytag's novels or Strauss's late life reflections. Biedermeier painters thus elevate the tranquility of domesticity to a model of the good life. Carl Spitzweg's 1856 painting of a "Cactus Friend" is a typical Biedermeier image of unpolitical life: a wealthy man in his house jacket is busy smoking a good pipe while potting plants inside the closed gate to his pleasant yard. Who in one's right mind would want to change such a comfortable setting?

The Biedermeier state of mind, in other words, is the precise opposite of the critical stance. Biedermeier characters "build and sow for their own day": they are miles away from any thought of overturning a most comfortable state of affairs.[20] Their works — whether these be gardens, newspapers, books, or paintings — celebrate the current times, as they have no wish to renovate culture. To name this comfortable bourgeois and apolitical perspective Nietzsche in 1873 coined a term that he remained proud of until the end of his active years: *Bildungsphilistinismus*. The Bildungsbürgertum's education is "cultural-philistinism" since its culture itself, by turning professional, domestic, and unpolitical, has become an *Unkultur*, a "non-culture."[21]

To voice his critique of bourgeois culture, Nietzsche makes heavy use of industrial and economic metaphors. All four *Unfashionable Observations* insist on the fact that capitalistic demands and the language of economy have penetrated the cultural and intellectual spheres to such a degree that the conditions for genuine, disinterested thought, contemplation, and creation are asphyxiated. Nietzsche was not alone in denunciating these trends. The rapid industrialization and urbanization of Germany during the second half of the nineteenth century had a tremendous impact on educational policies and cultural life. It thus comes as no surprise that Nietzsche was one of many intellectuals from the Bildungsbürgertum who were considering the modernization of industry, scholarship, and universities as a cultural decadence. Indeed, Nietzsche was a Kulturkritiker during a vogue of cultural criticism and pessimism.[22]

But Nietzsche stands out. First, by denouncing other pessimistic critics of modernism, such as the novelist Gustav Freytag or the philosopher Eduard von Hartmann. Also, by mixing styles and thus thwarting expectations: he was, after all, a scholar writing as a polemicist and claiming a philosophical position outside of the canon and jargon. Finally, by denouncing academic philosophy and, soon enough, repudiating it completely and retiring from the university, as we saw in chapter 1. Indeed, Nietzsche was not looking to save the Bildungsbürgertum. He was hoping to spark the conditions for a different, higher type of culture. There had to be something else than the homogenizing power of the Prussian state! He believed that the way to do this was to honestly and directly show to the present what its faults were, in the hope of sparking outrage, discussion, and thought: this was the constructive, cultural aim of his *Unfashionable Observations*.

The success of this aim depended on the Kulturkritiker's capacity for honesty. In his essays Nietzsche defines truthfulness as being true to oneself and to others, "in both word and deed": "Only this truthfulness can bring to light the distress and internal misery of the modern human being, and only then can art and religion, as true helpers, take the place of that anxiously concealing convention and masquerade, in order jointly to plant the seeds of a culture that answers to true needs and that does not solely teach us — as does the universal cultivation of today — to lie to ourselves about these needs and thereby become walking lies."[23] That is why he ended his first *Observation* by saying that speaking the truth is "always timely":

the present time has more need of it than ever, for speaking the truth "is still considered unfashionable."[24] But perhaps more importantly, *living* truthfully — that is: truth in deeds — was even rarer.

Nietzsche's originality as Kulturkritiker rests in this definition of untimeliness and the concurring requirement for a new form of non-scholarly life. Being "unfashionable" is the opposite of the common assumption according to which "to write in conformity with this age amounts to exactly the same thing as being just."[25] Nietzsche writes that the drive to truth is the same as the will to justice, and that both have nothing to do with what is called objectivity and much to do, rather, with strength — that is, with the capacity to incorporate what is alien or new and the power needed to make a sound judgement. There is no *Gerechtigkeitstrieb* without *Urtheilskraft*: no drive towards justice without the strength for judgment. Strength is thus akin both to metabolization and resilience, and it will be expressed through one's actions, not only through one's writings.

This is an important point to stress in order to understand Nietzsche's philosophy in the four *Observations*. The criteria of honesty and truthfulness lead him to criticize precisely the type from whom one would first and foremost expect honesty in words and deeds: the scholar. Indeed, is a scholar not animated by a love of knowledge and a quest for truth in all domains? Nietzsche's criticisms stem from an observation: scholars may be professionals in matters of research and knowledge, they nevertheless lack the strength for judgment. Their love of truth is actually limited by a stronger one: the love of comfort. In other words, the scholar is unfortunately too much of a tame bourgeois character to be capable of honest and sound judgment.

An Anatomy of Scholarship

Nietzsche discusses this relationship between truth and objectivity most particularly within the context of his wider reflections on history. His second *Unfashionable Observation* famously invalidates the notion of objectivity in the historical sciences. The word objectivity "is understood as the condition in which the historian observes all the motives and consequences of an event with such purity that it has absolutely no effect on his subjectivity; it connotes that aesthetic phenomenon, that detachment from personal interest with which the painter, in a stormy setting among lightning and thunder, or on a tempestuous sea, contemplates his inner picture; it connotes that total immersion in things. However, it is a superstition that the image that things produce in such an aesthetically attuned person reproduces the empirical nature of these things."[26]

In this passage Nietzsche stresses that a receptor is never a purely passive medium. Rather, a receptor is but a metabolizing, organizational force. A historian should thus turn to how one subjectively constructs history. Writing history is an aesthetic process, and therein lies its value: "in its ability to intelligently circumscribe, to elevate a well-known, perhaps even commonplace theme, an everyday melody, heightening it into a comprehensive symbol, and thereby intimating in the original theme a whole world of profundity, power, and beauty." As the Wagnerian melody-metaphor in this passage makes clear, the talent and value of the genuine historian thus resemble that of an artist: they both "must have the power to recast what is age-old into something never heard of before."[27]

Nietzsche is thereby rethinking what doing history consists of — and by so doing he expands the realm of history beyond academic walls. Indeed, one's relationship to history can be much wider than that of the scholar. That is why he finds in Wagner an example of a healthy relationship to history, meaning a strong and creative relationship. He writes in the fourth *Observation* that Wagner's "abundance of knowledge ... did not crush his will to act, nor did the attractions of its individual aspects lead him astray." The way in which he created history shows that Wagner was at the same time a philosopher, a historian, an aesthetician, and a critic. His "exceptional" outlook inspired an elucidation "of past views of life."[28]

As creators, writers of history must also express their new views simply, because truth according to Nietzsche is always simple. One such simple truth is the fact that at all times, knowledge of the past is useful in the service of the present and the future: "we need it for life and for action, not for the easy withdrawal from life and from action."[29] In other words, it is obvious that history is always pursued inasmuch as it is believed to have a function for life. If not, why would we even be interested in the past? History thus answers specific needs for a culture and for individuals.

Nietzsche points out that Germany's famous academies of sciences — which were renowned throughout Europe — simply ignore this simple truth. For the academies, "the increase of knowledge is itself the goal." Indeed, the historian is led by blind mania, "a restless gathering together of everything that once existed ... Often he sinks so low that in the end he is satisfied with any fare and even devours with gusto the dust of bibliographical minutiae." History has become a science. Thanks to the German model of scholarship, learned men were narrowed down to being mere "walking encyclopaedias."[30]

By following "*the demand that history be a science*," historians and scholars show that they have accepted to become "laborers who cart, heap, and winnow."[31] Nietzsche laments that his age is essentially one of labour. This means that "human beings must be broken in to serve the purposes of the age, so that they can be put to work at the earliest possible moment; they are supposed to go to work in the factory of general utility before they are mature — indeed, so that they do not become mature — because allowing them to mature would be a luxury that would divert a great deal of energy away from 'the labor market.'"

Nietzsche quickly regrets to have to use such metaphors to describe scholarship and science, which "should be conceived free of utility."[32] But science in the German academies had become an increasingly specialized profession for which the Prussian state defined specific orientations, where results — then as now — had to be profitable in the economic sense, and in which academics and other professionals of knowledge were becoming more prone to thinking of their career in terms of social recognition, securing "honors and advantages for themselves" rather than choosing a path out of genuine passion. The result, according to Nietzsche, was terrible: "If you want to further scholarship as quickly as possible, then you will also destroy it as quickly as possible."[33]

The Strauss essay describes the effect of scholarship on individual persons. Fully taken by their specific work, the scholars' "soul is set aglow at the thought of counting the filaments of a flower." The scholar is busy with minutiae and other trifling details while laboring in frantic hurry: "his studies are no longer a calling but an affliction." The scholar is thus a "living paradox" whose days are spent working in half-consciousness and exhaustion, as though science were produced in a factory: "Our scholars are scarcely distinguishable ... from farmers who hope to increase the tiny property they inherited and are diligently occupied day and night in sowing the field, driving the plow, and prodding the oxen."[34]

Nietzsche asks: what type of drive is at work here? In the context of this drive-analysis of the scholar, Nietzsche turns to the seventeenth century French polymath Blaise Pascal: "Pascal believes generally that human beings pursue their occupations and their scholarship and science so zealously only so as to flee from those all-important questions that every moment of solitude, every moment of true idleness would force upon them."[35] That is to say that the scientist's daily activity is precisely a way of avoiding the most pressing questions — whither? Whence? Why? The pure drive to knowledge devaluates such questions while prioritizing results. But Nietzsche shows that since the whole enterprise of science rests upon the fundamental value-judgements that form a culture, scientific work makes sense only in relation to such questions.

For Nietzsche, an example (or specimen) of this type of drive organization was a soon-to-be German philologist: Ulrich von Wilamowitz-Möllendorff. This young scholar simply refused to consider the wider, aesthetic, and philosophical theses that Nietzsche defended in *The Birth of Tragedy*, and instead went on to criticize it publicly on the grounds of supposed philological errors and whims of fancy unworthy of a serious scholar.

But Wilamowitz was still a student, and Nietzsche and his peers considered him a young fool. Most importantly, Nietzsche saw that other established scholars had an impact both on the general public and on soon-to-be professionals like Wilamowitz. That is part of the reason why Nietzsche chose to attack Strauss, whom Wilamowitz had invoked to conclude his anti-Nietzsche pamphlets just as one quotes a high authority in one's first published paper. Wilamowitz may have been the one to launch the first polemic against Nietzsche, it is telling that it was nevertheless against Strauss that Nietzsche addressed his reply.

David Friedrich Strauss wrote that Darwinism shocked and subverted his Christian worldview and explained how and why he abandoned the "old" Christian faith in order to adopt a new stance, that of modern science. Strauss's *The Old Faith and the New* had a huge success: just three years after its publication it was already in its eighth printing. Both critics and academics revered Strauss's scientific honesty and moral courage, and all were quick in labelling him a classic. Yet for Nietzsche, Strauss was a sloppy writer of German — as the tedious final section of the first *Observation* makes clear, in which he makes fun of Strauss's written style.[36] More importantly, Strauss appeared to Nietzsche as a walking paradox: his embrace of Darwinism stopped short of asking what a Darwinian ethics could be. He did not fully grasp the implications of his new, scientific creed. In fact, Strauss clung to the Christian ethics of goodwill and universal altruism as though they were weaved in the very fabric of things.

Nietzsche reminded his own readers that Christian ethics and Darwinism contradict each other. For Nietzsche, the Darwinian worldview is summarized in Hobbes' most famous statement: "*bellum omnium contra omnes*," a war of all against all. In the fight of all species for the survival of the fittest, what is important for all individuals is to be strong in order to differentiate themselves from others. These facts, for Nietzsche, result from natural laws that any scientist or philosopher after Darwin must take into account if one is to understand what being human implies. Strauss, on the contrary, simply ignores "that it is just as easy to preach morality as it is difficult to establish it."[37] Strauss took no notice of the difficult but extremely important task of explaining, from a Darwinian standpoint, how existing phenomena such as compassion, love, or self-abnegation can have come to exist — especially given that at first sight, such altruistic behaviour seems contrary to the natural fight for the survival of the fittest.

Why did Strauss overlook this most important task? Nietzsche gives several reasons that explain the theologian's failure. For one thing, Strauss condemns competition and violence; but in so doing he is a bad scholar. An honest scholar would refrain from asserting the value of the laws of nature: "an honest natural scientist believes in the absolute adherence of the world to laws, without, however, making any assertions whatsoever about the ethical or moral claims of these laws." This refusal to judge a law of nature echoes the Stoic moral virtue of refusing to ascribe values to the events that are on our path. But also, for Nietzsche, the honest natural scientist "would recognize the supremely anthropomorphic demeanor of a reason unable to adhere to the constraints of what is allowed." Indeed, Strauss believes that any event "embodies a revelation of eternal goodness itself."[38]

For Nietzsche, this goes to show that Strauss does not love truth enough. Indeed, he loves something other than truth: namely, peace and harmony. In other words, Strauss is too bourgeois to be a good philosopher. Since he does not want to disturb anyone's peace of mind, his work is deprived "of anything offensive" so that it can be "universally appealing."[39]

Nietzsche's Questions

This critical portrait of a type outlined Nietzsche's own philosophical position. Three aspects stand out, and it is striking to see how consistent Nietzsche has been throughout his philosophical career in respecting his basic views and completing the tasks that he identified early on in his early *Unfashionable Observation*.

A first aspect is the task that he frames: one must explain the origin of morals. How is it that altruism — that is, a moral care for the other — came to develop in a by-and-by natural creature who, like all living creatures, survives by feeding from, using, and eliminating weaker species? In asking these questions, Nietzsche articulated a task that he would come to pursue almost fifteen years later. Indeed, already in his 1873 essay he advanced the thesis that he developed in his *Genealogy of Morality*: a physical weakness may find other, more sublimated ways of expressing strength and domination. They may conspire "to confuse the nature and the names of things."[40]

A second aspect of Nietzsche's position is methodological: he defends explanation for the sake of honesty and always in relation to larger questions such as Pascal's, which must be taken seriously for the sake of culture. These questions cannot be shunned. Every young person asks these questions for themselves, and the way we answer them draws a path for education and culture.

Thirdly, one must take note of Nietzsche's personal warning: in a naturalistic spirit, he insists that there is no merciful God and that the universe is devoid of goodness and purpose in the human sense. The cosmos is but a "rigid mechanism," in which one must take care not to be crushed.[41] This is the message, says Nietzsche, that an honest Darwinian philosopher should transmit. Ethics is a problem, and it first and foremost needs to be clarified and explained as to its origins and functions for culture and for the survival of humankind and of certain types of human beings. Once this is understood, only then could we consider the cultural question: What type of types should we want?

Almost a hundred and fifty years after the publication of Nietzsche's polemical essays, one could say that Nietzsche has both won and lost his battle. He has won in the sense that his books and many of his ideas are well known to us: they are studied, analyzed, caricatured, deformed, criticized, praised, and even copied by writers, academics, artists, and other public figures. Nietzsche, indeed, is a cultural landmark and sometimes even a pop icon. But he has lost in the sense that the cultural trends against which he warned his readers have not disappeared. He criticized tendencies that have simply grown stronger since his time. In many ways, his unfashionable observations are still untimely today in that they still go against the current — and perhaps especially his observations that concern scholars, academics, and all students and seekers of knowledge.

Indeed, we are all descendants of his time. We, citizens aspiring to middle-class comfort and security, in states that promote some career paths to the detriment of others by subsidizing certain activities and domains of research rather than others; we, democrats in an age of a mass-education that undervalues the study of classics, and bolsters more technical and quickly remunerated skills; we, who form our opinion on many public matters based on the journalistic writing that we read daily and hastily, and often without questioning the value-judgements that such news promote; we, scholars and academics who cobble up "a book out of bits and pieces" of research.[42]

It is we who bring our children to the nearby zoo on the weekend, and who like to show, over a pint or two at the nearby pub, that indeed we have read Hegel or Rousseau or Shakespeare, and that we have formed opinions on them all.

"Thus we live and go our way in bliss" — to recall a David Strauss sentence that Nietzsche laughed at.[43] Indeed, it is we who Nietzsche talks about: he offers us a mirror that we should not turn down if we are to know ourselves better.

There was surely a personal resonance to Nietzsche's *Unfashionable Observations*. As mentioned earlier, his cultural criticism was in large part a self-criticism. But also, his critical observations say a lot about his conception of philosophy. Nietzsche was far from a position of detachment or cold, clinical study. He was literally seized by the problems he depicted. In the opening to his second *Observation*, he wrote: "I have mainly drawn the occurrences that aroused in me those tormenting feelings from my own experiences."[44]

His writings were tied to his personal life. The public, unfortunately, did not seem to find interest in these. At the same time, Nietzsche was growing increasingly tired with the polemical style of his cultural struggle. He was tormented that he was "forced to address himself only to a sect, as it were" and "no longer needed by his people as a whole."[45] He did not want to "engage in polemics" any longer, and he thus abandoned his project.[46] (Yet he did not abandon the hope that his works and ideas would come to find a public, as will see in the last chapters of this book.)

Nevertheless, he could not do away with the personal resonance of cultural and philosophical questions, problems, and theses. And this is because Nietzsche was a philosophical question and thesis. Or differently put: Nietzsche — his works and his deeds — show how a human life can be lived as a series of possible answers to fundamental questions. In this way, Nietzsche was heir to the Hellenistic schools of philosophy and their idea that to be a philosopher is to be literally inhabited and sculpted by problems and tentative answers. In the age of the "walking encyclopaedias," as Nietzsche put it, philosophy, that "most truthful of all sciences," is reduced to "the learned monologue of the solitary walker, [to] the individual's chance capture ... or [to] the harmless chatter of academic[s]." Nietzsche lamented that "No one dares to fulfill the law of philosophy in himself, no one lives philosophically, with that simple ... loyalty that compelled an ancient, if he had once declared loyalty to the Stoa, to act as a Stoic wherever he was and whatever he did."[47]

That philosophy must be embodied and lived is perhaps what finally brought him to turn away from "the factory of scholarship" by resigning his academic chair at the University of Basel in 1879, at the very early age of thirty-five.[48] That decision, back in the late nineteenth century and still more today, is a most unfashionable one. It was a decision to pursue a life of philosophical enquiry and experimentation as a non-scholar and a non-professional, to continue learning and experimenting outside of the official educational institutions, in a most individual way.

Chapter 4

The Individualist

ON BECOMING WHO YOU ARE

I must be myself.
Emerson, "Self-Reliance"

In October of 1874 Nietzsche's third *Unfashionable Observation*, titled *Schopenhauer as Educator*, was printed by his new publisher, Ernst Schmeitzner, in Schloss-Chemnitz. (His three previous books had been published by Ernst Wilhelm Fritzsch, Wagner's publisher, in Leipzig.)

Nietzsche had already developed some ideas on education two years before, in a series of five public lectures that he delivered between January and March 1872 at the University of Basel, under the title *On the Future of Our Educational Institutions*. He had planned on writing a sixth lecture, reworking the complete series' manuscript, and publishing it as a short book that spring. "It will be my second book," he had announced to his friend Erwin Rohde in a March 1872 letter. But the talks — mostly written as a philosophical dialogue — were not as popular as he had hoped, and he never followed through on his publication project.[1]

Written two years after the talks, *Schopenhauer as Educator* pursues Nietzsche's 1872 critique of democratic education within the context of industrialization. But it does much more. It pinpoints the seat of education within the individual and it discusses what it means to live as a unique person. It proposes a model of virtues for leading a proper philosophical life and rejects purely academic endeavours. Importantly, the essay is also a witness to Nietzsche's pervasive — albeit often silent — dialogue with the American essayist Ralph Waldo Emerson. And while Schopenhauer appears in the *Observation*'s title, his magnum opus and even his philosophy seem conspicuously absent from Nietzsche's thoughts.

From the outset, the essay is energetically addressed to young persons who are about to enter university and who will therefore need to choose a profession. Nietzsche hopes to make them stop for a moment and think upon the meaning of education. The essay thus serves as an introduction to philosophy as a lived experience rather than an academic field or scientific endeavour. In this way, Richard Schacht was right to qualify *Schopenhauer as Educator* as Nietzsche's "first manifesto." As a professor, Nietzsche already stressed to his young philology students that they must "first study philosophy for one year, so as not to resemble factory workers who make screws day in day out,"[2] a worry he repeated in his 1872 talks and in his 1874 essay. Nietzsche hoped to entice young students to embark on a lifelong quest to be themselves — a quest that should lead them on a path other than the one carved out by the "factory of scholarship."

Professional Education and the Selfishness of Culture

Before opening his manifesto, let us return for a moment to Nietzsche's talks on education. The core of the 1872 public lectures criticized two prevailing educational trends. Nietzsche called them the extension of culture (meaning the democratization of education) and the reduction of culture (meaning specialized, professional education). Both are simultaneous phenomena, and both arise from industrialization. The fact that universities opened their doors to more students and the fact that they proposed new, specialized programs targeting specific professions went hand in hand.

The German empire of the mid-nineteenth century was undergoing a vast and rapid industrial development. The sudden diversification and augmentation of material needs and the number and preciseness of theoretical and technical skills necessary for production were such that Germany needed to train more professionals to fill an increasingly specialized and diversified workforce. Nietzsche saw that since they were tied to production imperatives, professions narrowed their pedagogical aims to specific competencies. Secondary and higher education thus became specialized and professionalized. Established professions reflect a prior decision as to what type of skills and capacities are efficient and effective in fulfilling the tasks that define it. In other words, they have already decided what is of value within an individual person. Academic specialization therefore targets certain abilities and maximizes their development in young people, to the detriment of other abilities that are now deemed useless — professional specialization is standardization by reduction.[3]

These observations lead Nietzsche to depict the university graduate as a cog in an industrial system rather than an agent in a cultural movement. He wrote that "a specialist in science gets to resemble nothing so much as a factory workman who spends his whole life in turning one particular screw or handle on a certain instrument or machine, at which occupation he acquires the most consummate skill." He was not overly surprised by this, since he already saw (through Schopenhauer's critical depiction of academic philosophy, for instance) and felt (especially through his own harrowing experience as a young professor) that "the exploitation of a man for the purpose of science is accepted everywhere without the slightest scruple."[4] Universities thus exploit persons for the benefit of a cold and lifeless abstraction. The newly increased access to higher education, then, was not fundamentally based upon humanistic arguments inherited from the classical tradition (as was still the case in the not-so-distant time of Goethe and Schiller). Essentially, higher education was economically driven.

Some of these thoughts from the draft of the 1872 talks made it into the 1874 essay on education, most notably in section 6. Nietzsche added to these criticisms by analysing the motives that underlie the dominant spheres of modern culture. As French philosopher Paul Ricoeur famously said, suspicion and critique are one of Nietzsche's most famous intellectual legacies, and it was already well developed in his early essays.[5] In his third *Observation* he suspected that the principal proponents who defended the importance of education in Germany were in fact all rooting for themselves. Culture, in other words, had become the objectification of specific economic and political interests.

Section 6 of the third *Unfashionable Observation* is by far the longest of the essay, and it is worth looking at in more detail. Nietzsche identifies four areas of cultural power and shows that when it favours education, each of these is in fact driven by its own interests. He thereby paints the culture of his time as a variety of selfishness.

First, there is the selfishness of the "money makers" — that is, the owners of the means of production. While favouring a "speedy" education but "thorough enough" to allow their children to soon become one of those money makers "who can rake in immense sums," they use education to dominate "all the ways and means." Then there is the state's selfishness. While promoting a democratic education out of "competition with other states," it expects universities to produce civil servants and officials who will serve existing institutions. There is also the cultural actors' mannerism. By favouring an education that defines rules of taste and offers an exotic variety "of piquant and spicy dishes," they produce the philistines who merely seek to consume and enjoy culture. Finally, there is science's own selfishness. By promoting education essentially through the guise of problems of knowledge, it produces the scientist who cuts nature up and thereby "ossifies his humanity" in the service of the scientific enterprise.[6]

Nietzsche's analysis strives to show that the tenets of all four of the main cultural powers favour education insofar as it allows them to maintain their economic and social position. He notes that industrials, civil servants, aesthetes, and scholars are at the same time products and mechanisms of production. Each group exploits culture and educational institutions to reproduce itself, and each one thus reveals just "how predatory in striving, how insatiable in acquiring, how selfish and shameless in enjoying" they are.[7]

While he may be interested in the state or the industry's motivations towards culture, Nietzsche is much more focused on the fourth actor depicted here: he wishes to understand the scholar's motives. He describes the scholar as "a confused tangle of very different impulses and stimuli; he is a thoroughly impure metal" within which "a host of very human drives and petty passions have been mixed together to form a chemical compound."[8] In order to better understand the scholar, he begins by identifying three impulses that are a source of pleasure for the scientist: that of knowledge, research, and contradiction, which he identifies, respectively, with the pleasure of finding novelty, with the fact of stalking, and with experiencing victory. Nietzsche then describes thirteen character traits that are specific to the scholar: conventionality, myopia, sobriety, aridity, modesty, loyalty to one's models, loyalty to precedent, flight from boredom, love of salary, collegiality, vanity, playfulness, and concern for justice. A scholar is a mixture of these impulses and traits: they may be very present or not in each scholar, but this mixture always makes it such that "the scholar is by nature *unfruitful*." A scholar does not create, but rather tracks, dissects, and classifies.[9]

Yet culture is not a dead artifact in a museum or a sample in a lab. Culture is alive and vivid. It is continually in creation and in flux. In light of the selfish trends that he discerns and of the "seductive voices of that modish 'culture,'" there is no doubt for Nietzsche as to the necessity for a "new fundamental principle of culture."[10] But where could one find the impetus for culture, the seed of creativity? In everyday social life, people generally conform to predefined tasks and absentmindedly play several roles. They "strut about in a hundred different disguises, as youths, young men, old men, fathers, citizens, priests, officials, and merchants, all entirely preoccupied with their common comedy and not with themselves in the least."[11] A new idea of culture cannot emanate from these predefined roles, nor from the masses, which embody and symbolize conformity, and which Nietzsche depicts as a sea of undifferentiation. A new cultural idea can only emerge out of "a productive uniqueness,"[12] a creative aspiration and will to something new. That is what the young person embodies, as a unique individual as yet not broken to conformity.

Cherishing Individual Uniqueness: A Dialogue with Emerson

In the very first paragraph of his *Observation* on education, Nietzsche cries out to the young person: "Be yourself!"[13] Upon reading it, some may recall the famous Socratic injunction: "Know thyself." However, Nietzsche's maxim in fact marks a major shift from Socrates's. Their two different verbs make for an important contrast: rather than knowledge, it is *existence* that Nietzsche conjugates in the imperative. He invites the individual to turn towards being, that is, towards realizing one's unique and singular life. As Alexander

Nehamas noted in his *Nietzsche: Life as Literature*: "The self, according to Nietzsche, is not a constant, stable entity. On the contrary, it is something one becomes."[14]

The fact that one must be incited to realizing one's singular life implies that unfortunately it seems easy not to be oneself. That is why throughout his essay Nietzsche sustains his exhortation to the "young soul" who "does not want to be a part of the masses." In order to advance towards one's true self, it is not necessary to target objective knowledge. Formal education for a profession can lead one astray. What is needed, above all, is to live: "There is one single path in this world on which no one but you can travel. Where does it lead? Do not ask, just take it."[15]

The text's introduction shows that the third *Unfashionable Observation* is a protreptic essay: addressing a young person from the outset, Nietzsche invites emancipation all while proposing a justification of philosophy based on a conception of the good life and a critique of other common models. What is at stake — and thus what prompts the author's publishing his thoughts on education — is *culture*, as is most clearly revealed by a quote that Nietzsche underlines as he inserts it in his conclusion: "*A new degree of culture would instantly revolutionize the entire system of human pursuits.*"[16] This hope obviously rests on a rejection of the dominant culture, a critique that unfolds in the central sections of the *Observation* (§4–6).

To clarify what is at stake here, one must understand what "a new degree of culture" means. The text that Nietzsche quotes specifies that another degree of culture means another "mental horizon"[17] leading to the emergence of new ideas and values — in other words, to new expressions of what it is to be human. To the question of how such a new mental horizon can arise, Nietzsche proposes that it can only happen locally, from within individuals who, through their own internal and external channels — that is, through their own judgments and actions — will have elaborated, tried, and finally embodied new values. Culture, in other words, rests upon the individual person. This in turn implies that the individual person has an eminent cultural task, which makes the question of culture even more precise: how can the development of creative individualities be promoted?

Culture is thus a question of education. Nietzsche specifically addresses this question to young individuals whom he tries to awaken to their uniqueness so that they may wish to develop their autonomy. That is why from the very first lines he exhorts young people not to abandon themselves, out of laziness, to conformity within the "herd,"[18] but rather to aspire to go beyond this by deploying their own capacities and giving voice to their uniqueness — so that through themselves, the human world may perhaps reach a new possibility in its development.

Nietzsche's individualism is closely related to that of the author with whom he is discreetly discussing in his third *Unfashionable Observation*. Curiously, it is not Schopenhauer, to whom the title of the *Observation* draws our attention. Rather, that person is the author of the sentence that Nietzsche quotes in his conclusion. That author is Emerson.[19]

Nietzsche read Emerson when he was himself a young soul. In 1862, at the age of seventeen — before he discovered Schopenhauer, in 1865, and even before he read Plato — Nietzsche immersed himself in Emerson's works. First, *The Conduct of Life* (1860), which he read repeatedly, and then the *First* and *Second Series* of Emerson's *Essays* (1841 and 1844, respectively), as well as his *Representative Men* (1850). Emerson is one of the authors whom Nietzsche read the most. As Benedetta Zavatta shows in her rich studies on both authors, "Nietzsche read, reread, and commented on Emerson's essays constantly, and their influence can be traced throughout his published and unpublished works."[20] The year of Emerson's death, Nietzsche selected a sentence of his to use as epigraph to his new book, *The Gay Science*, and he named Emerson amongst the nineteenth century's five greatest masters of prose.[21]

The American philosopher sets the tone for several passages of Nietzsche's third *Observation*. Nietzsche's maxim "Be yourself!" echoes the famous essay "Self-Reliance" in which Emerson twice states: "I must be myself."[22] In his *Essays*, Emerson describes the individual person as the natural form of the mind and the will. He describes the individual through a series of synonyms: self-sufficiency, autonomy, independence. The collective good depends on one's individual will and capacity to follow one's own ways in the "perfect sweetness of independence proper to solitude."[23] The responsibility for one's own education lies within ourselves.

Nietzsche' individualism in the third *Observation* follows the two senses of Emerson's individualism. First, the individual is primarily given: each person is "unique" because "the power that resides in [each] is new in nature."[24] Second, the individual has a capacity for practical action because of one's "earnest experience of the common day" and the uniqueness of one's inner power.[25] Both Nietzsche and Emerson urge their readers to develop their autonomy rather than yield to social conformity, and to accept solitude as the state that allows for self-realization.

Self-reliance, indeed, is the face of the supreme form of nature that is character, that "reserved force, which acts directly by presence, and without means." This leads Emerson to underline the importance of whim: "Suppose you should contradict yourself; what then?" The individual has a right to inconstancy. Emerson wanted the word *Whim* to be inscribed on the lintel of his door because he believed that this tendency to follow one's fancy is the heroic trait of the great individual. Since the heroic person who follows whim "will not condescend to take anything seriously," another trait characterizes the self-reliant individual: cheerfulness.[26] As George Kateb puts it, self-reliance may be summed up as "intellectual independence, reactive and responsive self-possession."[27]

Although the third *Unfashionable Observation* remains close to Emerson's descriptions of the inner tendencies and outer signs of the individual, Nietzsche emphasizes the individual's cultural role more than Emerson does. For the latter, each new mind offers a new classification of things, making possible a new mental horizon. Institutions are thus "the lengthened shadow[s] of one man." But while Nietzsche attaches the individual to the great task of reforming culture, Emerson rather turns to the presence within him of "the soul of the whole," which is beyond all singular beings and opens onto the depths of "inextinguishable being."[28]

Yet in both cases individualism does not imply a withdrawal of the person from society or culture, precisely because individuals must work to surpass themselves. It is important to note that this process is not teleological. Neither the way nor the goal for this process of self-development are known, or even traced in advance. By wanting to surpass oneself, the individual aspires to a new configuration of being human — "new" meaning higher than what is already commonly realized everywhere. What is certain, therefore, is the verticality of the movement. The individual who follows one's path of singular uniqueness rises above the mass of the herd, in the words of Nietzsche, or of the conformist society, in the words of Emerson.

While faced with the democratization of education, both Nietzsche and Emerson defend a conception of human excellence that rests upon a personal desire to aim higher, and thus upon a vertical effort. The German thinker goes further than his American counterpart by stressing that culture depends on this elitism, and that a paradigm shift is urgently needed. The cultural "elite," however, does not lie in a genetic heritage, a nation, an economic class, or a profession. On that point, Nietzsche again agrees with Emerson who repeatedly emphasized that heroism and greatness are neither given in advance nor guaranteed by education or occupation: "It is the avowal of the unschooled man that he ... knows that his will is higher and more excellent than all actual and all possible antagonists."[29] Without predestination or teleology, it seems that the individual effort for education is precisely that: a tension, a movement that does not find an end in a stable state or a definitive configuration.

Much of the consensus surrounding Emerson's philosophical and cultural importance in the United States rests upon this conception of the autonomous individual as the seat of creative uniqueness and resistance to conformity. Emerson, the son of a young democratic nation, is seen as one of its most prominent voices, as the straightener who, through his critique of mediocrity and his reflection on human strengths, can lead the individual to want to strive for what is best.

Emerson thus occupies a natural place within American debates in moral philosophy. Now it so happens that Nietzsche accompanied him along this path. *Schopenhauer as Educator* is indeed one of the most quoted texts in the debates on moral perfectionism, which may also explain why the reception of Nietzsche in the United States since the 1990s essentially happened in the field of political and moral philosophy.

The source of these American debates around the third *Unfashionable Observation* is John Rawls. In his 1971 *Theory of Justice* Rawls rejected moral perfectionism on the grounds that it is essentially elitist, anti-egalitarian, and, as such, unfit for a democratic moral theory. To provide a paradigmatic example of perfectionism, Rawls quoted in a footnote a passage from §6 of *Schopenhauer as Educator*: "Mankind must work continually to produce individual great human beings — this and nothing else is the task."[30] The footnote launched a tidal wave of commentary.

Indeed, in North American debates Rawls's quote has come to embody Nietzschean individualism as well as moral perfectionism. The actors in the debate on moral perfectionism are numerous and their positions are contrasted. The authors discuss one another's position and criticize the opposing camp. In this way *Schopenhauer as Educator* has become not only an obligatory reference in Nietzschean studies in the United States, but also the site of a debate on the place of elitism in democratic culture and the options that present themselves to those who tread the path of an internal critique of democracy. It seems that since then, the tendency to accept or reject perfectionism rests upon the same condition as the tendency to judge Nietzschean philosophy of culture and the individual as aristocratic, or as compatible with democratic culture. In other words, all depends on the meaning given to elitism.[31]

In a 2013 paper, Tracy Strong summarized the two meanings of elitism that are at stake in these debates: "The first consists in holding the position that some individuals are, by the nature of their endowments, simply superior to the others ... The other way of thinking about an 'elite' consists in asking why is it that most humans are content to, as Thoreau put it, 'live lives of quiet desperation,' that they are not more than they are." By relating this second conception to American transcendentalism, Strong made his position clear: in his view, Nietzsche presents a critical posture for looking at "the way in which a sense of possibility and transformation has been slowly erased from human capacities."[32] The point for Strong and others is to show that democratic elitism, far from being an oxymoron, is a consistent philosophical position that has its roots in the first American school of philosophy, Transcendentalism. By emphasizing the autonomy of the individual, democratic elitism can play a critical role in addressing some of the pitfalls of democratic ideas, chief among which is the flattening out.

In fact, elitist, democratic perfectionism is perhaps best described by Nietzsche himself, in the second half of the alternative that he describes in §300 of his 1878 book *Human, All Too Human*, entitled "Two Kinds of Equality": "The passion for equality can express itself by someone either wanting to pull everyone else down to his level (by disparaging them, keeping secrets from them, or tripping them up) or wanting to pull himself up along with everyone else (by giving them recognition, helping them, taking pleasure in their success)."

To rise: that is precisely the meaning of education and emancipation that Nietzsche repeats many times in his third *Unfashionable Observation*, for instance when he reminds his young readers: "for your true being does not lie deeply hidden within you, but rather immeasurably high above you, or at least above what you commonly take to be your ego."[33]

Schopenhauer as Model for a "Courageous Philosophical Life"

Given the important albeit somewhat silent dialogue that Nietzsche entertains with Emerson — the first philosopher whom he read — why is his third *Unfashionable Observation* entitled *Schopenhauer as Educator*? The question is legitimate.[34] What can Schopenhauer educate us to?

A clue as to the answer certainly rests in the meaning of "educator." Nietzsche uses the German word *Erzieher*, and an educator as Erzieher is not an educator as *Lehrer*. A Lehrer is a teacher or professor who transmits doctrines, typically within an institution such as universities or high schools. An Erzieher is one who pulls (the verb in German is *ziehen*) pupils towards something other than what they are "in precisely this Now."[35] The educator, in this sense, is closer to an emancipator, a force of liberation through self-becoming.

Indeed, education is a process by which one comes to oneself. It is through this definition of education as emancipation that we can see why the *Observation* puts forth Schopenhauer as an educator. The Frankfurt philosopher was a mentor for Nietzsche not only in matters of philosophy but also as concerns the model for a philosophical attitude and life. On the one hand, Schopenhauer is the philosopher who may have revealed to Nietzsche "the true primordial sense and basic stuff of your being, something that is thoroughly incapable of being educated and cultivated."[36] Schopenhauer, in other words, was his educator as liberator. On the other hand, Nietzsche proposes Schopenhauer as the figure of the educator precisely because he himself shed the influence of Schopenhauerian philosophy. By becoming himself thanks to Schopenhauer's impetus, Nietzsche left Schopenhauer's path and made his own.

But the third *Unfashionable Observation* is also something of a case study. Schopenhauer's life, which Nietzsche surveys in §7, shows "some of the conditions under which, despite the harmful counterforces, philosophical genius can at least come into being in our times."[37] Therefore, Nietzsche examines Schopenhauer's case as part of an investigation into culture. He presents Schopenhauer as more than an author, and more than a philosopher in the professional sense: he was an autonomous and creative individual whose works may have a transformative effect on readers thanks to his moral force.

Nietzsche also points out that reading Schopenhauer had an "immediate," "physiological" effect on him. To understand this effect, he notes that he "struggled all the more to peer through the book and imagine the living person."[38] In §2 and 3, he emphasizes the philosopher's moral qualities: upright, strong, and courageous, and also simple, constant, and honest. Moreover, like Montaigne, whom both Nietzsche and Emerson admired, Schopenhauer was free and cheerful.

Nietzsche portrays Schopenhauer in an exemplary light — which is also a wink to Emerson's *Representative Men*. This virtuous portrait of Schopenhauer shows that the third *Observation* is all about moral education: "What has actually become of all the reflection on moral questions that at all times was the occupation of every noble society?" Virtue, Nietzsche asserts, is a word to be taken seriously. If there has never been "a greater need for moral educators," then Schopenhauer's role in Nietzsche's protreptic essay is clear: Schopenhauer serves as model for the virtues that it is desirable to develop in young people if they are to become something other than members of a "lost platoon" such as the one that scholars and scientists make up.[39]

It should thus come as no surprise that an *Unfashionable Observation* "on" Schopenhauer says very little about the philosopher's 1819 magnum opus, *The World as Will and as Representation*. When referring to Schopenhauer's works, Nietzsche more often mentions shorter essays collected in the 1851 *Parerga and Paralipomena* — lesser-known works such as "Writers and Styles," "Some Archaeological Considerations," or "On Scholarship and Scholars." These essays show their author's character: his verve and humour, his curiosity and independence.

One of those essays had a particular effect on Nietzsche: "On University Philosophy," which he held as a theory on wisdom (or lack thereof) in the university. Nietzsche referred to this essay in his letters and paraphrased and quoted it as well in his third *Observation*. He takes up Schopenhauer's criticisms of academic philosophy, whether it be the state's claims to control the conditions of philosophical practice or the claims of professional philosophers to define the object of philosophy. While some do "ascend to the level of a little metaphysics," German professors are not prepared in the least to live "for the sake of [their] philosophy," busy as they are with establishing "an obscure empire."[40]

Against the idealism typical of those he would later disdainfully label the "academic 'cud-chewers' and other professors of philosophy,"[41] Nietzsche deplored that the universities were training a hybrid between a thinker and a civil servant: "'current' human beings," professionals who, "in the sense that one speaks of a coin being 'current,'" had an economic value that made them easily tradable on the market of science. "The individual must, so the demand goes, be able on the basis of such general education to appraise himself exactly, so that he will know what demands he can make of life."[42] Nietzsche thereby describes modern education as the source of one's market value. How then could "professional philosophy" even be possible? Is it not an oxymoron?

In his essay, Schopenhauer shows what a philosopher should be: he embodies the counter-model of the teacher as Lehrer and the scholar. In its pages Schopenhauer describes the philosopher as a person of uncompromising integrity and honesty, led by "the most disinterested sincerity of striving, the most irresistible urge to solve the riddle of existence, gravity of profundity, the struggle to penetrate the innermost core of being, and genuine enthusiasm for truth."[43] For Nietzsche, Schopenhauer thus presents a rare example of a visible philosophical life. One of the third *Unfashionable Observation*'s most often quoted sentences is undoubtedly the one that opens §3: "I attach importance to a philosopher only to the extent that he is capable of setting an example." Nietzsche paints a model of philosophy as an exercise that leaves its mark on one's "visible life" and that shows itself, like the philosophers of antiquity, "through facial expressions, demeanor, clothing, food, and custom, more than through what they said, let alone what they wrote."[44]

But why do young people dedicate themselves to higher education, rather than seek to experience a philosophical life? And why does the current era value the scholarly type? In asking these questions, Nietzsche argues that forces other than simple curiosity, love of knowledge, and intellectual honesty are at work. In the second half of his essay he describes thirteen characteristics showing that to value the scholar is to value a way of life that satisfies both the medieval ideal of the scholar and bourgeois aspirations. As we saw in chapter 3, Nietzsche insists on several traits — and most still characterize academics today: a respect for professional environments, the lure of salary and social status, and loyalty to teachers. He also describes trends for which the Anglo-Saxon culture now has precise terms: the tendency to be or become workaholic and the sociological fact known as path-dependency.

This portrait allows Nietzsche to note that the scholar does not so much serve the truth as serve certain "truths," that is those that have useful spin-offs, which are "capable of leading directly to a higher income and a higher position, or at least capable of winning the favour of those who have bread and honors to confer."[45] This is because some perspectives — in other words, some "truths" — are lucrative, while others are not exploitable and tradable on the global market. The academic world — and scholars themselves — limits itself to those that help maintain the professional intellectuals in their status and tasks, thereby ensuring their remuneration and reputation.

Nietzsche therefore finds that his milieu encourages young people to choose a field of study to work in a salaried profession, thereby reaping economic and social benefits, rather than to follow a passion. Moreover, as he wrote in his project for an *Unfashionable Observation* on philology, the young person "chooses his profession at a time when he is not yet able to choose, because he does not know the various professions, because he does not know himself."[46] Nietzsche sees that the result of such a situation is disastrous. "Granted, scholarship has been furthered at an astonishingly quick pace in the last decades, but just look at the scholars, these exhausted hens."[47] In this race for permanent positions at prestigious universities — a competition that Nietzsche knew from personal experience — some hens are already exhausted at the very beginning of their career, emptied of all creative energy, and nevertheless well-trained enough to continue the activities that will provide them with the bourgeois comforts likely to give them a few moments of respite.

And yet, in words reminiscent of Emerson, Nietzsche, in his notes for his unfinished *Observation* on philology, assures that "there is no institution which one should consider superior to one's own soul": that is why one should avoid "putting oneself at the service of."[48]

In the third *Unfashionable Observation* the exemplary figures of Schopenhauer and Emerson complete one another. Nietzsche discusses the education of the individual in democratic culture with Emerson. At the same time, with Schopenhauer he defines a model of philosophical life contra the model conveyed by German academia, because Schopenhauer shows how "to be *simple* and *honest* in thought as in life — in short, to be unfashionable in the most profound sense of the word."[49] The third *Observation* thus tackles properly philosophical problems about culture and education, with Emerson, all while proposing a model for spiritual and moral life, with Schopenhauer.

While publishing *Schopenhauer as Educator* in 1874, Nietzsche was still a young university professor. Yet his essay showed that he had become something other than a pure scholar or a perfect civil servant precisely thanks to the process of personal education for which Schopenhauer had provided him the opportunity and Emerson the questions. It is obvious, if only by the exhortations of §1, that the author of the third *Unfashionable Observation* hoped in turn to have a liberating effect on young souls. The issue at hand was to pursue the philosophical work of self-education in order to bring about a cultural renewal.

The third *Observation* could thus very well be entitled *Nietzsche as Educator*. And this is indeed what the author himself retrospectively noted: in his 1888 autobiography *Ecce Homo*, Nietzsche stated that his 1874 book "delivers an invaluable teaching" precisely on the way in which he conceives the philosopher, "miles apart" from academics.[50] The third *Unfashionable Observation* thus participates to Nietzsche's incessant critical reflection on what it means to creatively practice philosophy.

Chapter 5

A Portrait of the Philosopher as Artist

You are the true "educational institution."
Nietzsche to Wagner, 25 July 1872

In the winter of 1875, after his essays on Strauss, history, and education, Nietzsche started writing yet another *Unfashionable Observation*. This new draft was on philology and the professionalization of knowledge — an issue, as we saw in the first chapter, that preoccupied Nietzsche from the onset of his career. But when a fourth *Observation* did come out in bookstores during the summer of 1876, it was something altogether different. Entitled *Richard Wagner in Bayreuth*, it was to be the last essay in the series. And it was perhaps the most timely: its publication was planned to coincide with the first presentation of Wagner's masterwork, the Bayreuth festival, which included the inauguration of its theatre and the very first performance of the four music dramas that make up the *Ring of the Nibelung* cycle.[1]

The projects on philologists and Wagner coexisted for some time in Nietzsche's mind. His spring 1875 work schedule shows that he planned writing the philology essay during the summer, while autumn and Christmas would be devoted to an essay on Wagner.[2] For Nietzsche the two themes were linked at least since Wagner had published an open letter in the *Norddeutsche allgemeine Zeitung* in support of *The Birth of Tragedy*. Wagner wrote of "waiting for a man to come out of this wonderful field [of academic philology] so that he may tell us, without scholarly language and dreadful quotations, what initiated people can see behind the veil of research, which is wholly incomprehensible for the uninitiated that we are, and tell us if it is worth entertaining such a costly cast."[3]

Greek tragedy was a model for Wagner's quest for a "total" work of art, and Nietzsche had often discussed classical scholarship while visiting Richard and Cosima Wagner. Although they did not take a liking to all of the young professor's projects — Nietzsche's draft for a book on the Pre-Socratic philosophers, for instance, seemed quaint and too far removed from pressing cultural issues — the Wagners were interested in a reflection on the heritage of the Greeks for a modern cultural regeneration in the context of the reform of German educational institutions.[4]

Writing *Richard Wagner in Bayreuth*, though, was not a straightforward task. Since 1870 and for about five years, Nietzsche had been at the forefront of Wagnerianism. He witnessed the birth of the Bayreuth project and the laying of the theatre's foundation stone in 1872. At the time, his admiration for Wagner was total and boundless. But Bayreuth took up all the maestro's energies between 1872 and 1876, and as the festival project progressed, Nietzsche's relationship with Wagner waned. In 1875, Nietzsche was also tired and ill. He had planned to attend the *Ring* rehearsals in Bayreuth during the summer, but instead he went to the Steinabad spa, in the Black Forest. (Nietzsche nevertheless made it to the inauguration of the *Festspiel* in the summer of 1876.)[5]

At the time, Nietzsche also held doubts regarding his writing activity and publication plans. One must keep in mind that his previous four books had either triggered harsh criticism (*The Birth of Tragedy* and the Strauss essay) or gone almost unnoticed (*Schopenhauer as Educator*) — or both (*On the Utility and Liability of History for Life*).[6] As for his other projects (he planned books on the Pre-Socratic philosophers and on the educational institutions), Nietzsche had left his manuscripts unfinished. And as we saw in chapter 3, the plan for his *Unfashionable Observation* series was so ambitiously long that he envisioned its end (which was nowhere in sight) as a "liberation."[7] Moreover, Nietzsche was labelled either as a Wagnerian or a Schopenhauerian. More often than not, he was labelled as both and shunned. Writing — at least, writing in the manner that he had favoured since 1872: cultural criticism joined with classical scholarship in essays with strong Wagnerian and Schopenhauerian overtones — was becoming more of a burden than a spontaneous mode of self-expression.[8]

And now, in 1875, was he really to write an essay specifically on Wagner? Was he to prepare to join the boisterous crowds in Bayreuth? And was there no other form for his philosophical thoughts than yet another essay of cultural criticism?

Milestones on a Blazing Path

Nietzsche's 1880s harsh criticism and derision of Wagner and his music has been the focus of much scholarly attention. It is well-known, for instance, that he turned away from all things German and developed an admiration for French culture during the last years of the 1870s; that he was fond of Georges Bizet's French opera *Carmen* and scorned Wagner's last opera, *Parsifal*; and that he scoffed at the sight (and, later, the souvenir) of Bayreuth as the reunion grounds for large masses of beer-drinking philistines. This cynicism is probably best seen at work in *Ecce Homo*, where Nietzsche reflects upon the conditions that enticed him to write *Human, All Too Human*, in 1876–77:

> one of its preconditions was a deep alienation from everything that surrounded me there ... I woke up in Bayreuth one day ... So where was I? I did not recognize a thing, I hardly recognized Wagner ... The incomparable days of laying the foundation stone, the small circle who *belonged*, who celebrated it and whose dexterous delicacy left nothing to be desired: not a shadow of similarity. *What had happened?* Wagner had been translated into German! The Wagnerian had become master over Wagner! — *German* art! *German* master! *German* beer ... In fact, for the instruction of posterity, a genuine Bayreuther should be stuffed ... with the inscription: the "spirit" on which the "Reich" was founded looked like this.[9]

What is not as often discussed, on the other hand, is Nietzsche's infatuation with Wagnerianism and the extent of his involvement in Wagner's projects in the first half of the 1870s. To recount Nietzsche's position towards the composer, it is not enough to show how *The Birth of Tragedy* calls upon a Dionysian renewal of tragic art through Wagner's music. In fact, arguably all of Nietzsche's writing and projects in the first half of the 1870s was engaged with Wagnerian culture. Wagner had been a complex figure for Nietzsche: a friend, certainly, but more importantly a mentor and inspiration, and even his leader in cultural rejuvenation — perhaps too much for one person alone to represent.

Wagner's role in Nietzsche's early projects is multifarious, and the magnetism of the maestro's personality was instantaneous. Nietzsche met Richard Wagner in Leipzig on 8 November 1868. The next day Nietzsche wrote a long letter to his friend Erwin Rohde in which he described the meeting as a "wonderful adventure." He was immediately seduced by the composer and spent those days in a somewhat "novelistic atmosphere": having the occasion to meet this great man was like "something out of a fairy tale."[10] Wagner casually invited the young philologist to pay him a visit in Tribschen, Switzerland, where the composer had moved after leaving Munich. Whether the composer thought that Nietzsche would really take him up on his invitation or not, what may have been a simple polite gesture turned out to be the start of a relationship.

For Nietzsche, the invitation to Tribschen was more than an honor: it was a sign of fate. After their paths crossed in 1868, Richard Wagner appears in all of Nietzsche's endeavours between 1870 and 1876. Their meeting may have even had an effect on Nietzsche's career path. Curt Paul Janz, in his now classic intellectual biography of the philosopher, believes that the proximity of Wagner was an important factor in Nietzsche's decision to accept an early nomination to the chair of philology at the University of Basel in 1869.[11] In truth, as soon as he was living in Switzerland, Nietzsche travelled many times to Tribschen, about a hundred kilometres south-east of Basel, on the banks of the pristine lake Lucerne.

Retrospectively, their encounter indeed appears fateful, as the chronology makes clear. Even before writing his book on tragedy, Nietzsche diligently sent his first writings to the Wagners, including copies of his February 1870 Basel talk on "Socrates and Tragedy" and his summer 1870 essay "The Dionysian View of the World," so that they could discuss these works when they met in Tribschen. As a Christmas present in 1870, Cosima Wagner offered to Nietzsche Montaigne's *Essays*, a book that he would come to revere. Already in 1871 Nietzsche cherished the idea of founding a cultural and literary newspaper for Bayreuth, which would be edited by Wagner himself. Such a journal would eventually be published as of January 1878 under the title *Bayreuther Blätter*, but Nietzsche played no part in it.[12]

When it came time to publish *The Birth of Tragedy*, which Nietzsche wrote in 1870–71, Wagner recommended his own publisher, Ernst Wilhelm Fritzsch, in Leipzig.[13] Unsurprisingly, Nietzsche dedicated his first book to Wagner. As we saw in chapter 2, references to musicological debates of the time are numerous in Nietzsche's first book, and so are references to Wagner's writings and compositions — if not in an explicit manner, then symbolically. One such example is the image of the bird that comes up in the last two sections of Nietzsche's book. The bird is an allusion to Act 2 of Wagner's *Siegfried*, where a *Waldvogel* saves Siegfried and becomes a messenger of the hero's happy fate. And indeed, Nietzsche in 1872 envisioned his near future as closely entwined as possible with Wagner's cultural projects. He wrote to Erwin Rohde in April that he would soon tour Germany and lecture on the *Ring* cycle for the Wagner Societies, a task (although it never materialized) that he likened to doing "one's duty in time of conflict."[14]

Nietzsche paid his last visit to Tribschen in the spring of 1872, before the Wagners moved, in May, to Bayreuth to oversee the construction of the theatre and their new house, Villa Wahnfried. Nietzsche closed the Tribschen chapter of his life reluctantly: "On this day, Tribschen is over. I spent a few days more here, it was like living within ruins; days of melancholy."[15] Tribschen had been a place of intimacy, where a few friends were admitted and shared in the pleasure of amiable and stimulating discussion with the maestro. At Villa Wahnfried, things would be quite different. Nietzsche travelled to Bavaria for the May ceremonies in Bayreuth, and the laying of the theatre's foundation stone. The 22 May 1872 event unfolded in full grandiosity, with Wagner directing Beethoven's Ninth Symphony on his own birthday.

In October 1872 Nietzsche wrote that "for a unique spectator such as Wagner I abandon all laurels with which the present time could wish to crown me."[16] In his eyes, Wagner was his principal reader, the magnet that attracted all his finished and even unfinished work, and the amplifier that would ensure that Nietzsche's cultural thought would have an effect thanks to a tight network throughout Germany.

Nietzsche did continue to present his writings to the Wagners for comments and discussions. Later that same year, he offered as a Christmas gift to Cosima Wagner a manuscript of five "Prefaces to Five Unwritten Works," a gesture intended to pursue discussions that they had had in person and in writing. These short essays — which Nietzsche never published — are directly related to his other writings of the time. They interrogate philosophy's innermost drives such as its "passion for truth," they reflect upon the future of educational institutions and the importance of Schopenhauer for German culture, and they develop issues pertaining to Greek political culture and ethics.[17]

But the young philologist also took on more specifically Wagnerian missions. In January 1873 he published in the *Musikalisches Wochenblatt* — his and Wagner's publisher's musical magazine — a short article defending Wagner against psychiatric accusations of megalomania: this was Nietzsche's "A New Year's Word to the Editor of the Magazine *Im neuen Reich*," the only article he ever published in a cultural newspaper or magazine. During the spring of that same year he wrote his first *Unfashionable Observation*: the fact that it was on David Friedrich Strauss was to the liking of the composer. Since Strauss had publicly criticized Wagner and supported the conductor Franz Lachner, Wagner had a score to settle with Strauss and encouraged Nietzsche to write against him.[18]

Also in 1873, Nietzsche composed "A Call to Germans," a thirteen hundred words essay intended to stimulate private funding for Wagner's Bayreuth project. It was written at the behest of Emil Heckel, whom Nietzsche had met during the 1872 Bayreuth ceremony and with whom he discussed the possibility of founding a Swiss Wagner Society (another project that did not materialize). The short essay was printed in October 1873 so it could be distributed to members of the Wagner Societies across Germany.[19] In its pages, Nietzsche emphatically wrote that "the word 'Bayreuth' is not only addressed to large numbers of people or to specific musical taste": for Nietzsche that word concerned first and foremost the German nation and culture.

Nietzsche in the 1876 Wagner Essay

In October 1874, exactly six years after meeting Wagner, Nietzsche was still praising the composer in his third *Unfashionable Observation* and naming him alongside other German geniuses, "those constitutions made of iron, such as Beethoven, Goethe, Schopenhauer, and Wagner."[20] Yet the tone changed within less than a year.

His 1875 notebooks and correspondence show that Nietzsche alternated between days during which he felt a pressing need to write an essay on the figure of the artist and moments when he was seized by cramps upon hearing echoes from the upcoming Bayreuth festival. In the early 1870s, Wagner was the herald of a new culture, the creator who brought about a cultural metamorphosis for Germany. The Bayreuth Festival finally showed to Nietzsche that the formerly revolutionary artist had metamorphosed into a composer for a bourgeois audience. Disillusioned, Nietzsche advised his friend Carl von Gersdorff in September 1875 not to expect new work from him: "Publications disgust me above all else!"[21]

Nevertheless, he was writing. Nietzsche exerted himself: by the mid-autumn 1875, he had finished the Wagner essay's first eight sections. He took a break, uncertain that he would finish at all; but pressed by the publisher, the composer, and the unprecedented cultural event that was unfolding, he finally wrote the last sections in 1876. He was able to send the complete manuscript to his publisher, Schmeitzner, so that 1500 copies appeared in time for the opening of the Bayreuth Festival, in July 1876. Relieved, Nietzsche could attend the opening of the Bayreuth festival while knowing that he was closing the eight-year-long Wagner chapter of his life.

At first glance, the fourth *Unfashionable Observation* seems completely entwined with Wagnerianism. That may explain why it is rarely read and little commented upon today. *Richard Wagner in Bayreuth* can indeed give the impression of a purely contextual and at times falsely laudatory essay, useful only to historians of Wagnerian music or those interested in Nietzsche's intellectual biography. But a first glance is always a rapid one — surely one must peer longer to see what the essay has to offer.

Ironically, the current readership's disinterest might in part be triggered by Nietzsche's own retrospective assessment. Twelve years after its publication, he pointed out in *Ecce Homo* that the *Observation* on Wagner cannot help the readership understand or even articulate the problem that Wagner represented for him.[22] Why, then, should we read it today?

Two facts point to the importance of *Richard Wagner in Bayreuth*. One is that it was the first of Nietzsche's works to appear in a translation. This shows that the European circulation of his Wagner essay was important for its author. Surely Nietzsche saw something there other than its Wagnerianism, especially at a point of his life when he was turning his back on Bayreuth. Unfortunately, the 1877 French version by Marie Baumgartner had a limited circulation because it was issued by the German publisher Schmeitzner rather than by a French publisher.[23] The second fact, again found in *Ecce Homo*, is that Nietzsche retrospectively asserted that the essay was "just basically ... about me."

What, then, can we learn about "Mister Nietzsche" and his philosophy from reading the Wagner essay? Quite a bit, it turns out — and this is worth looking into.[24]

A close reading of *Richard Wagner in Bayreuth* shows that Nietzsche expands on his conception of philosophy as embodied cultural praxis by defining it as an art. He does so through an examination of two related themes: an isochronal conception of history inspired by the historian Jacob Burckhardt, on the one part, and a critique of writing and conceptual language, on the other. In this respect, the essay is noteworthy for its performative aspect: Nietzsche uses language in creative ways to a degree that he had not reached in his previous books. Reading the Wagner essay therefore helps to pinpoint Nietzsche's original conception of creative philosophy.

Isochronal History and the Cultural Task of Philosophy

Richard Wagner in Bayreuth opens and closes on allusions to Jacob Burckhardt, the famous Swiss historian who was a colleague and friend of Nietzsche's in Basel. Nietzsche thereby inscribes his reflection on Wagner within a larger context: that of a reflection on the nature of history and cultural events. The essay thus complements the more famous second *Unfashionable Observation* on the uses and abuses of history.

In the second sentence of his essay, Nietzsche writes that "In and of itself no event is great, even if entire constellations disappear, nations perish, vast states are founded, and wars are waged with tremendous forces and tremendous losses; the breath of history has blown away many such things as though they were nothing but snow-flakes."[25] One could perhaps hear echoes of Marcus Aurelius or Emerson in these musings on the passage of time. But Nietzsche is alluding to a talk that he had heard Burckhardt deliver in Basel on 6 November 1870. While reflecting upon the notion of historical greatness, the historian stressed that "greatness remains a relative concept, and we can never hope to attain an absolute concept of greatness."[26]

By alluding to Burckhardt, Nietzsche asserts throughout his essay a conception of history as isochronal rather than teleological, thereby pursuing his disagreement with the dominant conceptions of history as progress (Hegel) and newness (Marx). The teleological (from the Greek *telos*: end or goal) conception of history views time as a continuous, chronological progression towards higher levels of cultural, intellectual, moral, and political developments that, in turn, are considered new; whereas isochronism (from the Greek *isos*: equal, and *chronos*: time) focuses on the recurring configurations of events through historical time.

An isochronal view of history therefore sees patterns through time, similarities in values, social structures, or modes of living, and considers that history does not progress nor augment: newness, in fact, is rare. To make sense of history, the isochronal historian therefore identifies similar events that reoccur through time. That is why Nietzsche, for instance, is more interested in pinpointing "affinities and kinships between Kant and the Eleatics, between Schopenhauer and Empedocles, between Aeschylus and Richard Wagner," rather than considering each only within its past context and dissecting it into specific and unique characteristics. These kinships sketch cultural configurations through which, as Nietzsche writes in a Burckhardtian way, "we are almost tangibly admonished about the extremely relative nature of all conceptions of time."[27]

In this view, the important factor of change is not simply the passage of time: it is the recurrence of event configurations that are culturally rich in that they have a resonance or effect within their context and generate an increase in the variety of cultural forms and events. And indeed, if historical time is not teleological and if, to return to Nietzsche's opening statement, "no event has greatness in itself," then that which has greatness — understood as cultural effect and, thereby, meaning and posterity — is the inscription of an event in a context within which it resonates and can be diffused. The context may give its thickness to an event.

Greatness thus depends on the capacity of the acting individual to seize the right moment for action. This is why it is necessary "to take precise enough aim," and to "recognize and choose the proper time."[28] If the individual is not attuned to context, personal strength may well be exhorted and forces spent here and there, they may nevertheless be simply squandered while thus thrown at random. Nietzsche therefore calls for a conscious effort at being well-attuned to cultural context in order to prepare historical change. In later works he repeated this belief that the development of humanity must not be left to pure chance. *Human, All Too Human*, for instance, proposes that cultures could orient their development towards desired paths, and this more efficiently than nature, which in reality spends a lot but wastes as much by shooting its arrows blindly.[29]

This dependence of historical change on contextual events implies a dependence, in turn, on uncommon individuals whose greatness lies in their awareness of history, desire for cultural change, and force and timeliness of action. We saw in the previous chapter how Nietzsche hoped to entice the individual person to remain independent of cultural trends, typical modes of life, and social uniformity. Indeed, since history is not oriented by predetermined progress, the singular event (as well as the singular person who triggers it) is of primary importance as concerns its cultural role: the event can inflect the course of history. But above all, the non-linear unfolding of history means that events are not predestined. As Nietzsche puts it, "There were no portents, no transitions, no intermediary stages that pointed to an enterprise such as that of Bayreuth."[30] Wagner seized the moment — and acted.

Perhaps the most important aspect of this isochronal view of history for the development of Nietzsche's philosophy is that the resurgence of past configurations within the present times informed him as to the changeable nature of human beings. In other words, his historical thought opens onto a philosophical anthropology that asserts the malleability of humanity. In a passage of the Wagner essay, Nietzsche gives voice to a would-be advocate of art as entertainment: "'Given how human beings are,' someone might say, 'such art is sufficient and appropriate — and they have never been different!'" Nietzsche's answer to the entertainment advocate is firm: "They [human beings] have certainly been different." Against the idea of a fixed and unchanging human nature, Nietzsche asserts that the modern, Western way of being human can indeed be "changed and reformed," "transformed and rejuvenated." Subverting metaphors that German philosophy conveys at least since Kant's *Foundation of the Metaphysics of Morals*, Nietzsche believes that the foundations of modern culture are not so solid that "the entire edifice" cannot "shudder and collapse" under the impact of a new event or the return of a previous cultural configuration.[31]

The notion of human malleability in turn leads Nietzsche to the important position which concludes the essay's §3: "It seems to me that the most important question in all of philosophy is the extent to which things possess an unalterable nature and form, so that, once this question has been answered, we can with relentless courage set about the *improvement of that aspect of the world recognized as being alterable*. This is also taught by the true philosophers through their actions, in that they work toward the improvement of the very alterable insights of human beings instead of keeping their wisdom to themselves."[32] This passage commands attention. First, it is worth noticing that it is one of the very few parts of the fourth *Observation* where Nietzsche uses the first person singular. Here, he is clearly stating his position as to what philosophy is and must do. Nietzsche explicitly affirms — even underlines — what he considers to be philosophy's task: philosophers must seek to enhance human beings through targeted improvements of that which is modifiable. This, says Nietzsche, is what prompted philosophers of antiquity to publicize and transmit their wisdom, rather than keep it private. Philosophy must henceforth recognize that human beings are modifiable and work to create richer cultural configurations than those currently valued, embodied, and transmitted through education in the Western world. Soon pursuing this reflection on history in his next book, *Human, All Too Human*, Nietzsche writes that "the lack of historical sense is the hereditary defect of all philosophers ... They do not want to learn that the [human being] has become." His message is clear: it is time to stop considering human beings as though they had a fixed nature. All evolves and becomes, as "there are *no eternal facts*."[33]

For Nietzsche isochronal history is clearly a window into the creative, cultural task of philosophy. By linking Wagner to this reflection, Nietzsche unites art with history and philosophy. He shows that the composer "perceives qualities in contemporary human beings that do not belong to the unalterable character and bone structure of human nature, but instead are changeable, indeed, transitory, and that it is precisely *due to these qualities* that art must be homeless among them and he himself [must be] the messenger of another age."[34] Not only does Wagner thus appear as one of those great individuals capable of bringing about cultural renewal, Nietzsche also shows him as producing his art in full awareness that cultural effort is not a question of recovering a golden age, nor of aiming for a utopia, nor deciphering a future that would already be written. Cultural effort consists in giving a new present-day form to the past.

A Question of Medium

The task of a historically informed philosophy — the "improvement of that aspect of the world recognized as being alterable" — poses the question of medium: through what can the philosopher hope to modify culture? For centuries in Western culture, philosophy's medium has been verbal language and most precisely — in the case of German philosophical thought, which has dominated the conception of philosophy in Western culture at least since Kant — a language of conceptual abstraction used for the construction of metaphysical systems. But that is not the only model for a philosophical medium. As we saw in the previous chapters, Nietzsche favours an embodied practice, making a case for a lived, holistic philosophy. This is most visible, for instance, in the opening sentences of *Schopenhauer as Educator*'s §3: "I attach importance to a philosopher only to the extent that he is capable of setting an example ... the philosopher must supply this example in his visible life, and not merely in his books; that is, it must be presented in the way the philosophers of Greece taught, through facial expressions, demeanor, clothing, food, and custom, more than through what they said, let alone what they wrote. How far Germans are from this courageous visibility in our philosophical life; here the body is just beginning to be liberated after the spirit long seems to have been liberated."[35]

It is striking that discourse ("books," "writing") are not at the forefront of Nietzsche's conception of philosophy. Rather, the body ("facial expressions, demeanor") and embodied cultural practices ("food, custom") are. In his notes and in his next books, Nietzsche turns to another example of non-systematic and non-conceptual philosophy: that of the French moralist thinkers of the eighteenth century, such as Chamfort and Vauvenargues. These gave an example of philosophy as psychological observation of social life, written through short, often humoristic epigrams destined to have an effect on the reader's mind and body (for instance, through surprise and laughter).[36] Evidently, Nietzsche's models for philosophical practice are far removed from the leading academic definition of philosophy.

An essay on Wagner was of course a perfect occasion to reflect upon the praxis of philosophy and the question of its medium. In his fourth *Observation* Nietzsche specifies that art and philosophy are both languages — and as such they are first and foremost communicative: they enable human beings to inform one another "about their most basic necessities of life."[37] How can a philosopher ensure the reception and impact of his message in this respect? There certainly are ways of communicating that are more efficient and precise than others. Whereas philosophy does not generally regard style as worthy of attention, Nietzsche believes that this aspect of discourse cannot be set aside or ignored.

Nietzsche is adamant that art is much more effective than the verbal language on which philosophy usually relies. His 1876 reflection on language repeats but also completes the critique that he had started three years earlier in an unfinished essay *On Truth and Lies in a Nonmoral Sense* — yet another of his 1870s abandoned manuscripts — and testifies to his long-lasting interest for written style and constant concern with the communication of his ideas. He deplores that through the domination of abstract, conceptual thought, "everywhere in this civilized world [verbal] *language* is diseased." He uses metaphors of health, but also subjugation to express the effect of the dominion of conceptuality on philosophical thought: moderns have become "the slaves of words," they "are seized by the madness of general concepts, indeed, by the pure sounds of words."[38]

Clear, abstract concepts do not efficiently serve communication. Although we can pronounce and use them, they do not succeed in naming our inner states or expressing the minute nuances of our feelings. Nietzsche perhaps best expressed this in his 1880 book *Dawn*: "Wrath, hate, love, compassion, craving, knowing, joy, pain — these are all names for *extreme* states: the milder middle degrees, and to say nothing of the lower ones that are constantly in play, elude us and yet it is precisely they that weave the web of our character and destiny ... *We are none of us what* we appear to be solely in those states for which we have consciousness and words."[39] To efficiently convey notions of feelings, intimacy, and bodily states, concepts must be helped by a wide range of stylistic devices: narration for a description of lived context, evocation through metaphors or allegories, impersonation through characters, to name but a few. These are devices that novelists, essayists, and all authors of literature know well, and that Nietzsche himself, as we will see in the next chapters, made extensive use of as of the 1880s. The 1876 Wagner essay shows that Nietzsche was already developing his specific and, in a way, unphilosophical art of writing philosophy in the mid-1870s.

The Wagner essay shows that Nietzsche was clearly in favour of art over essay writing. Unlike philosophy, "art cannot be transported in the ship of written records."[40] For one, because it does not depend on verbal language art avoids the traps of conceptual thought in which philosophy is entangled. Echoing ideas from *The Birth of Tragedy*, Nietzsche asserts that through tragic drama, Wagner "thinks in visible and palpable events, not in concepts." *The Ring of the Nibelung* is indeed "an immense system of thought without the conceptual form of thought." The artist thereby avoids the "greater danger" that "*verbal language* awakens in us the theoretical human being."[41]

But more importantly, art speaks to the body. It speaks to our senses (whether hearing, seeing, or touching, etc.), and often with synesthetic force — that is, it affects many senses at once (precisely as Wagner's *Gesamtkunstwerk* was aiming to do by linking music to poetry, rhythm, gest, space, architecture, etc.). By reaching the body through our senses, art affects the individual more directly and completely than verbal language can. For Nietzsche, art is therefore much more likely to have a cultural effect. Works of art have more possibilities of action than philosophical works do. The fourth *Observation* is thus an essay on artistic means and action as well as a reflection on philosophy as art. And what better way to observe the action of art on the body than to examine a specific artist?

In his first three *Unfashionable Observations* Nietzsche set about understanding the type of the scholar by examining the drives behind scientific and academic modes of living. Now, in the fourth *Observation*, he conducts the drive-analysis of an artist through the person of Richard Wagner. The composer, in other words, is for Nietzsche an occasion for fieldwork.

Trieb, the term for drive, appears no fewer than seven times in *Richard Wagner in Bayreuth*. Although his terminology varies — he sometimes speaks of "drives or sides," "profound forces," or "tyrannical omnipotence"[42] — he narrows down his drive-analysis of the artist to two impulses that, from within the deep obscurity of our internal urges, aspire to externalization — or, as he puts it, to light, power, "bright air and sunshine." These internal thrusts push the artist Wagner through "all paths, crevices, and ravines" that he experiences. The first impulse is agitated, violent, and wild: it expresses a "limitless, tyrannical desire"[43] and opens a combative path. The second impulse is soft, tender, and purifying: it is "a protective, as it were, motherly impulse" that opens onto creativity.[44]

These passages show that Nietzsche describes the artists' drives as violence and care. This gendered analysis was frequent in nineteenth-century musicological analysis. But Nietzsche also describes Wagner himself as a human being who is both masculine and feminine: "Each further stage in Wagner's development is marked by the fact that the two basic forces of his being joined ever more closely together."[45] The artist's strength lies in the rare balance of these drives, in their interrelation and "submission of the one to the other."[46] Creation comes from coupling these drives. Nietzsche thus takes up an image that he explored in *The Birth of Tragedy*: that of creation as an ecstatic manifestation of internal drives, a discharge of internal forces in a "joyful self-renunciation." The Wagner essay repeats these images of Dionysian frenzy, its "ecstatic gestures," "floating dance," "shuddering," and "love."[47]

Nietzsche thus interprets art against a backdrop of biological creation: procreation. And indeed, the matter on which this impulsive expression acts is the very place where drives are expressed: the body — both the individual, physical body and the larger, collective body that is culture. Creation, then, is not only about "the arts" strictly speaking. It is about culture, "a rejoicing of humanity at the guaranteed cohesion and continuation of all that is fundamentally human. —"[48]

Nietzsche's 1876 Wagner essay proposes a conception of philosophy as a praxis that strives to alter culture. Its holistic impact depends on the medium that it will use. Nietzsche believes some impact may be achieved through lived example — in other words, by living philosophically, as did the Hellenistic philosophers that he had in mind in *Schopenhauer as Educator*. But the impact of concrete, lived example is surely limited to the circle of people surrounding the philosopher. (As we saw in the first chapter, Nietzsche hoped for a time to unite something akin to a "cultural sect," but to no avail.) A philosopher may certainly hope to reach a wider audience through what has become philosophy's principal medium for centuries: writing.

For its reception and impact philosophy depends on how the author will affect its readers. Nietzsche believes that for philosophical writing to do so it must be freed from the dominion and narrowness of conceptual language and use art's supra-linguistic means of conveying meaning through the body. The more a philosophical text triggers one's senses, the more reception, effect, and transmission its messages should have. Philosophy, for Nietzsche, must therefore aim for an embodied, synesthetic understanding. A book could thus have a rich mood, as he wrote in an 1874 notebook: "Of a book I demand *mood* [*Stimmung*] as unity and measure; this determines the choice of words, the type and number of metaphors, the path and the end."[49]

The fourth *Unfashionable Observation* is Nietzsche's first firm encounter with the issue of philosophical style. In this sense, the essay is not only a reflection on the creative nature of philosophy's cultural task: it is also a performance. Nietzsche puts synesthetic writing into practice, thus paving the way to a renewed style. The essay indeed uses a wide array of creative linguistic tools to reach the readers' senses. For instance, Nietzsche uses certain stylistic devices to give rhythm to sentences. He praises Wagner for his own use of *Stabreim*, the alliterative versification, based on repetitive consonants (rather than vowel rhymes) and syllabic accentuation for memorization purposes, that is typical of Germanic and Anglo-Saxon texts of the late Middle Ages (e.g., in the *Edda* or in *Beowulf*).[50]

Also, Nietzsche often illustrates his positions through a value-laden vocabulary. For instance, to speak of a work of art's impact he uses two words in German: both the word of Germanic origin, *Wirkung*, and the one of Latin origin, *Effect*. Whereas the first is used positively, the second is used negatively and often in quotation marks. "Effect" thus symbolizes the derivative, artificial, and even fake impact of certain works of art (most notably, the composer Giacomo Meyerbeer).[51]

The *Observation* on Wagner makes a rich use of metaphors that construct semantic webs. Some are used in a typical fashion: for instance, the architectural metaphor to speak of culture in terms of edifice and foundations, the political to speak of power relations (e.g., in §5), the economic to speak of cultural works as resources. As in many texts of Nietzsche's from this period, the dominant metaphor remains the medical, in both its positive (therapeutic) and negative (pathological) meanings. Wagner, for instance, is praised for his "*astringent* power,"[52] and art is described as a means for healing but also as an undue anaesthetic. These metaphors suggest the difficulty of finding a balance between agitation and apathy: art is a precarious equilibrium that can tip towards pathology.

Through their evocative power, metaphors draw semantic webs — sense-rich scenes within which the reader grasps the meaning that Nietzsche strives to convey to our embodied understanding. *Richard Wagner in Bayreuth* is rich in landscape contexts — as are many later texts of Nietzsche's, such as many scenes in *Zarathustra* or several aphorisms in *Dawn*. The garden evokes the flow of life at springtime; the cave evokes depths; the sea evokes the forceful flow of the current and drives; mountain summits recall that from an overhead position "the yearning to descend out of the heights into the depths"[53] may be strong.

In §9 Nietzsche stressed that "the most powerful aspect of Wagner's talent" was his ability "to coin a new language for every work and also give the new inwardness a new body, a new sound."[54] Wagner, in other words, had created a mood — the mood of his Gesamtkunstwerk. How does one construct the mood of a book, an idea, a philosophy? What could be the artistic tools ensuring that a work of philosophy have an embodied effect on its readers? What could a "new language" for philosophy look and sound like?

In the mid-1870s, Nietzsche was just starting to enrich his artistic palette. The issue of style and the aesthetics of philosophical discourse was soon to be the focus of much reflection, effort — and craft.

Chapter 6

His Best Prose

NIETZSCHE'S PREFACES

My books are hooks; if they don't attract anyone to me, then they are meaningless!
Nietzsche to E. Förster-Nietzsche, mid-August 1885

Friedrich Nietzsche was a prolific author. He published seventeen books between January 1872, when his first work appeared in bookshops, and January 1889, when his last one did. Seventeen books in as many years? Surely enough to satisfy any author.[1] Nietzsche also wrote many prefaces — more, even, than books. During the same seventeen-year period, he completed twenty-six prefaces. He put about a third of these texts aside, along with manuscripts that he never finished, but he published the other two-thirds. What was it about prefaces that compelled Nietzsche to write so many?

Although he had written some eleven prefaces before the mid-1880s, it is only as of *Beyond Good and Evil*, published in 1886, that he systematically opened his books with a preface. The most striking in his prefatory corpus are perhaps the five prefaces that he composed during the spring, summer, and autumn of 1886. These five prefaces are similar in tone, style, and intent, as we will see later in this chapter. Nietzsche conceived them with the explicit aim of "rejuvenating" those of his books that he deemed to be his most important.[2] And he was extremely satisfied with the outcome: in a letter to his friend Franz Overbeck in November of that year, he declared that these prefaces were "probably the best prose that I have written to date."[3] The simple fact that Nietzsche wrote so many prefaces shows that he ascribed value to a literary form that, as we will soon see with Derrida and Hegel, is rarely prized by philosophers. This is certainly worth looking into.

As Richard Schacht noted, Nietzsche's prefaces "may have been to little avail in his attempt to make himself understood at the time; but they are of considerable value to those who seek to make sense of him today."[4] Unfortunately for Nietzsche's philosophical project, however, commentators have often considered his prefaces inasmuch as they were autobiographical texts. These readers were perhaps spurred by his acknowledgement that his 1886 prefaces contained "a sort of 'developmental history.'"[5] Two French scholars appear as opposites on this interpretative spectrum. On the one side, in the 1920s Charles Andler, arguably the first Nietzsche scholar, read the 1886 prefaces to see how "Nietzsche interprets his own past," while on the other, aesthetic theorist Jean-Marie Schaeffer disregarded Nietzsche's prefaces precisely for what he deemed to be their "self-laudatory" tone. In a study of philosophical prefaces, Schaeffer refused to take Nietzsche's prefaces seriously as philosophical texts because he read them as signs of "mania," "narcissism," "megalomania," and on the other hand, also, "supreme self-deprecation."[6]

It is certainly true that Nietzsche abundantly speaks of himself in his 1886 prefaces. But Schaeffer's judgment is not only caricatural; it is also a misreading that entirely misses why the author presents himself the way he did. Nietzsche crafted his prefaces much as he crafted his works. So why did he make a point to speak of himself in the third person? Are we to take this "Herr Nietzsche" seriously?[7] This authorial staging is a literary device that can be interrogated.

Some scholars did judge Nietzsche's prefaces to be worthy of attention. In the Anglophone world, Richard Schacht and Marta Faustino devoted essays to Nietzsche's 1880s prefaces, as did some European scholars: for instance, Wojciech Simson studied Nietzsche's typographic and phonetic devices in his 1886 prefaces, and Paul van Tongeren examined how Nietzsche uses prefaces as an experimental form of writing. Furthermore, in some languages — German, Italian, French — scholars (myself included) have republished Nietzsche's collected 1886 prefaces as a book, thereby proposing to readers that they consider them as a coherent work.[8]

Surely, we must take Nietzsche's prefaces seriously as writings and as parts of his philosophical works. An investigation is called for: What do his prefaces do and how are they crafted to do so? But to start off, do we already know what, exactly, is a preface? To clarify this, one may turn to literary theory and discourse analysis.

Attempt at a Definition

Etymologically, a preface means to "speak before": it is "the author's introduction to a book usually explaining the object and scope of what follows." (A preface is thus almost synonymous with a foreword, except that the latter is "commonly written by someone other than the author of the text.")[9] Yet, literary theorists distinguish between preface and introduction on at least four fronts: length, timing, quantity, and relation to the whole.

As for the first two, a preface is shorter than an introduction and it is written after the work is completed. In fact, "a foreword is thus always an afterword" — yet many literary theorists do not make a difference between a preface inserted in a book as a *fore*word and a preface inserted as an *after*word.[10] As concerns their quantity, the difference is clear: an introduction is unique. There cannot be more than one introduction to a book — indeed, a development needs only one introduction and one conclusion — whereas an author can (and often does) write many prefaces for a same work. The French literary theorist Gérard Genette therefore distinguished *original prefaces* — written for the first edition of a book — from *ulterior prefaces* — written for reprints, expanded editions, translations, etc. And just as there can be multiple prefaces to one work, there can also be none. It is not necessary that a work have a preface, and many books are published without their author having written one.

A preface's status in relation to the whole work is therefore different from that of an introduction. The preface stands, as it were, "outside" the completed work that it presents to the readership. A preface, in short, is generally not considered a part of the development: it is optional. That may explain why prefaces often go unnoticed in the philosophical corpus. One exception is Jacques Derrida. In his 1972 book *Dissemination*, Derrida examined the practice of writing prefaces in philosophy and asked an apparently simple question: "But what do prefaces actually do?"[11] That question appears, of course, in his book's preface.

Genette, who sought to dissect and classify all literary aspects of a written work, answered Derrida's question in a practical way: the aim of an original preface is to explain *why* and *how* one should read the book. "The two objectives imply, therefore, despite all the customary disavowals, that the reader begins by reading the preface." Prefaces relate to authorial intent: with the preface the author makes sure that the book be read, and especially that it be read in a certain way, because "a book that in its first edition is read improperly, and *a fortiori* not read at all, risks having no other edition."[12]

Wolfgang Leiner, who was a scholar of seventeenth-century French literature, added to Genette's answer to Derrida: he stressed that a preface is a text in which the author speaks to the reader. "Beyond their many possible differences, all prefatory discourses have a common trait: someone is always addressing themselves to someone; in these texts one sees the presence of an *I* concerned with getting its word and message to a reader, the addressee of the preface, who is present as a *you*." In this way, a preface is similar to a conversation — and as such it is very much alive.[13]

However, in asking what prefaces *do*, Derrida had a more philosophical question in mind: what does the fact that a philosopher wrote a preface tell us about the work at hand? Derrida agreed that a preface is different from an introduction — in fact, he believed them to be radically at odds. He pointed out that the introduction to a philosophical work is wholly part of that work and its development, whereas a preface remains on the periphery. He would thus agree with Schaeffer that it is the person as philosopher who writes the introduction, whereas it is the person as author who writes the preface.[14] This point echoes both Derrida's and Schaeffer's inspiration in all matters anti-prefatory: Hegel.

Hegel expressed his dismissal of prefaces in these terms: "In the case of a philosophical work, such clarification [as that which a preface usually presents] not only seems superfluous, but also improper and inadequate to the nature of philosophical research." (This dismissal was of course written in his preface to his magnum opus.) According to him, all that a preface would say about philosophy — such as "historical considerations" regarding the content and results of the work at hand, or the circumstances that brought the author to write this work, or the author's view as to the work's relationship to other contributions to the field — "would have no value as a philosophical mode of exposition." Derrida (who in his own 1972 preface was commenting on Hegel's preface to the *Phenomenology of Spirit*) appears to agree: "Philosophical exposition has as its essence the capacity and even the duty to do without a preface."[15]

For both Derrida and Hegel, then, prefaces are considered worthless because they remain outside of the philosophical development. Derrida thereby describes a preface metaphorically as "an empty husk, a piece of formal refuse, a moment of dryness or loquacity, sometimes both at once."[16] Yet Derrida seems irritated by something more than a preface's supposed "exteriority." Literary theorists generally consider prefaces to be a "continuation and emphasis of the enterprise towards finalizing" a work.[17] Derrida believed it was "ludicrous to attempt a preface that is truly one" precisely because we "*know* semantic saturation to be impossible."[18] The writing of a preface, for Derrida, is an absurd attempt at finalization — but it is also a precious window enabling one to better appreciate the radical openness of a written work. The very first sentence of his preface to *Dissemination* expressed both that belief in infinite interpretation and his concurrent irritation with prefaces: "This (therefore) will not have been a book."[19]

But is a preface really an attempt at finalization? It seems that something is left unnoticed in Derrida's reflections and in Schaeffer's and others' comments on Nietzsche's prefaces: its active and even performative aspect, made evident through the fact that a preface is a "communication act," an "enunciative event."[20] As such, a preface has an inherently active dimension that does not boil down to the fact that the author is therethrough speaking to the reader, as Leiner pointed out. The active dimension rests upon the fact that evidently, by writing a preface the author is clarifying one's place and position within the world of discourses.[21] In other words, the narrow communication act (from author to reader) is also a wider social act (of the author within the field).

As the scholar of discourse analysis Frédéric Cossutta has written: "Any philosophy, no matter how it philosophically solves the issue of its own expressiveness, must satisfy the requirements that are inherent to communication and negotiate a relationship with its audience and the social institutions that regulate the distribution of discourse. In short, a philosopher must develop strategies for recognition, make alliances, address oneself to specialists, be accepted by one's peers, and seek to formalize one's doctrine."[22] Whether Hegel or Derrida acknowledged it or not, by writing prefaces they were participating in this "distribution of discourse" in their own society, institution, and field. And both their prefaces served to clarify for their intended audience the status that they ascribed to their philosophical work.

The same goes for Nietzsche — with a philosophical twist.

Nietzsche's Prefaces

Before investigating the literary construction and philosophical effect of Nietzsche's "best prose," it will be useful to size his prefatory corpus. The chart in table 6.1 presents the complete prefaces (numbered #1 to #26) that Nietzsche wrote in the seventeen years between the publication of his first and last books.[23] Some of Nietzsche's works are missing from this chart. He published ten books without a preface: the *Unfashionable Observations* I, III, and IV; *Human, All Too Human* and its two "Additions" (*Mixed Opinions and Maxims* and *The Wanderer and his Shadow*); *Dawn*; the second and third parts of *Thus Spoke Zarathustra*; and *The Gay Science*. The preface to *Beyond Good and Evil* (#12) is heavily highlighted in the chart because it is a tipping point: one can see that as of the publication of this book Nietzsche wrote an original preface for all his new publications (#18 to #26), thereby showing, as Tongeren pointed out, that "the preface as a genre gradually became more important" for him.[24] The five 1886 prefaces (#13–#17) are lightly highlighted in the chart to make them stand out as a whole.

A quick glance at this overview reveals that most prefaces written during the 1870s were published only posthumously (eight out of ten). In other words, Nietzsche either did not conceive them for publication (#5–#9)[25] or abandoned the projects and manuscripts they related to (#2–#4). This shows that he valued prefatory writing

Table 6.1 Tally of Nietzsche's complete prefaces, 1871–88[1]

	Indication of date when the preface was written	*Work prefaced*	*Title of the preface*	*Type of preface*	*Indication of place where the preface was written*
1	End of 1871	*BT*	Vorwort an Richard Wagner	Original	Basel, Switzerland
2	[Winter 1872]	*FEI*[2]	Vorrede, zu lesen vor den Vorträgen, obwohl sie sich eigentlich nicht auf sie bezieht	Original (posthumous)	[Basel]
3–4	[Spring 1872]	*PTAG*[3]	[no title] [no title]	Original (posthumous)	[Basel]
5–9	29 December 1872		Fünf Vorreden zu fünf ungeschriebenen Bücher[4]	Original (posthumous)	[Basel]
10	[1874]	*UO* 2 (*UL*)	Vorwort	Original	[Basel]
11	[1882]	*Z* 1	Zarathustra's Vorrede	Original (actorial)	[Sils Maria, Switzerland]
12	June 1885	*BGE*	Vorrede	Original	Sils Maria, Upper Engadine

1 In this table, information that was not supplied by Nietzsche himself in his preface is given in square brackets. Dates indicate when the preface was written, not when its corresponding book or manuscript was published.
2 Unfinished manuscript.
3 Unfinished manuscript.
4 This is the title of the collection. Each of the prefaces has a title: *On the Pathos of Truth*, *Thoughts on the Future of Our Educational Institutions*, *The Greek State*, *The Relationship of Schopenhauerian Philosophy to the German Culture*, and *Homer's Contest*.

Table 6.1/*continued*

	Indication of date when the preface was written	*Work prefaced*	*Title of the preface*	*Type of preface*	*Indication of place where the preface was written*
13	Spring 1886	*HAH* I	Vorrede[5]	Ulterior (2nd ed.)	Nice, France
14	[August 1886]	*BT*	Versuch einer Selbstkritik	Ulterior (2nd ed.)[6]	[Sils Maria]
15	September 1886	*HAH* II	Vorrede	Ulterior (2nd ed.)	Sils Maria, Upper Engadine
16	Autumn 1886	*D*	Vorrede	Ulterior (2nd ed.)	Ruta, near Genoa, Italy
17	Autumn 1886	*GS*	Vorrede zur zweite Ausgabe	Ulterior (2nd ed.)	Ruta, near Genoa
18	July 1887	*GM*	Vorrede	Original	Sils Maria, Upper Engadine
19–21	[Spring 1888]	*CW*	Vorwort Nachschrift Zweite Nachschrift	Original	[Turin, Italy]
22	30 September 1888	*TI*	Vorwort	Original	Turin
23	[Autumn 1888]	*AC*	Vorwort	Original (posthumous)	[Turin]
24–5	[Autumn 1888]	*EH*	Vorwort [no title]	Original (posthumous)	[Turin]
26	Christmas 1888	*NW*	Vorwort	Original (posthumous)	Turin

5 The first edition (1878) proposed a quotation from Descartes “in lieu of a preface” (“An Stelle einer Vorrede”). In the second edition (1886), the Descartes quotation was replaced by this preface.
6 2nd ed., but 3rd printing (see Schaberg, *The Nietzsche Canon*, 132).

from an early stage on — and it also points to his (enduring) habit of launching book projects, as evidenced by the numerous title ideas, plans for tables of contents, and drafts that appear in his many notebooks.

As concerns the books published in the first half of the 1870s, only *The Birth of Tragedy* and one of the four *Observations* received an original preface (#1 and #10). When he decided to prepare a reissue of his main works, in 1886, he wrote a new and long preface for *The Birth of Tragedy*, titled "Attempt at Self-Criticism," which then replaced the short original preface. In 1886 he also reissued his *Unfashionable Observations*, but he opted to simply unite them under one book cover, with no preface. This suggests that he considered these cultural criticism essays to be finished works to which he had nothing more to add. Indeed, they were not part of the philosophical experience that his other 1886 reissued works describe — and to which we will soon turn. (The preface to the second edition of *The Birth of Tragedy* confirms that Nietzsche distanced himself from his early cultural criticism: in §6 of #14, he claims to have "*spoiled*" with the *Observations* "the grand *Greek problem* ... by mixing it with the latest issues of modernity.")

This brings us to Nietzsche's prefaces of the next decade. Before *Beyond Good and Evil*, the only one of his 1880s books that received an original preface was the first part of *Zarathustra* (#11). However, following Genette's terminology this is an "authorial" preface. In other words, it is presented as having been written by one of the characters of the book — in this case, the narrator.[26]

The most striking moment in this corpus remains the year 1886, when Nietzsche wrote five prefaces (#13 to #17) for the republication of his main works. Claus-Artur Scheier first published these prefatory texts in German as a self-standing book. He thereby wished to show that they form a "microcosm" that offers the "key" to interpreting Nietzsche's later writings. Indeed, according to Scheier Nietzsche's most important work of the mid-1880s was not *Beyond Good and Evil*, as is often claimed, but these five prefaces taken together.[27]

A Sizeable Editorial Enterprise

The five 1886 prefaces were a battle cry. They were part of large-scale publishing enterprise: Nietzsche became his own publicity agent, graphic designer, and publisher.

These prefaces are the work of a European without a homeland or passport, a traveller who followed the sun from the French Riviera to Liguria, passing through the canton of Graubünden in the Swiss Alps. They are the work of a prematurely retired professor in his mid-thirties who had already published thirteen books in Germany. They are the work of a specialist in Greek and Latin texts, who had been following his philosophical vocation for nearly fifteen years. But they are also the work of an author who found himself extremely isolated: he had no disciples, not even any real readership.

While Nietzsche's first two books had featured in the cultural and specialized press in Germany and Switzerland in 1872 and 1873, as we saw in the first chapters, as of *Human, All Too Human*, in 1878, his books sold poorly and almost stopped being reviewed. In fact, Nietzsche simply had no audience: after fourteen years of assiduous publication, almost two thirds of all the copies of his thirteen published works to date were accumulating dust on his publishers' shelves. In short, his work was in danger of falling into oblivion, and he knew it.[28]

Nietzsche was distressed, as he wrote to his sister during the summer of 1885: "I am forty-one years old and isolated, I have *no* pupil, but every day I feel that I am in the best position to exercise a great scholarly activity as a philosopher ... My books are hooks; if they do not attract anyone to me, then they have no meaning!"[29] And indeed, what is a book without readers? Nietzsche knew that without reception, there can be no effect and thus no impact. But he also knew that publishers will not reprint or even push a book that has not succeeded in attracting a readership. If a book does not sell in its first printing run, it will certainly not be reissued: it will die. Nietzsche stated his worry bluntly to his friend Overbeck: if it is not republished "my 'literature' no longer exists."[30]

So Nietzsche had to buckle down: he needed to act quickly and strongly if he hoped to find readers before his death. To do so, he decided to show that his work existed by presenting it to the public in a "rejuvenated" form.[31] How can one give visibility to decade-old unsold books? By rebranding them and then flooding the market with these "new" books. This was the admittedly somewhat crazy project that Nietzsche embarked upon between 1885 and 1887. He wanted to show to the public that he indeed had "complete works" that were worthy of attention.

Given the number of unsold copies, Nietzsche's publisher refused to collaborate in this grand enterprise. (And what publisher would have agreed, really?) Nietzsche therefore sought to regain control over his work. He was in fact battling on many fronts. After buying his large unsold inventory back from his former publisher, Ernst W. Fritzsch, in Leipzig, he sued his other publisher, Ernst Schmeitzner, in Chemnitz, and proceeded to rebrand and reissue his works himself.[32] He had already decided to self-publish his new book, *Beyond Good and Evil*. (From then on Nietzsche often paid his publications' printing costs.) As for his previous works, he made sure to uniformize their graphic and material presentation: typography, front cover font, even the hue of the cardboard. Nietzsche's concurrent letters to his publisher Fritzsch and to his friend and proofreader Peter Gast reveal how important these material issues were to him: he wanted his books to stand out in bookstores.

He also asserted the official chronology of his complete works, as is evident from the back cover of *Beyond Good and Evil*'s first edition, where they are listed following their composition rather than publishing year. He even announced his forthcoming publication projects: he named three books that were "in preparation" and revealed that *Thus Spoke Zarathustra*, which had come out in three separate volumes two to three years earlier, had a fourth part that had not yet been published. In his reissues he even quoted or mentioned his unpublished works. For instance, in the preface to the second volume of *Human, All Too Human* (#15-§1) he mentions that he has "kept hidden" his 1873 manuscript on *Truth and Lies in the Unmoral Sense*. In these ways he was announcing to his hoped-for public that he not only had "complete works" that were now being reissued, but also esoteric works that no one had had access to because they were not meant for a large public. Members of the

German readership could indeed measure to what degree they had not read Mr Nietzsche ...

The "rejuvenation" of his books was achieved, however, not solely through visual and material means. Nietzsche singled out his five most important works and revisited or expanded them. He started by writing a preface to *Human, All Too Human*. But also, to mark the continuity between his three 1878–79 books, he combined *Mixed Opinions and Maxims* and *The Wanderer and His Shadow* into a single book (with a preface), under the title *Human, All Too Human, Volume 2*. He then wrote a prefatory autobiographical essay to present his very first book, *The Birth of Tragedy*. He finally wrote prefaces for his two 1881–82 books: *Dawn* and *The Gay Science*. The latter was also much expanded thanks to a new part ("Book V") and poems added as an appendix.

In short, the prefaces written in 1886 for his five most important books were at the core of a strategy for achieving visibility, attractiveness, reception, and impact. Nietzsche was presenting himself — as author *and* as philosopher — to the German public in the hope of sparking interest in his philosophical perspectives. It was no longer strictly a question of typography and printing: it was a question of philosophy.

Of Pronouns and Fiction

Through his prefaces Nietzsche presents his philosophy as an "attempt" or "experiment" (*Versuch*: #15-§4 and #17-§2, e.g.) and as "lived experience" (*Erlebnis*: #13-§7 and #17-§1, e.g.). In this way he presents philosophy as a practice rather than a theory. In his prefaces he seeks to not only transmit the experience that the author of the books has gone through — the experiments that his philosophy expresses and to which his books testify — but also to spark new experiments. He hopes that the reader may also live such experiences, provided one may "*learn* to read me well! —" to quote the last words of the preface to *Dawn* (#16-§5).

To read him well, it is important to observe how Nietzsche writes. We need to take style into account if we are to understand his philosophy. Stylistically, one thing stands out in the five 1886 prefaces: pronouns. The many and diverse pronouns that he uses ensure that all grammatical persons are reunited — sometimes in one paragraph, sometimes in one sentence.

As Leiner pointed out, in a preface "someone always addresses someone." These two *someones* are typically the *I* of the author and the *you* of the reader, "a partner who is sometimes explicitly called upon, sometimes implicitly convened."[33] While Nietzsche uses these pronouns profusely, he blurs the traditional lineages. For instance, he refers to himself not only as an *I* but also as a *he*, in the third person. He moreover pluralizes his first person through a *we*, thereby including the reader when relating past experiences or making observations.

Nietzsche's prefatory pronoun population is complex. In fact, the multiplicity and variety of pronouns are directly linked to the performativity of the prefaces. By ignoring the classic boundaries between author, work, and reader, Nietzsche shows the interweaving of production and reception in a work that is open to the reader's participation. His prefaces stage the exercise of philosophy in such a way as to encourage the reader to have an Erlebnis — a lived experience — similar to that of the author. The writing of prefaces is thus a philosophical task: for Nietzsche, far from being external to philosophy a preface is rather its epitome.

Pronouns are also a key to deciphering the fictionalized account that Nietzsche gives of himself as author. By speaking in many voices, he walks onto a stage upon which he wears different masks. The philosopher thus presents himself as a fiction. This is all the more apparent if one notices that when speaking of himself Nietzsche switches from one grammatical person to another within the same text. To underline this, a look at the first of the five 1886 prefaces — the preface to *Human, All Too Human* (#13) — will be useful.

This preface starts and ends with an *I* — but in between Nietzsche uses all grammatical persons, to different effects. The third person singular *he*, for instance, allows for some distance (#13-§3) from this "Mister Nietzsche" whom he names as such in other prefaces (see #17-§2). But the *he* also permits him to call in a hypothetical reader

(#13-§1). This one grammatical pronoun, the third person singular *he*, thus refers to many persons: the pronoun as signifier relates to more than one signified.

Similarly, a signified is often referred to by many pronouns: the reader, for instance, appears here as a *you*, there as a *we*. By tracking pronouns, it becomes obvious that the preface engages in a complex staging. This staging concerns not only the author or the reader, but also their interaction. By using *we* Nietzsche includes his reader within his assertions (#13-§7). This is a stylistic trait that he has often used to much effect in many aphorisms and section titles.[34] As for the *you*, it may refer to the reader, but Nietzsche also uses it to call upon his critics (#13-§1): *you* can thus be the good reader as well as the bad reader to whom Nietzsche speaks. (When he does not speak directly to them, he also refers to present and future readers in the third person plural as *they* [#13-§2]). Nietzsche uses *you*, moreover, for himself. He constructs dialogues in which a figure — presented in the first person — addresses the author of the book as a *you* (#13-§6).

Without explicitly naming himself, Nietzsche describes the path that led him to thoughts "outside of morality" (#13-§1) as one of "great emancipation" (#13-§3). This path led him to his becoming a free spirit. Nietzsche is thereby telling his readers that he himself is a free spirit, but he also admits that the "free spirits" of which he spoke in his 1878 book[35] did not exist at the time: he reveals that he had invented these characters to embark upon his own healing, as a means of making himself believe that he was not the only person to adopt a perspective "beyond good and evil" (#13-§1). The author presents himself as a former convalescent who lived "*as an experiment*" by "adventurously" following the path leading him to the person who he was. Thanks to the path taken he is now experiencing "*great* health" (#13-§4). The *free spirit* thus appears as both means and result of a therapeutic process, and in both cases, it is linked to the threats posed by loneliness. Nietzsche's address to readers in the 1886 prefaces could thus also be a fictional device against isolation.

The complex fictionalization of the author through pronouns reaches a high point in #13-§6. There, the author's *I* invokes a *he* (the free spirit) to whom the status of *I* is finally granted. This new

I delivers a monologue in which he addresses the initial authorial *I* as a *you*. Are we reading a dialogical monologue? Finally, this new *I* is silenced by the first *I*: the "real" author regains control of the text. The reader thus witnesses a peculiar event: the author interrupts the speech of his own mask. Therewith, multiplicity is brought back to unity.

Of Quotation Marks and Experience

This example shows that the author is behind each grammatical person used. He is in the classic prefatory *I*, but also in the substance of the book's descriptions and metaphors, since the book admits of speaking of the author's "treatment" and "cure" (#13-§1). Moreover, the readership's figures appear as many authorial masks. The author is present in the *you* because Nietzsche includes his reader in his assertions (#13-§7) and invents critics so as to better voice his own position.

Knowing that Nietzsche's works had close to no audience at the time, it is astonishing to notice him respond to his critics in the first 1886 preface. From the very first paragraph (#13-§1) he describes the impression that his books have been told to give ("One would leave my works with this sigh"); his works' supposed common thread ("I have been told often enough, and always with great displeasure, that all my works have something in common"); the label that has been affixed to him ("My works have been called a school of suspicion"); and a criticism that he actually would be ready to acknowledge ("Perhaps in this respect could one blame me for a number of 'artifices'"). Yet by the end of the paragraph, Nietzsche must also acknowledge the limits of the readers' capacity to evaluate his experience: "— but assuming that all this is true and rightly advanced against me, what do you know about it, what *could* you know about it?"[36]

Is Nietzsche inventing his readership? More to the point, he is defining a reading practice. One of the few commentators to have pondered this observation is Paul van Tongeren. He emphasized the role of the 1886 prefaces in defining Nietzsche's "art of reading" — reading as "*rumination*," as Nietzsche metaphorically describes it at the very end of his preface to *On the Genealogy of Morality* (#18-§8).

According to Tongeren, the prefaces are not simply a means of attracting readers. They clearly testify to the way in which Nietzsche understands his works: he "shows how one should read by describing how he reads so as to discover himself" in his works.[37] The supposed "criticism" that Nietzsche exposes in #13, then, is beside the point. Rather than focusing on the work, one should focus on the author inasmuch as he testifies to an experience that is worth recounting, metabolizing, and living.

Yet — who is this author? It appears that he is not reducible to the events of his biography. The author, in fact, is perhaps best represented by means of punctuation: the quotation marks within which Nietzsche enfolds himself.

In his third 1886 preface Nietzsche writes: "My books speak *only* of my conquests; 'I' am therein" (#15-§1). It is worth noting that this *I* is in quotation marks: it is the "me" as "self-experimentation" (#17-§2), Erlebnis (#13-§7, #17-§1), and process. As Tongeren puts it, the 1886 prefaces are more about "Nietzsche" than they are about Nietzsche: "They are *not* about Herr Nietzsche in the sense of the *particularity* of the accidental individual person Friedrich Nietzsche, who would be sharing (or not) his experiences and his thoughts."[38] The *I* that is present in these texts is a self as a singular process — but this process could well be experienced by another self, provided that one makes a similar journey, thus solitarily walking "on his 'own paths'" (#16-§2).

The multiplication of prefaces should help foster such experiences. Indeed, in the preface to *The Gay Science* Nietzsche famously defines philosophy as the unconscious expression — the "disguise" — of "physiological needs" (#17-§2).[39] Because drives are in perpetual motion, more writing opens onto more perspectives and increased possibilities of experiencing and embodied understanding on the part of the reader. The almost infinite variation of affects (#17-§1) may thus be an epistemological tool for the philosopher. The work of philosophy, from Plato to Nietzsche, thereby testifies to the states and needs of the author. It invites one to try "exercises of self-mastery" from which one emerges changed, "another person" (#17-§3).

But importantly, as Nietzsche emphasizes, the experiences that he describes are not only personal (#15-§6). They are intended as baits and hooks for any individual because they are philosophical experiences: they pertain to understanding and knowledge.[40] The 1886 prefaces thus illustrate the task that Nietzsche formulated in §110 of *The Gay Science*: "To what extent can truth stand to be incorporated? — that is the question; that is the experiment."[41] Nietzsche is hoping for readers who will read and experiment in this embodied way. Such an enterprise "cannot be everyone's" (#16-§2), but it is certainly not solely the enterprise of the author. The prefaces demonstrate that although it initially seemed an entirely fictitious type, the "free spirit" (again in quotation marks: #13-§3) qualifies the author, and the path that is described in his books show this. The path of the convalescent invites a solitary process, but one who has lived such an experience will be able to find one's place in a philosophical community — or so Nietzsche hopes. Then can the *I* become a *we*: it is with this aim that he addresses his reader as *you* and *we*.

Through his prefaces, Nietzsche seeks to reach readers who will be "friends" in this way,[42] readers who will share at least some of the many qualifiers that the author gives himself: immoralist and psychologist; solitary and pessimist; philosopher and philologist; poet and artist; Greek and German. The readers Nietzsche portrays are "good Europeans," adventurous free spirits whose time will undoubtedly come.[43]

These remarks show that it becomes impossible to distinguish the author from the good reader and friend (whose epithets are precisely those that Nietzsche gives himself) but also from the bad reader and critic (who Nietzsche mimics and mocks). Just as he expresses himself through all grammatical persons, the author fully embraces the experience of reading. He inhabits and performs the act of interpreting. Writing is thus inseparable from an interpretative act. The prefaces testify to this philosophical experiment, which consists in inviting robust but varied reading and interpretation.

"But what do prefaces actually do?" Nietzsche answers Derrida's question by saying that prefaces do quite a lot. In fact, his prefaces do everything that a work of philosophy does, while also showing that they are doing so. Nietzsche's prefaces are performative philosophical texts, whose short length makes for a condensed presentation of philosophy as exercise.

Literary theory, therefore, has it both right and wrong. It has it right in that it considers a preface as a discursive act and event that exceeds the work's boundary. But it has it wrong when it considers prefaces as attempts at completing or "finishing" a work. As we saw, that was in part what prompted Derrida to disqualify a preface's relevance. However, Nietzsche's prefaces rather intend to show that all work is an "open work" precisely because the work is an act. This act needs a reader: a written work is thus never a completed object, even once it is published and presented in bookstores.[44]

While preparing the reissue of his most important works and writing his "best prose," Nietzsche made sure to emphasize the openness of his works. He showed to what extent his books went beyond all typically perceived boundaries. Indeed, a book is not limited to the volumes available in bookstores: some works have not been published, which should raise questions concerning their topic, number, aim, and public. But also, a book is not limited to biographical or editorial chronology: in his third 1886 preface Nietzsche specified that all his works should be "retro dated" (#15-§1) and stressed that the *Unfashionable Observations* were in fact older than *The Birth of Tragedy* — although all had their origin in the 1870–71 Franco-Prussian war (#15-§1 and #14-§1). A book, moreover, is not even limited to the author's words: Nietzsche specified that his ideas did not emanate from a purely personal experience (#14-§6). Finally, a book is not limited to its reception: thus Nietzsche could reissue his works despite the public's initial lack of interest.

The author must truly prepare the conditions for his works to be found, read, and metabolized by readers who will make epistemological experiences similar to those that the author has been through. Reception, experience, and impact are stages of interpretation and understanding. A useful way to account for this conception of a work and the pivotal role that reading — reception and impact — has for a work is to turn to the school of reception aesthetics and reader-response theory that was developed in the 1960s and 1970s by German literary scholars around the University of Konstanz. Inspired by Gadamer's hermeneutics, but even more so by Ingarden's philosophical aesthetics, Jauss and Iser developed a definition of a literary work as a dynamic structure. Jauss insisted that the actualization of a work by the reader is a constitutive element of that work. A work, therefore, is never closed or finished: the work is indeed the convergence of text and reception.[45] For a work to have meaning, it must be received (i.e., read and interpreted) by and have an effect (i.e., work) on a reader. These two elements, effect and reception, are "constitutive" of the work.[46] It is this openness of the literary text that allows the reader to "participate in the constitution of meaning."[47] It would thus be misleading to deduce the completeness of a work from the materiality of the book at hand. As Nietzsche's prefaces make clear, a work is an act whose experience is made in the present — if someone is willing to become its reader.

A preface also adds a layer of meaning to a work. It testifies to a new layer of experience, and opens possibilities of interpretation. In other words, it points to the openness of the text, which is why prefaces can be multiplied. A work that receives a new preface could well receive another one a few years later — and why not a third preface, and so on? Nietzsche did not get to go that far. But he did open his preface to the second edition of *The Gay Science* with this observation: "Perhaps this book needs more than a single preface ... and still there would always remain, in the end, a doubt as to the possibility that someone, without having lived something similar, would become familiar with the lived experience of this book through prefaces." (#17-§1)

In other words: reading is one thing, living is another. But experience — lived, diversified, repeated — trumps reading.

Chapter 7

An Unlikely Hero

NIETZSCHE'S DASHES

All that I have written until now is foreground; as for myself it always starts first with the dashes.
Nietzsche to his sister, 20 May 1885

In §218 of *Human, All Too Human* I, Nietzsche lamented that "We have outgrown the symbolism of lines and figures, just as we have lots the habit of recognizing the effects of rhetorical tone."[1] In this final chapter, we will take him up on this challenge: we will take visual lines seriously and turn our ears to the sound of rhetoric and the effect of signs as symbols.

In one of his last books, literary theorist Gérard Genette wrote that the true hero of Gustave Flaubert's novel *Sentimental Education* was not its famous central character, Frédéric Moreau, but rather a punctuation sign: the semicolon, of which Flaubert made heavy and diversified use. Although we may not always devote much attention to it, punctuation is central to style: it aids clarity, supports the logic of expression, and imposes rhythm. It perhaps does much more: Genette wished that someone would one day embark on a study of the "stylistic and moral function" of Flaubert's semicolon.[2]

An admirer of the French theorist wrote in a book on Genette's style that "For many writers, punctuation is the locus of specific stylistic effort."[3] This is certainly true of Nietzsche. In fact, the translation theorist Peter Newmark believed that Nietzsche was nothing short of "a master of punctuation."[4] Yet this aspect of Nietzschean style has not been the focus of many studies. It seems that once again, close to fifty years on Richard Roos's remark according to which much has yet to be done in the field of a stylistic-philosophical Nietzsche commentary still stands.

Some punctuation signs have indeed interested readers of Nietzsche. Éric Blondel, for instance, studied Nietzsche's important use of quotation marks. Also, in a paper on punctuation in the five 1886 prefaces, Simson noted that a heavy use of question marks assures the philosopher "of an agreement with his discussion partner that is more emotional than rational." In this way, punctuation is at the service of philosophy, whether for its role of criticism and distancing (as Blondel shows with quotation marks) or its intended effect and impact (as Simson shows with question marks).[5]

Although Simson's study suggests that awareness to punctuation informs us as to how a text affects the reader, most favourite punctuation signs of the philosopher have not been the focus of much study. One example is the ellipse: as one sample among others, it is noteworthy that almost a third of the aphorisms (twelve out of forty-four) that make up part I of *Twilight of the Idols* end with ellipses rather than a period. Another example is the dash. As a follow-up of sorts to Genette's musings, this chapter focuses on an improbable hero of Nietzsche's works: the em-dash — or *Gedankenstrich*, as it is called in German.

The best place to look for his Gedankenstrichen are the writings that Nietzsche published or prepared for publication between 1882 (the year during which he published *The Gay Science*) and 1888 (the last year during which he prepared books). The 1882–88 works are today the most read and studied of Nietzsche's corpus, and in their pages dashes abound. In fact, the heavy use of em-dashes as of the 1883 *Zarathustra* books is a turning-point: after these works Nietzsche used em-dashes frequently. But, as we will soon see, he also used them in unconventional ways or unusual settings. In short, dashes became a dominant tool of his "new" language and philosophy.[6] (Nietzsche certainly also used many em-dashes in his notebooks, which are now published as the posthumous fragments that make up his Nachlaß. While these are useful to follow the author's cogitation, self-reflection, projects, and drafts, his published works, however, are more revelatory since they present the extremely polished form through which Nietzsche wished his philosophical ideas to be received, experienced, and interpreted.)

Although punctuation signs follow grammatical rules and typographical norms, these standards do not dictate their complete use.[7] This is even more the case with signs whose functions are less rigid than others. The semicolon or the em-dash, for instance, are more likely to become means of personal stylistic expression than is the period. It will certainly be telling to see how Nietzsche personalizes his use of em-dashes and how these distinguish his written style. Yet a focus on Nietzsche's dashes is also justified, and doubly so, by commentators and, most importantly, by Nietzsche himself.

Why the Dash?

Nietzsche believed that a concept is a poorer means of signification than a metaphor.[8] Could a punctuation sign be even richer in symbolism than a metaphor can be in meaning? A few commentators have noted Nietzsche's extensive use of em-dashes. These include the German poet and literary scholar Ernst Bertram in his seminal 1919 *Nietzsche: An Essay in Mythology*, and the philologist Richard Roos, whom we already encountered in the introduction to this book, in his Cérisy-la-Salle talk titled "Rules to a Philological Reading of Nietzsche."

Bertram and Roos both notice a peculiarity of Nietzsche's style: his use of dashes to separate a terminal element from the development that precedes it. Roos writes: "Often the Gedankenstrich abruptly interrupts the aphorism, mostly at the end of the main argument, just when we await a conclusion, which indeed comes but only after the em-dash and under the guise of a brilliant, concise, and more general proposition. *In fact, that is the real aphorism: the preceding development was preparing us to understand it.* That dash asks readers to pause for a moment, take some distance, and seek on their own the significance and scope of what precedes — then the author finally presents his own results, clearly set apart from the rest and sometimes surprisingly so."[9] Indeed, Nietzsche's writings offer numerous examples of this tactic. Often he uses a dash to conclude his observations, but he also uses some to refrain from concluding — thereby halting, destabilizing, and stimulating the reader all at once. Surely this triple effect deserves attention.

The only study devoted specifically to Nietzsche's em-dash is a 2010 essay published by Rainer Hanshe in the journal *The Agonist*. However, by focusing exclusively on the double dash (— —) in Nietzsche's *Zarathustra*, Hanshe's interpretation is perhaps too narrow.[10] Yet, before looking into Hanshe's study, let us start by tracking Nietzsche's dashes. A good place to start are his own words on the Gedankenstrich.

Although he uses the punctuation sign extensively, it turns out that he has not written much about it. In his spring of 1885 to early 1886 notebooks — the period during which he wrote his famous book *Beyond Good and Evil* — Nietzsche was toying with the word Gedankenstrich to come up with ideas for a book subtitle. The fragment 1[232] is one such example: "*Das Problem der Rangordnung. Vorläufige Gedanken und Gedankenstriche. Von Friedrich Nietzsche.*" This idea for a book title can be translated thus: *The Issue of Rank: Preliminary Thoughts and Dashes*. There are six notes from the same period that play in this way on the German assonance between Gedanken and Gedankenstriche: "thoughts" and "dashes" (Gedankenstrich literally means a line or a streak of thought).[11]

Three other 1885 excerpts are noteworthy. First, the fragment 34[147] goes as such: "I have thought so many forbidden things, and I have been well at home there, where righteous and efficient spirits run out of breath: thus, I am always astonished when I find something else to communicate. Whether I know right away that I prefer my dashes to my communicated thoughts." Here, Nietzsche seems to be asking himself a question to which he in fact gave an answer in a concurrent letter to his sister. Dated 20 May 1885, it reads: "All that I have written until now is foreground; as for myself it always starts first with the dashes." Finally, a third note, the fragment 34[65], hints at the fact that Nietzsche considered himself as "one who places the highest value on the background thoughts [*Hinter-gedanken*] and who prefers above all the dashes [Gedankenstriche] to what is asserted in his books."[12]

These three excerpts are not a mere play on a rhyme. Indeed, Nietzsche situates dashes within a larger idea, that of an opposition between what an author publicizes and what he does not explicitly show — that is, the opposition between exoteric and esoteric

Table 7.1 Tally of Nietzsche's use of initial, terminal, double, and triple em-dashes in his 1882 to final works[1]

		Tally categories[2]						
Year	*Work*	*A* *Initial*[3] —	*B* *Terminal*[4] —	*C* *Initial and terminal*[5] —	*D* *Within the textual units*[6] — —	— — —	*E* *Totals*[7] — —	— — —
1882	GS books I–IV	0	9	0	3	0	2	0
1883–85	*Z*	4	56 9 — —	2	30	1[8]	39	1
1886	*BGE*	7	63 4 — —	3	4	0	8	0
	Five prefaces	9	11 7 — —	5	1	0	8	0
1887	GS book V	0[9]	15 1 — —	0	0	0	1	0
	GM	20	14 2 — —	7	1	0	3	0
1888	*CW*	7	5 1 — — 1 — — —	2	6	0	7	1
	TI	8	38 1 — —	2	0	0	1	0
	AC	17	17 5 — — 2 — — —	5	5	1	10	3
	EH	12	27 3 — —	7	2	0	5	0

1 A note of sincere thanks to Flora Roussel, who with her keen eye and attention to detail and to language had the patience to double-check the count of em-dashes in Nietzsche's works. These numbers are based on the Colli and Montinari *KSA* critical edition of Nietzsche's complete works. We should also not forget that in five of Nietzsche's earlier books (*HAH* I, the two books that make up *HAH* II, *D*, and *GS*), dashes separate the theme or "title" of each textual unit from its development.

2 Numbers in columns A and B include numbers from column C; numbers from column E include numbers from column B for double and triple dashes and numbers from column D.
3 By "Initial," I mean that a textual unit starts with an em-dash; numbers in column A thus include the numbers from column C, i.e., textual units that start and also end on a dash.
4 By "Terminal," I mean that a textual unit ends on an em-dash; numbers in column B thus include numbers from column C and take into account as well all textual units ending on two or three dashes (precisions are given below the numbers in each row) or on a dash followed by another punctuation sign, e.g. —. or —? or —".
5 This category means that a textual unit starts and ends with an em-dash; i.e., the textual unit is so to say "ensconced" by dashes. Numbers from this column are also counted in the totals appearing in columns A and B.
6 This category means that two or three concurring em-dashes appear somewhere in the book other than right at the start or at the very end; column D thus does not include numbers from columns A, B, or C.
7 For each category (whether — — or — — —) these totals include double or triple dashes that appear anywhere in the book; numbers in column E thus total double or triple dashes numbers from columns B and D.
8 The sole appearance of a triple em-dash in *Z* is in book III, "Der Genesender," §1. Its rhythmic and illustrative functions are apparent through the triple repetition of the word Ekel just before the triple dashes.
9 All textual units in Book V of *GS* start by a title which is followed by a period and an em-dash. One could argue that these textual units, then, all start by that dash. But starting a text by a title phrase is not the same thing, visually and rhythmically, as starting a text directly by a dash.

discourse. In his 1885 notes this boils down to an opposition between two types: on the one hand, the "democratic Zeitgeist" (represented by the writing and reading of newspaper articles), and, on the other, an aristocratic attitude through which one distances oneself from the multitude and strives to select an audience. That is why in the third note, Nietzsche directly scoffs at the "democratic habit" of writing "as though speaking before an unselected company."[13] Dashes are similar to backstage thoughts that are selected and kept for a few readers.

Because Nietzsche says that he embraces his Gedankenstrichen more than his "communicated thoughts," we may consider that the dash has a semantic function. It serves to expose philosophical ideas within Nietzsche's elements of style. This could explain why the em-dash takes so much space in his mid- to late-1880s works, where he indeed uses them in almost all his short essays and textual units. (His three last books contain the most.)[14] These books also contain many special uses of dashes, such as initial and closing dashes, and double and triple dashes.

A tally of the em-dashes' special uses in the middle to late 1880s works (see table 7.1) calls for some comments. A first number that may be striking concerns the double dashes in the four *Zarathustra* books: there are thirty-nine in total, with nine acting as terminal double dashes. *Thus Spoke Zarathustra*'s two last books contain the most, with seventeen double dashes in book III and twenty in the privately printed book IV. The literary form of the *Zarathustra* may certainly explain this choice of punctuation, but so can its intrinsic rhythmic quality and oral style.

The numbers in Nietzsche's subsequent works are also noteworthy. 1886–87 was an extremely prolific period: Nietzsche published *Beyond Good and Evil* and *Genealogy of Morality* and wrote and published book V of *The Gay Science*. And as we know, this was also when he wrote five prefaces for the new edition of what he deemed to be his most important books to date: *The Birth of Tragedy*, *Human, All Too Human* I and II, *Dawn*, and *The Gay Science*. In all these 1886–87 writings, thirty-six textual units start with a dash, one hundred and three end with at least one dash, fourteen end with two, and fifteen are ensconced between an opening and a closing dash.

Reading the tally against the actual length of Nietzsche's texts is even more striking. One sees an increase in the frequency of dashes. For instance, in *Beyond Good and Evil* more than one in five textual units end on a dash, whereas in Book V of *The Gay Science*, this proportion jumps to more than one in three.[15] In *The Case of Wagner*, from 1888, as much as three quarters of textual units start and/or end on a dash (12 § out of a total of 16 §) — and §7 even ends on three dashes. In *Twilight of the Idols*, one in four textual units end on at least one dash (37 § out of a total of 147 §). *The Antichrist*'s ten double dashes are certainly striking, as are its two terminal triple dashes. Finally, in *Ecce Homo*, more than one in three textual units (27 § out of a total of 72 §) end on one or two dashes.

As these numbers and instances show, not only does Nietzsche use dashes conventionally — to separate a part of a sentence from the preceding development or to introduce a conclusion, say — he also places them in unusual settings such as these: to start or to end a line or textual unit; within parentheses, thereby doubling their conventional effect (which I will discuss below); to end a paragraph without a period; to separate a pronoun from its verb; to ensconce a single word; or to accompany, side by side, one or even two other dashes or other punctuation marks.[16]

In these settings, the dash certainly does many things. It may bring the reader to a stop, while at other times encouraging one to read on — and fast! The dash's pure horizontality in our vertically aligned writing certainly catches the eye. Perhaps that is even more the case in English, since typographical norms dictate attaching the dash to the preceding and following letters, while in German and French the em-dash is preceded and followed by an accompanying non-breaking space. If it is somewhat difficult to separate the semantic and visual dimensions of the em-dash, it may be because it works both as a punctuation mark and typographic sign. Let's take a quick look at why, and how, that is.[17]

Attempt at a Definition

In typography, an "em-dash" is the widest type of dash. Much wider than a hyphen, the size of an em-dash's width *is* the size of the font that is used. In Times New Roman 12, for instance, the width of the em-dash would be 12 points (a "point" is the measure of the font's height). Importantly, this usually means that the em-dash's width will be the maximal possible width for a typographic sign in the font that is used. This is why it is called the "em-dash": this specific type of dash was thought to have the width of a capital M. (Simple typographic experiments, however, show that in Times New Roman, the em-dash rather has about the width of the capital W: an M is somewhat narrower.)[18]

The space that the em-dash takes up in a text may explain its visual attractiveness. Indeed, the em-dash is the punctuation sign that takes up and thereby shows the maximum space possible for any letter or written sign in the font that one is writing in or reading.

Hence its French name: *le tiret cadratin* refers to a letter's square frame-space (*cadre*). The em-dash thus delineates a typographic proportion within which the letters are set. It is a proportion, also, that our eyes and our brain work with when they read a text, even though it is never really seen or shown — except when the cadratin and its full frame-space suddenly appear within the text.

As with all punctuation signs, grammatical rules apply to the em-dash. Punctuation theory is written in a similar way to lexicons: it proposes prescriptive remarks (which specify how one ought to write), tallies (which enumerate actual uses), and, sometimes, specific case studies.[19] Let us look first at the prescriptive side.

Punctuation treatises define punctuation marks according to their function. The general function of an em-dash is similar to that of parentheses: it "emphasizes a word or expression by separating it from the rest of the context." (Yet punctuation scholars agree that em-dashes draw more attention to what is being separated than parentheses do.)[20] In their famous *Elements of Style*, William Strunk and E.B. White suggest to "use a dash to set off an abrupt break or interruption and to announce a long appositive or summary."[21] When combined with other punctuation, such as the comma or exclamation and question marks (combinations that Nietzsche multiplies), the dash may mark this separation even more firmly. By doing so, it also marks a pause more clearly than a comma does, since the comma's first role is rather to logically organize statements.[22]

In short, punctuation treatises generally permit a great deal of freedom to a writer wishing to know how to use em-dashes, since their grammatical norms are flexible. Perhaps because of this flexibility, which may come off as vagueness or unreliability, the *Elements of Style* caution one to use the dash "only when a more common mark of punctuation seems inadequate."[23]

As the prescriptive grammar suggests, uses of em-dashes vary. A tally of those uses, as noted in punctuation treatises, is informative. Thanks to a large overview of the em-dash's presence in literature treatises we can enumerate its conventional purposes.[24] These may be summarized in six categories.

The most cited purpose of an em-dash is that it marks an interruption within the sentence. Scholars say that "in a way, it includes by force another phrase in the sentence," a phrase that is almost exterior to the sentence itself. The dash thereby "breaks the flow of the syntax." It is in this sense that the French novelist Julien Gracq (a self-professed fan of the dash) wrote that the cadratin "obliges the sentence to hold the reins for a moment," or that the 1876 *Dictionnaire Larousse* said that the dash "lets in the light of day."[25]

Two other uses focus on disjunction. By separating a semantic unit from the rest of the sentence, the em-dash may in fact emphasize that unit. (Punctuation theorist Jacques Drillon stresses that French poet Charles Baudelaire was very strict about this purpose of the cadratin in his 29 March 1866 letter to his publisher.) Through separation the em-dash may also mark surprise, for instance by adding a complement to a sentence or development that appeared to be finished.[26] (Bertram and Roos alike considered that it was a trademark of Nietzsche's style. They interpretated it as a sign enabling the reader to take better notice of his intended point.)

Two other common em-dash uses concern the re-enactment of speech. The dash may serve to introduce interior dialogue. It can signal that the author is raising an objection to their own points, talking to themselves, or engaging in a dialogue with their reader. It may also serve as "a graphic mark for the voice." In this sense, the dash is a device for showing or even stressing the rhythm of the text and reminding the reader of the textual presence of the living and thinking author.[27]

Finally, an em-dash can function as a conclusion. It sometimes acts as a period to conclude sentences (for instance, in Heinrich Heine and Jack Kerouac — and Nietzsche) or it may appear after a period as a "magnificent mark of achievement" (for instance, in Stéphane Mallarmé and, again, Nietzsche).[28]

Nietzsche's Dashes

A reader of Nietzsche will immediately notice that his dashes do all the above. Yet he also does more: he emphasizes those purposes. For instance, not only does he end sentences on dashes, he also concludes complete aphorisms with them, and sometimes even without using a typical conclusive period.[29] Strikingly, Nietzsche also multiplies em-dashes, sometimes aligning two or three of them within or at the end of an aphorism.[30] (Three is less common: table 7.1 shows that there are only five — — — in Nietzsche's published works).

In short, Nietzsche uses dashes to expand the syntaxial prescriptions. And yet again, he does much more with his dashes than merely break with grammatical conventions. A punctuation case-study of Nietzsche's use of the em-dash is now called for. In the writings that he published or prepared for publication between 1882 and 1888. Nietzsche's em-dashes may be deciphered in six ways: as image (or symbol), silence, voice, fermata, rhythm, and synesthesia. Let us now turn to his unlikely hero's preferred purposes.

(1) Ernst Bertram opened his famous Nietzsche book with a quote in which Goethe lamented: "All of us, we talk too much. We should talk less and draw more."[31] Goethe's point (and the impetus to Bertram's book) was that we should consider all beings and things as symbols needing deciphering. Once we would know how to do so, we would not need so many discourses.

Perhaps Nietzsche's dashes could be understood as a symbol in this way. And that is precisely Rainer Hanshe's thesis in his paper on the double dash in the *Zarathustra*. Hanshe calls the double dash (— —) "Nietzsche's emblem." He asserts that — — functions "as a *graphic illustration* of the Moment or Augenblick, the Eternal Return, and the Great Midday." The double-dash would thus be "an invisible and inaudible code alerting astute readers to [Nietzsche's] allusions to the Eternal Return and the Overhuman [in *Zarathustra*]."[32]

Although this makes for an attractive interpretation, it is far from convincing, and this for several reasons. First, Nietzsche was a musician and a specialist of ancient rhetoric — one could thus rightly assume that the dash alludes to other senses than only the visual one. Second, why should one surmise that Nietzsche "hid" meanings in codes and formulas, moreover in a book that in part was already intended only for specially chosen "astute readers"? (We should remember that Nietzsche had only forty copies of the fourth and final part of the *Zarathustra* privately printed to be distributed to chosen friends and readers.)[33] The double-dash, also, is hardly "invisible," as its lines are visually striking in a page composed of alphabetical letters. Finally, it is hard to understand why the double dash would have a specific connotation in one book (the *Zarathustra*) that it would not have in other books where it is also used.[34]

Nevertheless, typographically speaking the em-dash is indeed a visual sign. Followingly, in some aphorisms the dashes do serve to visually illustrate part of the aphorism's message. A perfect example of this appears in *Beyond Good and Evil* §280, where the final double dash suggests the exact move of preparing to jump forward that Nietzsche has just put into words. Another such example appears in *Thus Spoke Zarathustra* (book III, "Der Genesender," §1), where a — — — immediately follows a triple repetition of the word *Ekel* (disgust), thereby emphasizing the word's signification and rhythm.

(2) The em-dash is a typographic symbol that also has manifest auditory and physical qualities, one of which is to represent silence. Nietzsche ends his preface to *Human, All Too Human* by writing that "in certain cases ... we only *remain* philosophers by — keeping silent."[35] It is striking to see that the last words are introduced by a dash. In many cases the purpose of Nietzsche's dashes is precisely that: to symbolize silence. Silence is found everywhere in his philosophy, under the guise of not saying something, stopping short of a conclusion, self-interrupting, or even doubting the possibility of knowledge. Now the dash does and says all of these. In *Beyond Good and Evil* §281, for instance, Nietzsche writes of his mistrust in the idea of self-knowledge, and ends his thought on a dash.

In this sense, the dash may be interpreted as symbolizing the great educator. As the scholar of ancient philosophy Pierre Hadot underlined in his foreword to Bertram's book, the great educator "never says what he thinks": like Socrates, he "is great in his silence."[36] Nietzsche's dashes certainly function as a quite Socratic way of leaving questions unanswered, suspending judgment, and perhaps also frustrating readers. But by so doing dashes also invite readers, as interlocutors, to tread their own interpretative paths — again in a

Socratic manner. As such, the em-dash is both ancient and modern: it echoes a classic Hellenistic approach to philosophy while at the same time acting as a performative symbol for the ongoing act of interpretation.

(3) The dash also plays a role opposite to that of silence: sound. The dash first resonates by incarnating voice. Punctuation scholars note that with dashes, the sound of the author's and reader's voices makes its incursion into a written text. Indeed, it is useful to remember that many punctuation marks evolved in written languages from the initial need of consigning oral speech. As Simson wrote in his paper on Nietzsche's typography, "Behind Nietzsche's style there is a firm feeling for and understanding of the spoken." This appears through dashes when they are used to introduce Nietzsche's voice or his characters' voices in dialogues or interjections, or when he mimics the rhythm of speech.[37]

Inasmuch as some dashes introduce questions or exclamations into the main clause, we can also consider these dashes as proposing a different tonality in the musical sense.[38] Now, a way in which the dash symbolizes musical sound is as fermata.

(4) In musical writing a fermata is a stay of unspecified length on a musical note or silence. When a dash closes a textual unit, it may serve to resonate the author's words. The dash's effect in this case is close to an echo: the sound of what one has just read resonates, and thus the reader cannot go on reading just yet. In this sense, Simson qualifies some of Nietzsche's final em-dashes as being "thought climaxes through which the public is sent on a break."[39] Indeed, some interruptive dashes (and Nietzsche uses many) force the reader to pause, since the flow of the author's thought process is stopped — whether temporarily, during the echo and resonating sound (dashes thereby serve as short speaking breaks similar to those in oral discourse and music), or permanently.

This resonating sound (or even silence) is certainly an invitation for us readers to start thinking by ourselves. That is the way in which Richard Roos interpreted the blank space that follows the end of Nietzsche's aphorisms. For Roos, rather than a mere silent, meaningless space, the blank between aphorisms or textual units is a fermata through which Nietzsche solicits the reader's interpretative act.[40] The dash itself, however, seems to me to be a quite direct, because visual, symbol of this invitation to interpretation.

(5) This alternation of sound, pause, resonance, and flow is a rhythmic phenomenon. And Nietzsche's dashes often fill rhythmic purposes. In *Beyond Good and Evil* §246 Nietzsche writes that "there is *art* in every good sentence. A misunderstanding about its tempo, for instance: and the sentence itself is misunderstood!"[41] He then lists the rhythmic qualities that a reader must sense in a text in order to understand it: its *staccato*, *rubato*, rhymes, and diphthongs. In §247 he adds that to read, one needs more than eyes! One needs ears, larynx, and good old antique lungs.

In other words, Nietzsche invites us to remember that reading is far from a purely visual activity. It is an embodied act, and written style, in turn, is a translation of physiological rhythm, as he explains in *Beyond Good and Evil* §28. That is also why in that same §247, he qualifies phrases as being "physiological wholes." The dash, then, as an integral part of Nietzsche's style, is an expression of rhythm that calls for an embodied practice of reading. We can thus consider the em-dash as an integral part of Nietzsche's philosophy, in which writing and speaking, as Blondel importantly noted, "must not be distinguished from physiological activities."[42]

(6) With this last point we turn directly to the idea of synesthesia. Synesthesia is the experience of simultaneous stimulation of more than one sense. (The title of Richard Cytowic's 2003 book on the phenomenon illustrates it well: *The Man Who Tasted Shapes*).[43] As a visual symbol that represents silence, evokes the author's voice, entices our own inner voice, provokes resonance, and represents and imposes rhythm, the em-dash certainly is a tool for synesthetic understanding.

Near the end of his preface to *Human, All Too Human* I, Nietzsche laments that his book "has been read most carelessly and *heard* the worst." (§8) Given what was just said about rhythm, this remark is not to be taken metaphorically. Quite literally, Nietzsche is saying that Germans do not have their senses turned on when they read. As he writes in *Beyond Good and Evil* §247, readers need to take their ears out of the drawer and approach books with their senses of speech and hearing, not only with their eyes. Nietzsche's texts therefore call upon most of our senses: while he says that writing is embodied, his writing style indeed encourages us to read with our ears, voice, and rhythmic bodily pulsation.

The dash conveys meaning that we may miss if we obliterate the typographic sign or pass over it too quickly. In this respect, one cannot overstate the importance of keeping all em-dashes in translations of Nietzsche's texts. In his study of the double-dash, Hanshe pointed out that "in many translations, Nietzsche's punctuation is frequently dishonored," and on this point he and I agree.[44] Unfortunately, one sees all sorts of missteps: some translators have simply done away with the dashes, others have left some in but taken many out, and others still have replaced them with other punctuation marks. Yet as we have seen, a dash does not have the same purpose and effect as other punctuation marks. If Nietzsche consciously chose single, double, or even triple dashes to stylistically express and provoke an embodied thought experience, then as readers we should be able to see, feel, and interpret the dashes where Nietzsche intended them to be in the exposition of his philosophical ideas.

Roos stressed the importance of reading Nietzsche literally.[45] This chapter on Nietzsche's em-dashes was perhaps a somewhat radical way of reading him "à la lettre": this enquiry indeed attempted to read him *au signe*. It thereby showed not only the diversity of Nietzsche's use of this punctuation sign, but also the semantic richness of this symbol.

The dash is a pure line that surely appealed to modernist artists. In his unique 1899 typesetting of *Thus Spoke Zarathustra*, for instance, the art nouveau artist Henry van de Velde tellingly inserted handmade designs near many of the texts' dashes, thereby enhancing their visual presence. Perhaps artists have been particularly attuned to the effect of punctuation symbolism, thanks to their intrinsically synesthetic practice of translating a text or an insight into another sense-language — whether visual or auditory.

Indeed, one wonders whether the dash also found auditory form in musical works. Did Gustav Mahler, for instance, in his rendering of Nietzsche's "Das Nachtwandler-Lied" §12 (from *Thus Spoke Zarathustra*, book IV) in his own 1896 Symphony no. 3, 4th movement, interpret the six dashes that appear in Nietzsche's poem? Four of them appear at end-lines:

Oh Mensch! Gieb Acht!
Was spricht die tiefe Mitternacht?
"Ich schlief, ich schlief —,
"Aus tiefem Traum bin ich erwacht: —
"Die Welt ist tief,
"Und tiefer als der Tag gedacht.
"Tief ist ihr Weh —,
"Lust — tiefer noch als Herzeleid:
"Weh spricht: Vergeh!
"Doch alle Lust will Ewigkeit —,
"— will tiefe, tiefe Ewigkeit!"

One could argue that Mahler indeed took note of these dashes within his composition. At the first end-of-line-dash, he wrote in a long pause with winds (horn, clarinet); there is no pause at the second one, but a change of colour, with flats; on the third dash he marks a short pause while two violins make their entrance; finally, on the fourth end-of-line dash, Mahler writes a key change, from D minor to E minor. Could this be a musical interpretation of the effect of punctuation symbolism?

My favourite interpretation of Nietzsche's poem is its unique voice through Jessye Norman's masterful 1980 rendering on Deutsche Grammophon, conducted by Claudio Abbado. It is perhaps not too bold to believe that Nietzsche would have been enthralled at this reading, hearing, and interpretation of dashes, his perhaps unlikely yet not-so-silent heroes.

Epilogue

Aesthetic Reception

ON READING AND CURATING NIETZSCHE

> Should I compare [the Nietzschean philologist] to a museum director who conserves, takes care of, and enhances the art works, and who makes sure that visitors do not tear up paintings or smear statues?
>
> Richard Roos[1]

This book showed how Friedrich Nietzsche's written style evolved out of his disenchantment with the requirements of professional philosophy and his concomitant and growing critique of a form of life: that of the scholar. By opting out of academia, Nietzsche resolutely tuned in to the crafting of an expressive, performative, and synesthetic style through which his philosophical ideas could have richer and surer means of affecting many different readers. Style is thus a multiplex: it is an expression of the embodied quality of thought and a sign as to the openness of interpretation, it is a bait and a gift, it is a show of resistance and an act of creation.

As such, Nietzsche's style is an integral part of his philosophy, and it must be the focus of attention if we are to understand his philosophical points, critiques, and aims. Indeed, the issue of style shows how critique and creation go hand in hand in Nietzsche's works as well as in his own personal evolution as a thinker. His style spells out but also stages and invites experimentations in such a way that reading Nietzsche makes for an embodied reception of his thoughts. His works thereby participate in a larger discussion on the scope of aesthetic experience, the act of reception and interpretation, and the nature of a work of art. This epilogue will be devoted to delineating this enquiry.

When Nietzsche, in his 1882 "Doctrine of Style" letter to Lou von Salomé, stressed that "Style must live,"[2] he meant that a work must have a life not only in the author's hands, but also — and perhaps even mostly — in the reader's eyes and ears. Style, in other words, lives alongside interpretation. The "Doctrine on Style" thus not only gives advice on how to write, but also on how to read.

An enquiry into style invites a larger reflection upon our relation to texts. As a philologist, Nietzsche was a professional reader, one who peruses ancient treatises, who is versed in the art of deciphering and using rhetorical tactics, who hears the creative effect of rhythms or rhymes and sees their epistemological implications. Professional readers do many things with texts. Scholars for whom texts are research objects as well as tools may rhetorically scrutinize a book's language, contextually situate its author, philosophically comment upon its theses, or critically appreciate its literary form or cultural or scientific effect.

The texts that we examine, praise, or critique have been passed on to us through processes that shape our reading and understanding. These processes may be editorial, cultural, even political. Am I picking up this book because it is mandatory for my studies, recommended by a friend, or deemed a classic by the culture I take part in? Or perhaps the dust jacket or type font simply attracted my attention. Is it presented as a contribution to a specific field, political struggle, scientific endeavour? Was the book even intended to be published by its author, was it perhaps self-published against editorial advice, or is it the product of other people's wishes and toil, possibly against the author's last intentions?[3] How many authorial voices are speaking between its covers? That of the author, of course, but also that of the translator, the writer of the preface, the editor ... in fact, how many languages were used in its making?

As these questions suggest, a book is the result of many decisions and operations. It is rarely the act of one person alone. Moreover, it is always the result of staging. Nietzsche's style — his characters, his humour, his dialogues — continually reminds us of the fact that a book is a curated object.

Editorial Curating

Etymologically, "curating" is related to "caring." The *curatus*, in Latin, is the person in charge of the care of souls.[4] Today, the word is mostly heard between the walls of museums. A curator cares for a gallery's artworks by conceiving ways to organize and show parts of its collection through exhibits. In so doing, a curator oversees that which in its initial state is but a disparate totality.

Upon visiting a gallery, visitors may have the impression that what they see on the exhibition floors is the collection. In fact, exhibition rooms show only parts of it. When my long-time friend Nathalie was curator at a downtown contemporary art gallery in Montréal, I had the opportunity to visit the vault where the complete art collection was stored. My first reaction was one of surprise, though not because of the sheer number of art works that were stored. Above all, I was astounded to realize that many of those works were not contemporary at all. But the older and more classical art pieces were almost never shown, as they did not fit the niche that the gallery had carved out for itself.[5]

That example reminds us that exhibits are the surface phenomena of underlying decisions through which curators follow a precise thread to prepare a reception of the individual works within an exhibit context. This context is meant to enhance the works' aesthetic value (and economic worth). Through selection and staging, the curator participates in defining the gallery's identity, but also in shaping the context within which we receive, interpret, and appreciate works of art. Yet the proposed curatorial staging is one amongst several possible. The selected works of art could very well be assembled differently, were other parameters chosen as threads, thereby creating new reception contexts. This goes to show that "to curate" is not only "to care," it is also to sort, to select, to associate, and to stage — actions through which a new whole is created and defined.

The parallel between curatorial and editorial work experiences is striking. By inserting an artwork within a context[6] a curator asserts a thesis on how it may or sometimes even must be semantically received and defined as to its sense, status, or impact. The same process happens in the editorial field. As readers we may tend to forget that by sorting and assembling someone's written works editors not only care for texts in multifarious ways, they also prepare and stage the contexts within which the works will be received and read.

Using curation as a metaphor may help us better investigate the relationship between editor, text, and reader. All past editors of Nietzsche's works have acted as curators in the sense of caring and in the sense of defining, choosing, and staging. But what is the metaphor's extent? As curators, are editors also aware of staging one possible iteration of an author's works? Perhaps in theory, but the practice and its discourse often say quite the opposite. Editors — especially ones who work on critical editions or new, modern translations with numerous explicatory footnotes — generally affirm that they are assembling and presenting the accurate (and thus objective) state of an author's work.

The curatorial metaphor certainly invites editorial self-reflection. More largely, it opens onto interpretative and methodological questions concerning the definition of a written work, our knowledge of and access to authorial intent, or the context and means of editorial and translation practice. These questions call for the contribution of different disciplines that have taken act of and part in what is now called the linguistic turn in the humanities and social sciences in the twentieth century.

Philosophy, for one, has contributed to these reflections. Philosopher Roman Ingarden, for instance, launched a life-long investigation into the nature of the literary work of art through phenomenological aesthetics and ontological enquiry. The field of hermeneutics, in turn, has produced studies on the nature of understanding and the limits of interpretation. Scholars in the philosophy of translation, a small although not so narrow subfield, propose theoretical reflections on translatability as a sign of interpretation and communication.[7]

The fields of philology, literature, and literary theory have also contributed to these questions. Scholars have analysed a text's inner workings or specified the conditions and limits of reading response and editorial practice, while others have engaged in meta-reflections on these practices.[8] This enquiry also interests researchers in the ever-growing field of digital humanities who focus on the relationship between our technological means and our reception and definitions of textual objects.[9] While these multiple angles share a common interest in the relationship between author, text, and reader, perhaps this interconnectedness concerns one field first and foremost: aesthetics.

Aesthetics may be understood as the philosophical discipline that analyzes the relationship between a producer, an actively perceiving person, and a certain type of object that finds its meaning through its reception (rather, say, than through its use). That is Ingarden's definition of philosophical aesthetics, which he proposed in his 1969 conference paper "Phenomenological Aesthetics: An Attempt at Defining Its Range." Ingarden describes a literary work as a dynamic relational structure that rests upon what he calls the indetermination (or openness) of the initial schematic form produced by the author. To exist, a work of art needs a creator, but also a receptor who actualizes the schematic form's potential elements through one's own experience. The work of art is not the form produced by the author and it is not only the receiver's experience. It is at the intersection of these forms and experiences: the work of art is an "intentional object."[10]

It is worth noting that Ingarden points to lived experience at every moment of that dynamic relational structure. Not only do the author and reader produce and actualize the work from within their own experience, but also a work itself has a "life" in reference "to a whole community of such readers, observers, or listeners."[11] A written work is therefore a social and cultural object that is never finished or "closed." A new reading, a new commentary, or a new translation shows a new actualization of the initial form produced by the author, depending on the reader's historical, social, cultural, or linguistic position. The reader's receptive role is therefore never a matter of "purely reconstructing the work." If it were so, the work would be "dead, aesthetically inert." Quite the contrary, a work functions as a power reservoir or an energy source.[12]

There have been few investigations into the reception and effect of specific works along Ingardian lines. (One reason may be that Ingarden limited his theory to works of fiction.) One rare example is the French philosopher Claude Lefort's monumental 1972 essay *Machiavelli in the Making*. In his magnum opus Lefort not only proposed an interpretation of what Machiavelli may still bring to contemporary political philosophy, he also studied the varied interpretations and definitions of Machiavelli throughout the ages. Moreover, he situated his own interpretation of Machiavelli within this historical community that *makes* Machiavelli what he is *as a work*. (The original French title of Lefort's book is *Le travail de l'œuvre Machiavel*, a strange grammatical construction in French, which says something akin to: "The work of Machiavelli as a work" or "Machiavelli's work at work.") Lefort claimed that his interpretation had two methodological advantages. On the one hand, it was self-conscious, in that it was aware of its inheritance and its status, and of being part of a whole that is the ongoing, ever-in-the-making "Machiavelli as work"; on the other (and concomitantly), it was continually questioning its own interpretative procedure.[13]

In the United States Lefort's book is deemed an important contribution to the understanding of the locus of power in democratic societies, while in France it is said to contribute to 1970s interpretation theory. That is certainly a striking difference. Perhaps even more astonishing are the underlying editorial practices: in 2012, the American editors of the English translation left out about three hundred pages of Lefort's book, which constitutes the core of his interpretation theory. This shows how academic cultures may have different expectations as to what counts as a contribution to a field. Apparently, American political theory does not care much for reception theory but does care for a new appropriation of the Machiavellian notion of power. In other words, the field is open to an expansion of the "*œuvre Machiavel*," but has little to do with a meta-discourse on hermeneutics.[14] Interestingly, Lefort's book in English not only shows cultural differences in its reception, it also reveals the impact of editorial curating.

The Illusion of an Intact Object

Interdisciplinary reflections on editorial curating; Ingarden's notion of a work of art as a relational structure; Lefort's hermeneutical understanding of a work forever in the making; and even the adventures in reception and translation of Lefort's own piece — these discussions all point to the fact that upon opening a book, we are not in front of an intact object. What, then, are we to make of the editorial hopes of attaining the "accurate" state of an author's work? Perhaps philology may help us address this question.

During his 1972 talk at Cérisy-la-Salle, while discussing the issue of Nietzsche's notes and unfinished manuscripts — the sum of which is now called the Nachlaß — Richard Roos underlined that an important advantage of the critical edition of Nietzsche's complete writings (assembled as of the 1960s by philologists G. Colli and M. Montinari) was precisely that it gives the reader access to Nietzsche's Nachlaß as notes (rather than as finished texts, which they obviously were not). A message was thus immediately transmitted to readers of Nietzsche's *Posthumous Fragments*, a message that could be formulated as such: *You are now perusing traces of the author's personal writing activity, and please keep in mind that these unfinished texts were not originally intended for readers.*

In comparison, Heinrich Köselitz's (aka Peter Gast, as Nietzsche preferred to name his friend), Elisabeth Förster-Nietzsche's, or Friedrich Würzbach's editions of Nietzsche's notes — all prepared between the 1890s and the 1930s — did not acknowledge the falsity of their reconstruction of the Nachlaß, most notably because they used their editorial voice to give the illusion of "an intact object."[15] Indeed, they used a book title: "*The Will to Power*, by Friedrich Nietzsche"; they constructed a table of contents, thereby conveying an impression of order and comprehensiveness; and they avoided editorial notes, which could have explained the extent of their creativity in putting together and presenting Nietzsche's so-called "*magnum opus*." In other words, not only did they act as though the author had written such a book as *The Will to Power*, the editors also acted as though this work contained Nietzsche's definitive philosophical ideas and aims.[16]

In truth, the illusion of "an intact object," Roos warned, is a fault that philologists and art restorers alike should always try to avoid. As Benedetta Zavatta reminds us in her research on Emerson and Nietzsche, the effect of Montinari's editorial enterprise was to show "that good philology transforms a static text into a dynamic object."[17] Roos shared the same optic. His talk gave philological advice to philosophers working with Nietzsche's notes. But perhaps more importantly, he also proposed a meta-reflection on editorial work:

> philology cannot hold a claim to complete objectivity. The times are behind us when philologists could imagine applying their research methods to any domain, intellectually, mathematically, mechanically, while resting assured of the scientific quality of their results. It is precisely because philologists are conscious of being guided by their interest, character, needs, and because they know that they are also unwillingly dominated and lead by the needs and concerns of their society, that they may now *attain a maximum of objectivity*. For this to happen, every answer must be interrogated again, and the choice of a question or method must in turn be the object of an interrogation.[18]

Roos' point was in fact very Nietzschean. He was stating that objectivity is not to be thought of as an undividable whole. Rather, if we may strive to "attain a maximum of objectivity," it is precisely because there are degrees of objectivity. He was also stating two conditions for a researcher to attain a high degree of objectivity in one's research field. The first is cultural self-reflection — that is, our knowledge of the cultural values of our time and our insight as to how these values drive research. The second is methodological meta-reflection — meaning our capacity and willingness to question our standpoints and tools. In this sense, Roos's talk (given the very same year when Lefort's *Machiavelli* was published) is a meta-discourse on methodology.

Interestingly, although Roos's talk was not well received by the philosophers to whom it was addressed (such as Pierre Klossowski, Derrida, or Philippe Lacoue-Labarthe), the advice that he gave has now come to define serious editorial scholarship. It is worth quoting its concluding remarks on what philology could bring to Nietzsche studies:

> a correctly established text; a critical apparatus containing all versions and corrections; linguistic and historic explanations; clarifications concerning the different levels of meaning that could be as complete as possible thanks to synthetic interpretation and a genetic study of the text: that is how philology can contribute to founding a philosophical interpretation that could go further and with less risk because it would be better assured of its basis. Such a philosophical interpretation requires a respect for and prior understanding of the text before it can propose an up-to-date commentary ... One's own interpretation that does not rely on a correctly established text is inadmissible.[19]

That quote precisely sums up the research ethos that drives Nietzsche scholarship today. Indeed, Nietzsche is now an object of science — a very dynamic object, in fact — and this is a rather recent phenomenon.

Thanks to Colli and Montinari we believe we have access to a robust edition of his writings. Their critical edition continues to inspire rich and reliable scholarship in many countries. But why do we feel that it is of the utmost importance to foster the conditions for high degrees of objectivity in the reception of Nietzsche's ideas — for instance through new, complete translations into French (currently undertaken by Garnier-Flammarion) or English (currently undertaken by Stanford University Press), or through an immense (and costly) endeavour to digitize his complete manuscripts and notebooks?[20] In other words, why has the reception of Nietzsche shifted from Jacques Derrida and Bernard Pautrat to, say, Patrick Wotling and James Porter? Is it simply the expected extension of the logic of scientific inquiry into an author that the philosophical field took some time to treat "academically"? Is it a reaction to interwar attempts to nationalize and Nazify his thought? Is it a way for scholars to simply keep busy (and for publishing houses to stay afloat)?

Perhaps the scientific drive to a complete presentation of (almost) all written traces left by Nietzsche is all of the above — a cathartic procedure, an endeavour to carve out a subfield for academic philosophers, an application of digital tools and public funds to the democratization of research. We can frame this phenomenon in ideological, sociological, or technological terms, but surely it is a phenomenon that we should interrogate if we are to better understand ourselves as readers or scholars, and to attain a higher degree of objectivity — and self-awareness.

Self-Awareness: The Text Is Not Enough

Translation is a particularly self-conscious practice. When one needs to transpose a sentence into another language, one is confronted by the oft-overlooked act of interpretation that ordinary reading consists of. Indeed, one must decide which foreign words can best render the author's philosophical meaning, practical intent, cultural reference, and rhetorical effect — all at once.

Nietzsche's use of language is a constant reminder that writing is an intrinsically creative act. Expressing oneself is never a matter of simply stating facts. Indeed, a text bears witness to the author's sensibility and experience of the world through the specific language used.

This point was made by the German Romantics in the nineteenth century. The theologian Friedrich Schleiermacher, for example, applied it to translation in his 1813 lecture *On the Different Methods for Translation*. Schleiermacher insists that translation has two objectives. One is to transmit an understanding, the other is to transmit pleasure (*Genuß*). These two cannot be separated if the translator is to communicate a "vivid sense of [the] cohesiveness" of the text — one that may show how the author created something through a use of language, thereby also creating "a new moment in the life of the language."[21] Indeed, language itself evolves — not only in the long run, but also within an author's own lexicon.[22]

If we take that to be a sound rendering of the plastic nature of language, then the act of translation constantly reminds us that the original text is no "intact object": it is a dynamic, quasi living entity open to the reader. In the act of translation, one is aware of the transitory nature of the strange object that a text makes for. Its meaning changes with the culture receiving and treating it, as Lefort showed with Machiavelli — and as 125 years of Nietzsche reception continually shows.

Yet openness does not mean absence of boundaries. To say with Ingarden that a text is a dynamic relational structure open to the reader does not entail that the text may be interpreted any which way, as though its author could have said anything and everything (as Derrida infamously wrote of Nietzsche's *Ecce Homo*).[23] There are parameters according to which — or borders within which — it is possible to understand the text and say something meaningful about it, and outside of which it is possible to err as to the author's possible message and intent.[24]

It is therefore necessary for the translator, but also the interpreter, to have access to the actual material text that the author wrote. But the text is not enough. It is also necessary to have some notion of the cultural background upon which a writer speaks. This asks for knowledge of the author's sources, but also of commonplace references of the times. However, can we claim to have access to that enunciation context as to a fixed and stable collection of facts? Language acts do not reach us in a stable, "objective" form because they are culturally mediated. As philosophers or professional readers, we need to self-reflexively acknowledge this and know what it is we are working with if we are to enrich our praxis and its output. In sum, we need to pay attention to our interpretative acts, to our methods, and to our own cultural context as well.

In 2019, I was revising early French translations of Nietzsche for a partial reprint. I came upon the case of a translation by Bracke, a turn-of-the-century socialist who was a specialist of Herodotus. (How he came to Nietzsche, I have yet to discover.) I was struck by the fact that while translating *Human, All Too Human*, in 1899, he repeatedly chose to translate *große Loslösung* as "*un grand coup de partie*," using a French phrase that evokes casinos, cards, and a winning hand at *baccarat*. It is a mystery to me how a nineteenth-century socialist could not understand Nietzsche's große Loslösung as meaning, quite bluntly, a great liberation or detachment. He perhaps read that section of *Human, All Too Human* as an analogy, since in that precise section Nietzsche talks about spiritual and not strictly material restraint and liberation. But because of Bracke's choice of metaphor, parts of his rendition remain obscure to Francophone readers of our own times.[25]

This example shows the multifariousness of metaphorical thinking both in the writing and the deciphering of a text. It suggests, in other words, that analogy is central to reasoning. That was of course an important position of Nietzsche's, and it is also central to hermeneutics and twentieth-century interpretation theory. It was by using metaphors that Humboldt or Gadamer, for instance, could describe language as a "circle," a "horizon," or an "organ" for thought. Today, the centrality of analogy is often underlined by scholars of the digital humanities such as Willard McCarty. In a 2013 paper in the *Companion to New Media Dynamics*, he argued for the need to move away from "the dominant and highly positivistic 'idea of text'" and closer to "new figure[s] of thought" to describe our relation to the mediums through which we form, communicate, and access ideas.[26]

Our new text-editing technologies have transformed the images through which we comprehend and define what a text is.[27] It thus comes as no surprise that the field of digital humanities takes up the philologists' and literary theorists' critiques of the idea of the text as "an intact object." McCarty stresses that in our intellectual relationship to texts (as in many other contexts) we have "inherited a 'repertoire of images and concepts' of which we are only peripherally aware."[28] Indeed, prior definitions as to what constitutes a "book" influence how we consider it necessary to transmit and present an author's "work" to the public. But then, should we not ask whether the "book" and "text" by which we are so taken could perhaps be instances of inherited metaphors that also ask to be reconsidered — or that already are reconsidered through current discourses and practices?

Digital tools can help us create new occasions for thought through new images. Perhaps in doing so, we may move closer to Nietzsche's lived experiences and thought experiments. By inviting us to view some of our traditional definitions and decisions through different lenses, studies in digital humanities seem well adapted to Nietzsche's writing.

Nietzsche's use of novel metaphors, his shunning of linear argumentation in favour of aphoristic writing, his invocation of the importance of an embodied experience by the reader, even his self-curating — his self-quotation or desire for typographical unity, for instance — all these habits make him well-suited to the tabular, that is, non-linear ways of presenting information that digital editing tools permit. Tabularity means the possibility for "readers ... [to] visually access data in the order that they choose, identifying sections of interest beforehand."[29] It generally points to a non-linear conception of reading, and even to a slowing down of reading habits, since the reader is no longer guided down an imposed linear narrative or argumentative path from beginning to end.[30] By espousing tabularity through his aphorisms and poems Nietzsche offers an active role to the reader. And readers have been grasping this invitation since the 1890s, whether through translation, artistic rendition, musical interpretation, literary copy, social and political discourse — and even through academic research and critical edition.

When reading Friedrich Nietzsche's works today, we are still making interpretative decisions. We receive his writings — their words and sounds, their metaphors and images, their dialogues and humour, their theses and insinuations — in our present cultural context, which rests upon layers of prior reception. It is impossible not to situate ourselves within or against these. It is also impossible not to contribute to the present culture and reception context with our own reading, creation, and judgment on the work and author at hand, provided we communicate our interpretation.

When using the linguistic or artistic tools of our own time, we refer to our culture while also enriching it through renewed reception. The current digitalized Nietzsche and the new translations are curatorial practices through which scholars, editors, translators, and readers participate in the ongoing "*œuvre Nietzsche*" — a Nietzsche perpetually in the making. We again build figures of Nietzsche as author and propose interpretations of his ideas. Through us, he is a philosopher forever being constructed out of our readings of his works — a phenomenon that perhaps would not have displeased him.

But will our "new" Nietzsches be accessible to future readers? This may depend on our willingness to achieve a "maximum of objectivity" through our dual awareness of the works' contexts and acceptance of their perpetual openness and incompleteness. Scholarly, editorial work is also an eminently creative way of answering the text's call to be read and interpretated. We should not forget how, as scholars, we are also artists.

Perhaps certain readings, translations, and editorial practices have more chance to stand the test of time. If so, surely an awareness of our own values and drives — whether we be scholars or artists or even occasional readers — is an asset. The understanding of a text, much like the knowledge we can have of the world that we take part in, goes hand in hand with an understanding of ourselves. All three are perpetually in the making.

A Very Short Chronology

Academia: The Professional Life

1868–70	Eleven philological papers (published in specialized, academic journals).
1869	Chair of Classical Philology at the University of Basel, Switzerland; inaugural lecture: *Homer and Classical Philology.*
1870	Three talks on tragedy at Basel: *The Greek Music Drama*, *Socrates and Tragedy*, *The Dionysian Worldview.*
1870–75	Basel lectures on Sophocles, Plato, the Pre-Socratics, Democritus, Greek religion, etc.
1871	Unsuccessful application to the Chair of Philosophy at the University of Basel.
1872	First book: *The Birth of Tragedy*. Five talks in Basel: *On the Future of our Educational Institutions* (manuscript prepared for publication, but left unfinished and unpublished). Gift to Cosima Wagner: *Five Prefaces to Five Unwritten Books*.
1872–73	Polemic around *The Birth of Tragedy*.
1873	Two short Wagnerian articles: "A New Year Word to the Editor of the Magazine *Im neuen Reich*" and "Call to the Germans." Unfinished and unpublished essay: *On Truth and Lie in the Unmoral Sense.* Unfinished and unpublished manuscript: *Philosophy in the Tragic Age of the Greeks.*

	Second book: *David Strauss the Confessor and the Writer* (first *Unfashionable Observation*).
1874	Third book: *On the Utility and Liability of History for Life* (second *Unfashionable Observation*).
	Fourth book: *Schopenhauer as Educator* (third *Unfashionable Observation*).
	Unfinished and unpublished essay: *We Philologists* (project for an *Unfashionable Observation*).
1876	Fifth book: *Richard Wagner in Bayreuth* (fourth *Unfashionable Observation*).
1876–77	Teaching leave from Basel, officially for health reasons.
1878	Sixth book: *Human, All Too Human*.
	Basel lectures on Hesiod and Plato.
1879	Seventh book: *Mixed Opinions and Maxims*.
	Eighth book: *The Wanderer and His Shadow*.
	Early retirement from the University of Basel.

Wanderings: A Philosophical Life

1881	Ninth book: *Dawn*.
1882	Tenth book: *The Gay Science*.
	Eight poems published in a magazine: *Idyllen aus Messina*.
1883	Eleventh book: *Thus Spoke Zarathustra*, part I.
	Twelfth book: *Thus Spoke Zarathustra*, part II.
1884	Thirteenth book: *Thus Spoke Zarathustra*, part III.
1885	Fourteenth book: *Thus Spoke Zarathustra*, part IV (private print run of forty copies).
1886	Fifteenth book: *Beyond Good and Evil*.
	Five prefaces written for the planned re-edition of his first, sixth, seventh, eighth, ninth, and tenth books.
	Essay: *We, Without Fear* (new section V of the *Gay Science*, for its re-edition).
1886–87	New publication of his "complete works": *The Birth of Tragedy* (with a new preface), *Unfashionable*

	Observations (in one vol.), *Human, All Too Human*, part I (with a new preface), *Human, All Too Human*, part II (*Mixed Opinions and Maxims* and *The Wanderer and his Shadow* in one vol., with a new preface), *Dawn* (with a new preface), *The Gay Science* (with a new preface, poems, and a new part V), *Thus Spoke Zarathustra* (parts I, II, and III, in one vol.).
1887	Sixteenth book: *On the Genealogy of Morality*.
1888	Seventeenth book: *The Case of Wagner*. Manuscript: *Nietzsche contra Wagner* (sent to the publisher, but Nietzsche stopped its publication).
1889	Eighteenth book: *Twilight of the Idols*. Nineteenth book: *Dionysus-Dithyrambs* (poems). Nietzsche falls and stops all activity.

Weimar and Beyond: The Posthumous Life

1890	First complete publication of *Thus Spoke Zarathustra* (the four parts in one vol.).
1894–1904	Publication of the first "complete works": *Großoktav-Ausgabe* (*GA*), 15 vols., Leipzig (2nd ed. in 19 vols., 1901–13), under the editorial directorship of Elisabeth Förster-Nietzsche.
1895	Twentieth book: *Antichrist* (from 1888, first published in *GA*). Twenty-first book: *Nietzsche contra Wagner* (first published in *GA*).
1900	Nietzsche dies in Weimar.
1901	Publication of the fake book *The Will to Power* (translated into French in 1902).
1903	In France, Nietzsche's works are on the professional exam (*agrégation*) for professors of German.
1908	Twenty-second book: *Ecce Homo* (from 1888–89, published posthumously).
1967	Publication (Italy-Germany-France) of the first critical, philological, and chronological edition

	of Nietzsche's complete works (including letters, unpublished manuscripts, and notes) based on the manuscripts and notebooks, edited by Giorgio Colli and Mazzino Montinari.
1970	In France, Nietzsche is on the professional exam (*agrégation*) for professors of philosophy.
1970–2020	Other posthumous publications: youth writings, *Philologica*, and music compositions.

Notes

PROLOGUE

1 On the relationship between Meta von Salis-Marchins and Nietzsche, see Stump, "Salis' Begegnung." For a general history of the Nietzsche archives in Weimar, see Hoffmann, *Geschichte*; and for an excellent overview of Nietzsche's presence in Weimar, see Naake, *Nietzsche und Weimar*.

2 On the "*Neue Weimar*" artistic and social movement, see Schütze, *Nietzsche and the Artists*.

3 On the beginnings of the 1890s to 1910s Nietzsche-Kultus, see Duboc, *Jenseits vom Wirklichen*, and Tönnies, *Nietzsche Kultus*; see also Cancik, "Nietzsche-Kult."

4 Henry van de Velde had already designed a type font for an exquisite edition of *Thus Spoke Zarathustra*, which he prepared and published in Weimar in 1899. On van de Velde's Nietzsche designs, see Fischer, "Birth of Modernity," and Hollis, *Henry van de Velde*, 125–34.

5 On Andler, Rolland, and the Nietzsche Archive, see Wartenweiler, "Charles Andler," 71–6, and Franck, "Anti-moralisme pacifiste." On the relationship between fascism, Nazism, and the Nietzsche Archive, see Hoffmann, *Geschichte*.

6 On the concentration camp, see the Buchenwald Memorial's website: https://www.buchenwald.de/en/ (accessed 9 August 2023).

7 President Obama's speech is available at https://obamawhitehouse.archives.gov/the-press-office/remarks-president-obama-german-chancellor-merkel-and-elie-wiesel-buchenwald-concent (accessed 9 August 2023).

INTRODUCTION

1 "Zur Lehre vom Stil": Nietzsche to von Salomé, 8/24 August 1882, in *KSB* 6, 243–5.

2 Herrig, "Moderner Freigeist." On the early reception of Nietzsche's books during his active years, see Béland, "Nietzsche avant Brandes."
3 See chapter 6, note 1.
4 *GS*, §381; see also *TI*, "Things I Owe to the Ancients," §1. On Nietzsche's use of aphorisms, see Ansell-Pearson and Bamford, *Nietzsche's* Dawn, 19–23.
5 Kofman, *Nietzsche and Metaphor*, 22. See also, e.g., *TI*, "Reason in Philosophy," §5, in *CWN* 9, 59–60. In the rich literature about metaphors, see, among others, Ricoeur, *Rule of Metaphor*, and Davidson, "What Metaphors Mean."
6 Neymeyr, "Sprache als Medium," 331. A simple and striking example of a metaphor in Nietzsche's oeuvre is the title of his 1881 book, *Dawn*. The book has nothing to do with an astronomical phenomenon. "Dawn" is a metaphor for a new cultural beginning. It names a new interpretative stance: that of "the philosophy of the morning" (*HAH* I, §638), which Nietzsche associates with independence, discovery, and joyfulness. The moment of dawn, when a new morning sun rises, thereby evokes the new epistemological position that Nietzsche proposes: perspectivism. On Nietzsche's *Dawn*, see Ansell-Pearson and Bamford, *Nietzsche's* Dawn.
7 See Nietzsche to Schmeitzner, 18 January and 6 February 1884; to Overbeck, 6 February 1884; and to Köselitz, 30 March 1884, in *KSB* 6.
8 See *WS* (*HAH* II), §87. For a precise commentary on the importance of the issue of style in Nietzsche's *WS*, see Lebeau-Henry, "Apprendre à bien écrire," 204–8.
9 *EH*, "Books," §4, in *CWN* 9.
10 See, e.g., Barthes, "Old Rhetoric," and Schopenhauer, "Art of Being Right."
11 Babich, *Words in Blood*, 23; Strong, "Defense of Rhetoric," 511; Stegmaier, *Nietzsche zur Einführung*, 98. See also Bertram, *Attempt at a Mythology*.
12 On Nietzsche's use of dialogues, see Zittel, "Der Dialog."
13 Nietzsche concludes *BGE* (§296) on the astonishment with which he notices the "new look" of his thoughts now that he has written them down: he compares writing to painting and enumerates hues that he wished to employ for his thoughts — "lots of yellows and brown."
14 Simson, "Typographie," 208. For all his emphasis on emotions, passions, and embodied experience, Nietzsche also stressed the importance of reason. This is evident through his use of many classical rational tools, for instance the principle of simplicity known

as Occam's razor (see *HAH* I, §10, or *BGE*, §36). For useful notes on Nietzsche and the role of reason, see Ansell-Pearson and Bamford, *Nietzsche's* Dawn.

15 *WS* (*HAH* II), §110, in *CWN* 4: 203.

16 On the phenomenon of synesthesia, see Cytowic, *The Man* and *Synesthesia.*

17 Ansell-Pearson, "Knowledge of the Sufferer," 15.

18 Examples are numerous: see, e.g., *HAH* I, preface, §1 and §8, or *GS*, §84.

19 See chapter 6 and Nietzsche's 1886 letters to his Leipzig publisher, Ernst W. Fritzsch.

20 See Blue, "Nietzsche's Nationality."

21 Maingueneau, "Énonciation philosophique," 40.

22 Derrida, "Langue philosophique."

23 The two last quotes are from Ruin, "Aesthetics of Philosophy," 324 and 328.

24 The situation was the same in American universities, as Ludwig Marcuse noted in the 1950s, where often, in scholarly or student publications, "Nietzsche was made the spiritual author of the nationalistic megalomania of Wilhelm II and Hitler" (Marcuse, "Nietzsche in America," 333). The multi-volumed *Nietzsche-Kommentar*, which is now being edited by the Heidelberger Akademie der Wissenschaften and published by de Gruyter in Berlin, is certainly a sign of the renewal of interest in Nietzsche's philosophy in German academia. On Nietzsche's legacy in Germany, see Aschheim, *Nietzsche Legacy.*

25 Since the 1990s several studies have examined liberal movements' relationship to Nietzsche's works and ideas. On feminists' reading of Nietzsche, see, for the United States, Ratner-Rosenhagen, *American Nietzsche*, and, for a wider reception, Oliver and Pearsall, *Feminist Interpretations.* On left-leaning readings of Nietzsche, see Gerlach and Caysa, *Die Linke.*

26 These are surely mistakes; but often translators are neither professionals nor philologists, and philosophers may often be attuned to theses more than they perhaps are to grammar. To their defense, it is useful to remember the fact, well-known to translators, that it is often difficult to respect the length of a sentence while translating it: for the sake of native syntax, e.g., many translators cut sentence-units or insert clauses where the author wrote none.

27 Fortunately, scholars, students, and the general public now have an open access to the complete German texts of Nietzsche's works

through the *Nietzsche Source* online edition: Nietzsche's books and complete unpublished works, letters, and fragments are available on the website *Nietzsche Source* in the original German (www.nietzsche source.org). I have participated in the ongoing retranslation of Nietzsche's works into French for Garnier-Flammarion (Paris) by translating the third and fourth *Unfashionable Observations* (forthcoming).

28 For an overview of this position, see Mash, "History of Philosophy."

29 See *BGE*, §36.

30 Roos, "Regeln," 22. See also Blondel, *Body and Culture*, 39.

31 Nietzsche advocates for this new philosophy and the need for a new language most notably in his 1886 works such as *BGE* (e.g., §4, in *CWN* 8, 7: "our new language sounds strangest in this respect") and his five prefaces (e.g., *BT*, preface, §3: 20; "It should have *sung*, this 'new soul' — and not spoken!").

32 Kofman, *Nietzsche and Metaphor*, 2.

33 See, e.g., *BGE*, §11, §23, §34, §36; or *GS*, §374 on the possibility of there being "infinite interpretations" of the world, and *GS*, §343 on the new perspectives for thought that this idea opens up. On Nietzsche's perspectivism, see Gerhardt, "Perspektivismus."

34 Norton, "Demythologization," xx.

35 Blondel, *Body and Culture*, 51.

36 Four last quotes are from Nehamas, *Life as Literature*, 4–5.

37 Ruin, "Aesthetics of Philosophy," 320.

38 Nehamas, *Life as Literature*, 8.

39 See, e.g., *BGE*, §25, where Nietzsche praises question marks more than philosophical doctrines, and *BGE*, §31, where he praises the art of nuances. On Nietzsche's influence on modernist artists, see Kowalsky and Phelan, "Modernist Art," and Schütze, *Nietzsche and the Artists*; on his influence on German expressionist artists, see Roy, *From Naturalism to Expressionism*, 58.

40 See, e.g., *UO* 3 (*SE*), §3, in which Nietzsche compares the model of Hellenistic philosophers to the model proposed by Kant through his life choices.

41 In *BGE*, §3, Nietzsche stresses that a value is always a value *for* something or someone: there is no absolute value, only relative value. He defines the fact of giving value to something (*Wertschätzungen*: "valuations," in the plural) as "physiological demands for the preservation of a certain type of life" (*BGE*, §3, in *CWN* 8, 7).

42 Compagnon, *Literature*, 123 (see also Turgeon, *Style de Genette*, 10); and see Spitzer, *Stilstudien*.

43 See Ingarden, "Phenomenological Aesthetics," and Iser, *Implizite Leser*.

44 *BT*, §19, 118.

45 Nietzsche to Overbeck, 14 November 1886, in *KSB* 7, 282.

46 NF 34[147] (April–June 1885), in *KSA* 11, 469.

47 *GS*, §381, 245.

CHAPTER ONE

1 *HAH* I, preface, §7, in *CWN* 3, 12.

2 On Nietzsche's published reviews and philological essays, see Schaberg, *Nietzsche Canon*, and Porter, "Rare Impressions." On his going to the University of Munich's jubilee, see *KSB* 4, 37. On the philosophical orientation of his philology, see *EKP* (which I discuss later in this chapter). On *The Birth of Tragedy*'s lack of scholarship apparatus, see Porter, "Wilamowitz contra Nietzsche," 73.

3 Nietzsche to Vischer-Bilfinger, January 1871, in *KSB* 3, 175. In a late letter, he told of this important crisis that happened in the middle of his decade-long career: see Nietzsche to Brandes, 19 February 1888, in *KSB* 8, 260; see also *EH*, "Human, All Too Human."

4 See Nietzsche to Ritschl, 2 August 1869, in *KSB* 3, 34; and to Gersdorff, 28 September 1869, in *KSB* 3, 61. On Nietzsche's workload, see Janz, *Nietzsche*, especially vol. 1, part 2, chapter 4.

5 See Schaberg, *Nietzsche Canon*, 8–14.

6 Daston, "The Academies," 69; see also Turner, "Prussian Professoriate," 460. On the modernization of the universities at the time, see Clark, *Academic Charisma*.

7 Daston, "The Academies," 77; see Turner, "Prussian Professoriate," 465. On the innovations in the field of philology, see Daston, "The Academies," 74; Turner, "Prussian Professoriate," 461; and Clark, *Academic Charisma*, 171.

8 Droysen is quoted in Reinhardt, "Klassische Philologie," 342. For previous quotes, see Mommsen, "Ansprache," 198, and Schelling, *On University Studies*, 42–50.

9 Reinhardt, "Klassische Philologie," 339 and 336. On the crisis in the German historical sciences, see Lloyd-Jones, "Introduction," xxviii–xxix; and Emden, "Invention of Antiquity," 372.

10 Porter, "Classical Tradition," 13. For previous quote, see Reinhardt, "Klassische Philologie," 342.
11 See Emden, "Invention of Antiquity," 378. On the transformation of the learned class, see Turner, "Prussian Professoriate." On philology's incapacity to confront its theoretical issues, see Reinhardt, "Klassische Philologie," 342.
12 Wundt, "Mission de la philosophie," 113.
13 Porter, "Classical Tradition," 12.
14 *HKP*, in *KGW* 2 (1): 249–50.
15 Schelling, *On University Studies*, XIV, 151; for previous quote, see III, 39.
16 *HKP*, in *KGW* 2 (1): 253.
17 See *UO* 2 (*HL*), §3.
18 Reinhardt, "Klassische Philologie," 351. On German classical philology's interdisciplinarity, see Lloyd-Jones, "Introduction," xi and xiv; and Turner, "Prussian Professoriate," 469.
19 *EKP* §7, in *KGW* 2 (3): 370.
20 Whitman, "Magisterial Tradition," 459.
21 *EKP* §7, in *KGW* 2 (3): 369–70. See Nietzsche to Ritschl, 10 May 1869, in *KSB* 3, 7.
22 Du Bois-Reymond, "Zustande der Gegenwart," 450.
23 *HKP*, in *KGW* 2 (1): 252.
24 Ibid.
25 Nietzsche to Vischer-Bilfinger, January 1871, in *KSB* 3, 175.
26 Nietzsche to Rohde, 29 March 1871, in *KSB* 3, 189.
27 See Whitman, "Magisterial Tradition," 463.
28 Porter, "Wilamowitz contra Nietzsche," 75. Rohde's review and both of Wilamowitz's pamphlets are reprinted in Gründer, *Der Streit*.
29 Porter, "Wilamowitz contra Nietzsche," 74. For the 1873 review, see Leutsch, "Review," 138; see Rohde to Nietzsche, 12 January 1873, in *KGB* 2, 4.
30 Wilamowitz-Möllendorff, "Zukunftsphilologie," 55.
31 See Anonymous, "Die Vertreter." For Nietzsche considered as a Wagnerian philosopher, see for instance Leutsch, "Review," 137–8. On the "immediate response of the profession" to Nietzsche's book, see Whitman, "Magisterial Tradition," 455.
32 Nietzsche to Rohde, 30 April 1872, in *KSB* 3, 314.
33 I look more closely at this project in chapter 3.
34 NF 3[19] (March 1875), in *KSA* 8, 20.

35 The two last quotes are from NF 3[19] (March 1875), in *KSA* 8, 20.
36 Weber, *Protestant Ethic*, 39–40. On Nietzsche and Lutheranism, see Large, "Bauernaufstand."
37 Weber, "Science as Vocation," 7–8 (as regards specialization) and 9 (as regards method).
38 Weber, "Science as Vocation," 31.
39 Weber, *Protestant Ethic*, 155n1.
40 On Schopenhauer, see chapter 4.
41 See, respectively, for "instinct," NF 3[62], March 1875, in *KSA* 8, 31; for "enigma," Reinhardt, "Klassische Philologie," 335; for "intoxication," Weber, "Science as Vocation," 9.
42 *HKP*, in *KGW* 2 (1): 253.
43 See, e.g., *EKP* §7, in *KGW* 2 (3): 369–70; and Du Bois-Reymond, "Zustande der Gegenwart," 450.
44 NF 3[62], March 1875, in *KSA* 8, 31.
45 *EKP* §7, in *KGW* 2 (3): 371.
46 Nietzsche to Rohde, 15 December 1870, in *KSB* 3, 165. For "*Bildungs-Sekte*," see NF 32[62] (early 1874–spring 1874), in *KSA* 7, 776.
47 Daston, "The Academies," 82.
48 Rohde to Nietzsche, 6 May 1872, in *KGB* 2, 4; see also Rohde to Nietzsche, 14 November 1872.
49 *EH*, "Human, All Too Human" §4, in *CWN* 9, 270. For an example of a Nietzsche scholar attributing a liberating effect to Nietzsche's physical state, see D'Iorio, "Naissance de la philosophie," 41.
50 Nietzsche to Rohde, 11 April 1872, in *KSB* 3, 304–5.
51 Rohde to Nietzsche, April 1872, in *KGW* 2, 2.
52 Rohde to Nietzsche, 6 May 1872, in *KGB* 2, 4.
53 Rohde to Nietzsche, 14 November 1872, in *KGB* 2, 4.
54 See Rohde to Nietzsche, 6 May 1872 and 14 November 1872.
55 See Brobjer, *Nietzsche's Philosophical Context*, 254–5. On Schopenhauer and Emerson, see chapter 4.
56 Nietzsche to Rohde, 15 December 1870, in *KSB* 3, 165.
57 Quotes in this paragraph are from Schopenhauer, *Parerga*, vol. 1, respectively 156, 152, and 141.
58 Wolf is quoted in Clark, *Academic Charisma*, 171. See Schelling, *On University Studies* 3, 23n6.
59 Schopenhauer, *Parerga*, vol. 1, 152.
60 See *UO* 2 (*HL*), §10, in *CWN* 2, 166. For the two previous quotes, see NF 3[63] (March 1875), in *KSA* 8, 32; and NF 32[73] (early 1874–spring 1874), in *KSA* 7, 780.

61 Nietzsche, *Die vorplatonischen Philosophen*, I, in KGW 2 (4): 215. See also Plato, *Theae*, 155c–d, and Aristotle, *Meta*, A, 2, 982b.
62 *UO* 3 (*SE*), §3, in *CWN* 2, 183.
63 *PTZ* I, in *KSA* 1, 805.
64 *UO* 3 (*SE*), §8, in *CWN* 2, 246. See Nehamas, *Life as Literature*, especially chapter 6.
65 Nietzsche to Rohde, 29 March 1871, in *KSB* 3, 190.
66 *HAH* I, §261, in *CWN* 3, 178; see also *PTZ*.
67 *UO* 2 (*HL*), §10, in *CWN* 2, 166.
68 Nietzsche, "Fünf Vorreden," I, in *KSA* 1, 758.
69 Wilkerson, *Nietzsche and the Greeks*, 3.
70 See Porter, "Wilamowitz contra Nietzsche," 90, and "Rare Impressions," 410.
71 A parallel could perhaps be drawn between Nietzsche and Swiss historian Johann Jakob Bachofen, who retired from his University of Basel chair in 1845 after holding it but four years. Bachofen pursued his research on archaic societies and published most of his work as an independent scholar. According to Cancik (*Nietzsches Antike*), Bachofen is to be counted among the four figures most important for Nietzsche while he was in Basel (along with Wagner, Overbeck, and Burckhardt).
72 Weber, "Science as Vocation," 8–9.
73 Regarding the rather common practice in Swiss and German universities of hiring very young scholars during Nietzsche's time, see Janz, *Nietzsche*. For other examples of artistic vocations in philology, see Whitman, "Magisterial Tradition." For another defense of a philosophical perspective in historical studies, see Schelling, *On University Studies*.

CHAPTER TWO

1 Chabanon 1785, quoted in Charlton, "L'orchestre," 108.
2 On Nietzsche's compositional imperfections, see Fabre, *Nietzsche musicien*, 253; on his imagination and improvisational capacities, see Liébert, *Nietzsche and Music*, 20–2.
3 Liébert, *Nietzsche and Music*, 1.
4 On the relation between these three essays and *BT*, see Sweet, "The Birth."
5 For instance, his 1871 lecture on Sophocle's *Œdipus Rex*. On Nietzsche's lectures, see Porter, *Philology of the Future*, 167–224.

6 *BT*, §19, 118.

7 *BT*, §19, 121.

8 For a concise overview of Nietzsche's use of the term "type," see Denat and Wotling, *Dictionnaire Nietzsche*, 257–62.

9 *BT*, §22, 132. The word *Trieb* (drive) appears twenty times in *BT*.

10 See "Trieb," in Ottmann, *Nietzsche Handbuch*, 339.

11 See *BGE*, §6.

12 That is the sense in which Nietzsche uses the term "type" as of his 1878 book *Human, All Too Human*, most notably in sections that he wrote while using his summer of 1875 notebooks. See, e.g., NF 6[7.23.27.28.43.47] (summer 1875), in *KSA* 8. For "type" and the idea of a "possibility of life," see *HAH* I, §261, in *CWN* 3, 178; see also *BGE*, §257. I discuss this in more detail in chapter 3.

13 *BT*, §19, 114 and 116.

14 Wagner, "Kunstwerk der Zukunft," in *GSD* 3, 17.

15 Meyer, "Beiträge," 653. Bruno Meyer (1840–1917) was Leipzig's *Deutsche Warte* editor and a professor in Berlin.

16 On "uncultural" utilitarianism and egoism, see Wagner, "Kunstwerk der Zukunft," in *GSD* 3, 206–7; on *Geldtendenz*, see Nietzsche, "The Greek State."

17 *BT*, §19, 119.

18 *BT*, §18, 110.

19 Nietzsche, "On the Future of Our Educational Institutions, Lecture I," 36.

20 Wagner, "Kunstwerk der Zukunft," in *GSD* 3, 25.

21 Wagner's critique of profit in the opera industry also revealed his antisemitism; this made its way into Nietzsche's critique of German Jewish composer Meyerbeer in the fourth *Unfashionable Observation*, §8. For more on this issue, see my French translation of and notes to §8 of *Richard Wagner à Bayreuth* (forthcoming at Garnier-Flammarion, in Paris).

22 Rousseau, *Dictionary*, 198. For more on music aesthetics of this era, see Cannone, *Philosophie de la musique*.

23 *BT*, §22, 133. On the French tradition, see Accaoui, *Éléments d'esthétique musicale*, 230.

24 Plato, *Rep.* III, 398d–400d.

25 Last quotes are from *BT*, §19, 114.

26 See Haskell, *Early Music Revival*.

27 Last two quotes are from *BT*, §19, 114 and 116.

28 Caccini, *Nuove musiche*, 3.

29 Rousseau, *Dictionary*, 334 (translation slightly modified). By "us," Rousseau means French composers and French music.
30 *BT*, §19, 115.
31 On Hanslick's music aesthetics, see Nattiez, "Introduction."
32 Hanslick, *Musically Beautiful*, 41, §74.
33 *BT*, §19, 119. For "forms" and "arabesques," see §16, 100, and §19, 119. For the "Socratic world view," see §19, 118.
34 Schopenhauer, *World as Will*, book III, §52, 283.
35 Ibid., 289. For studies on Schopenhauer's philosophy of music, see the collected essays in Koßler, *Musik als Wille*, and especially the chapter by Crocetti, "Instrumental Music as Universal Language."
36 For a comprehensive overview of Schopenhauer's influence on Wagner, see Berry, "Nietzsche and Wagner."
37 Hoffmann, "Rezension," 631.
38 Chabanon's 1779 treatise was published anonymously. He incorporated much of this work in a second treatise on music, which he published in 1785 under the title *De la musique considérée en elle-même et dans ses rapports avec la parole, les langues, la poésie et le théâtre*. For English editions and commentaries, see Lippman, *Musical Aesthetics*, and Lyall, *French Music Aesthetic*.
39 On Hiller, see Abert and Baumann, "Hiller," and Böhm, "Hiller."
40 Chabanon 1785, quoted in Guertin, "Universel et singulier," 46; for previous quote, see 44.
41 Chabanon 1785, quoted in Guertin, "Universel et singulier," 44. For previous quote, see 45. To read more about Chabanon on language, see Salomon, "Chabanon and Chastellux."
42 Guertin, "Universel et singulier," 45.
43 Otabe, "Chabanon et Hiller," mentions that Chabanon's *Treatise* had a "large influence in Germany." Perhaps Schopenhauer could have known of Chabanon's ideas via the composer and music theorist Friedrich Wilhelm Marpurg (1718–1795): see Dahlhaus, *Esthetics of Music*. Hiller's book does not appear in Schopenhauer's library (see Schopenhauer, *Handschriftliche Nachlass*, vol. 5). I wish to thank Marie-Michèle Blondin for her help on this matter. Lussy, "Chabanon," noted the filiation between Chabanon and Hanslick. I also wish to thank my friend and colleague, the musicologist Ghyslaine Guertin, for the rich discussions we have had on these issues over the years.
44 Accaoui, *Éléments d'esthétique musicale*, 160.
45 Born in Saint-Domingue, Chabanon was a student and later a friend of the Guadeloupean composer and conductor Chevalier de Saint-Georges (1745–1799). See McClellan, "Colonialism and Science."

46 *BT*, §16, 100.
47 Plato, *Rep.* III, 403c. For "aesthetic Socratism," see *BT*, §12, 83.
48 *BT*, §12, 83–4.
49 Wagner, "Beethoven," in *GSD* 9, 105.
50 Schopenhauer, *World as Will*, book III, §41, 234.
51 *BT*, §2, 38.
52 Schopenhauer, *World as Will*, book III, §38, 220; for "effect," see 221.
53 NF 14[47] (early 1888), in *KSA* 13, 241.
54 *BT*, §2, 38; for "aesthetic listener," see §22, 132.
55 *BT*, §2, 38.
56 Gould, "Glenn Gould Interviews Glenn Gould About Glenn Gould," in *Glenn Gould Reader*, 321. Gould says he made his peace with "the fact that no real aesthetic yardstick relates your performances as originally conceived to the manner in which they will be subsequently audited" (320).
57 In his famous self-interview, Gould refuses the art critics' right to aesthetic judgments. See Gould, "Glenn Gould Interviews," in *Glenn Gould Reader*, 321–2, and "Critics," in *Glenn Gould Reader*, 257–8: "The critic as aesthetic arbiter had, I think, no proper social function, no defensible criteria upon which to base his subjective judgments."
58 Gould, "Let's Ban Applause!," in *Glenn Gould Reader*, 246. "I believe that the justification of art is the internal combustion it ignites in the hearts of men and not its shallow, externalized, public manifestations."
59 *BT*, §22, 133–4.
60 See Gould, "Glenn Gould Interviews," in *Glenn Gould Reader*, 318–19. Here, Gould explicitly links the notion of "creative audience" to the ideas of Canadian philosopher of media Marshall McLuhan.
61 Gould, "Let's Ban Applause!," in *Glenn Gould Reader*, 246.
62 Nietzsche, *Introduction aux études de philologie classique*, §7, 103 and 101.

CHAPTER THREE

1 See Strauss, *Life of Jesus*. Strauss's book had an impact on Nietzsche's losing his faith as a teen: see Brobjer, *Nietzsche's Philosophical Context*, 43–4, and Schaberg, *Nietzsche Canon*, 32. On the impact of Strauss's book in Germany, see Beiser, *Father of Unbelief*, and Chapin Massey, "Literature of Young Germany."
2 On the reception of Nietzsche's Strauss essay in his time, see Béland, "Nietzsche avant Brandes," 564. For the sales statistics, see Schaberg, *Nietzsche Canon*. The currently available numbers show the scant

popularity of the essay today, at least in the Francophone world: in 1998 the two paperback volumes of the *Considérations inactuelles* in the widely popular and available Folio series published by Gallimard had the lowest total numbers of sale of all the Folio Nietzsche volumes (see Le Rider, *Nietzsche en France*, 44). For the letter to Wagner, see Nietzsche to Wagner, 18 September 1873, in *KSB* 4; for Nietzsche's insistence on the importance of his Strauss essay, see Nietzsche to Brandes, 19 February 1888, in *KSB* 8.

3 Both quotations are from *UO* 2 (*HL*), preface, in *CWN* 2, 86. English translators gave different titles to Nietzsche's book through the years, from A. Collins's 1909 *Thoughts out of Season* in the Foulis edition of Nietzsche's works, to R.J. Hollingdale's 1983 *Untimely Meditations* for Cambridge University Press, and the more recent *Unfashionable Observations* translated in 1995 by R.T. Gray for the complete edition of Nietzsche's works by Stanford University Press.

4 Again, for the essays' contemporary sales statistics, see Schaberg, *Nietzsche Canon*, 44; for their current sales statistics in France, see Le Rider, *Nietzsche en France*, 40–50; for their contemporary reception, see Béland, "Nietzsche avant Brandes," 559.

5 For the "We Philologists" notes, see NF groups 2 and 3 (March 1875), in *KSA* 4. For Nietzsche's wish to abandon his *Unfashionable Observations* project, see, e.g., Nietzsche to Gersdorff, 26 September 1875, in *KSB* 5. For the plans for nine *Observations*, see, e.g., NF 1[3.4] (Winter–Spring 1875), in *KSA* 4; see also Nietzsche to Bülow, 2 January 1875, in *KSB* 5.

6 See, e.g., Nietzsche to Gersdorff, 26 September 1875, in *KSB* 5.

7 For the statistics, see Béland, "Nietzsche avant Brandes."

8 Nietzsche to Gersdorff, 3 June 1872, in *KSB* 4. Nietzsche used the word "disenchantment" early on, in an 18 September 1873 letter to Wagner (in *KSB* 4).

9 *UO* 2 (*HL*), preface, in *CWN* 2, 86.

10 NF 19[259] (Summer 1872–Early 1873), in *KSA* 7.

11 *Die Gartenlaube* was the newspaper with the largest circulation in Germany between 1853 and 1880 (it had more than 380,000 subscribers in 1875). The literary newspaper *Literarisches Centralblatt* published nine reviews of Nietzsche's books in his time (including reviews of the first, third, and fourth *Unfashionable Observations*), which makes it the newspaper that gave the most visibility to his works (see Béland, "Nietzsche avant Brandes," 556–7). On these and other newspapers of the time, see Obenaus, *Literarische*.

12 NF 5[84] (September 1870–January 1871), in *KSA* 7.

13 *UO* 2 (*HL*), §3, in *CWN* 2, 105–6.

14 This is a question that Nietzsche developed in "The Passion for Truth," one of five short essays which he titled *Prefaces to Unwritten Works* and offered to Cosima Wagner in 1872. Nietzsche's notion of drive has had considerable influence in psychology; for a study of its impact from the perspective of Nietzsche scholars, see Golomb et al., *Depth Psychology*; for an example of its use in psychotherapy, see Bazzano, *Nietzsche and Psychotherapy*.

15 *HAH* I, §261, in *CWN* 3, 178. See also NF 6[7.23.27.28.43.47] (Summer 1875), in *KSA* 8, and *BGE*, §257.

16 On the importance and role of drive-analysis in Nietzsche's philosophy, see e.g., Müller-Lauter, *Nietzsche*, and Wotling, "Languages."

17 *UO* 4 (*RWB*), §3, in *CWN* 2, 272. I discuss this in chapter 5.

18 *UO* 1 (*DS*), §2, in *CWN* 2, 14.

19 See the edited volume by Ottomeyer, Schröder, and Winters, *Biedermeier*, which focusses on Biedermeier arts and simplicity.

20 *UO* 3 (*SE*), §4, in *CWN* 2, 199.

21 On Nietzsche's pride with the term *Bildungsphilister* see, again, his 19 February 1888 letter to Brandes. He uses the term in *UO* 1 (*DS*), §2 (*CWN* 2), to name David Strauss.

22 See Le Rider, *Allemagne*, 11 and 82–4.

23 *UO* 2 (*HL*), §5, in *CWN* 2, 118.

24 *UO* 1 (*DS*), §12, in *CWN* 2, 81.

25 *UO* 2 (*HL*), §6, in *CWN* 2, 125.

26 Ibid., 125–6.

27 Ibid., 128–9.

28 *UO* 4 (*RWB*), §3, in *CWN* 2, 269–70.

29 *UO* 2 (*HL*), preface, in *CWN* 2, 85.

30 *UO* 2 (*HL*), §4, in *CWN* 2, 110–11; for "goal," see 108; for "minutiae," see §3, in *CWN* 2, 105.

31 *UO* 2 (*HL*), §6, in *CWN* 2, 130; for the previous quote, see §4, in *CWN* 2, 109.

32 *UO* 2 (*HL*), §7, in *CWN* 2, 136; for "labour market," see 134.

33 Ibid., 136. On the general development of the universities in Germany, see Clark, *Academic Charisma*.

34 *UO* 1 (*DS*), §8, in *CWN* 2, 46–7.

35 Ibid., 47.

36 Until the new French translation now published in the GF series, the previous paperback translation of Nietzsche's Strauss essay, in

Gallimard's Folio series, did not include the long §12 in which Nietzsche lists and comments upon Strauss's stylistic mistakes.

37 UO 1 (DS), §7, in CWN 2, 40; for the reference to Hobbes, see 39.
38 Last quotes are from ibid., 41.
39 UO 1 (DS), §11, in CWN 2, 64.
40 Ibid., 69.
41 UO 1 (DS), §7, in CWN 2, 43.
42 UO 1 (DS), §9, in CWN 2, 53.
43 UO 1 (DS), §4, in CWN 2, 24 (the quote is from p. 294 of Strauss's book).
44 UO 2 (HL), preface, in CWN 2, 86.
45 UO 2 (HL), §4, in CWN 2, 114.
46 UO 1 (DS), §4, in CWN 2, 28.
47 UO 2 (HL), §5, in CWN 2, 118.
48 For "factory of scholarship," see, e.g., UO 1 (DS), §8, in CWN 2, 46; or UO 2 (HL), §7, in CWN 2, 136.

CHAPTER FOUR

1 The text of Nietzsche's five Basel talks on education was published posthumously. For the German edition, see *KSA* 1; an English translation will be published by Stanford University Press in the upcoming vol. 1 of *The Complete Works of Friedrich Nietzsche* series. In the meantime, the reader of English may consult the 1910 translation by J.M. Kennedy (Edinburgh and London: Foulis). For the quoted letter, see Nietzsche to Rohde, 15 March 1872 (see also his letter to Rohde, mid-February 1872), in *KSB* 3. Some months later, during the summer, Nietzsche still had the intention of working on his manuscript: he planned to finish it during the winter of 1873 (see Nietzsche to Rohde and to Wagner, 25 July 1872).
2 See Nietzsche's *Encyclopedia of Classical Philology* course (Summer 1871), §7. For a study of Nietzsche's philology course, see Porter, *Philology of the Future*, chapter 4. Schacht, *Making Sense*, chapter 8, qualifies the third *Observation* as Nietzsche's "first manifesto." For "factory of scholarship," see, e.g., UO 1 (DS), §8, in CWN 2, 46; or UO 2 (HL), §7, in CWN 2, 136.
3 On the industrialization of Germany in the nineteenth century, see Trebilcock, *Industrialization*, especially chapter 2; see also Blackbourn, *Long Nineteenth Century*, especially chapters 4 and 7. On specialization and professionalization, see chapter 1 and Daston, "The

Academies." On educational changes in Germany in the nineteenth century, see Blackbourn, *Long Nineteenth Century*, chapter 8, and on the "German model" in academia, see Rüegg, *History of the University*.

4 Both quotes are from Nietzsche, *On the Future of Our Educational Institutions*, first lecture, 62.

5 Ricoeur considered Marx, Nietzsche, and Freud as the three "masters of suspicion," by which he pointed to their methodological use of question and critique addressed at the surface signs of consciousness and culture. See Ricoeur, *Conflit*.

6 For this paragraph, see *UO* 3 (*SE*), §6, in *CWN* 2, 219–24.

7 Ibid., 223.

8 Ibid., 225 and 230.

9 Ibid., 230.

10 Ibid., 232–3.

11 *UO* 3 (*SE*), §4, in *CWN* 2, 206.

12 *UO* 3 (*SE*), §3, in *CWN* 2, 192.

13 *UO* 3 (*SE*), §1, in *CWN* 2, 172.

14 Nehamas, *Life as Literature*, 7.

15 Last quotes are from *UO* 3 (*SE*), §1, in *CWN* 2, 172 and 174.

16 *UO* 3 (*SE*), §8, in *CWN* 2, 255.

17 Ibid., 254.

18 *UO* 3 (*SE*), §1, in *CWN* 2, 171.

19 *UO* 3 (*SE*), §8, in *CWN* 2, 255. The quote is from Emerson's "Circles," the tenth of his 1841 *Essays: First Series* (407–8).

20 Zavatta, "Historical Sense," 372.

21 See *GS*, §92; the four other "masters of prose" according to Nietzsche are Goethe, Leopardi, Walter Savage Landor, and Prosper Mérimée. Nietzsche read Emerson's *Essays* in the 1858 German translation, *Versuche*, by G. Fabricius (Hanover). After his copy was stolen in 1874, he immediately bought a new one: this second copy is the one that the Nietzsche archives, at the Klassik Stiftung Weimar, possess, and it has many marginalia — which suggests an extensive, and repetitious reading. In fact, Brobjer (*Nietzsche's Philosophical Context*) states that it is probably the most heavily annotated book in Nietzsche's library. For a thorough study of Nietzsche's reading of Emerson, conducted from the standpoint of the Italian school of Nietzsche Studies' attempt to "reconstruct Nietzsche's ideal library" (Zavatta, "Historical Sense," 375), see Zavatta, *Individuality*.

22 Emerson, "Self-Reliance," in *Essays: First Series*, 273. Zavatta ("Historical Sense," 373) reminds us that at the time when Nietzsche was

working on his third *Unfashionable Observations*, "he never traveled without Emerson's *Essays* in his suitcase."

23 Emerson, "Self-Reliance," in *Essays: First Series*, 264–5.

24 Ibid., 259; see also 279.

25 Emerson, "The Over-Soul," in *Essays: First Series*, 293.

26 On character as force, see Emerson, "Character," in *Essays: Second Series*, 495; on self-contradiction, see "Self-Reliance," in *Essays: First Series*, 267; on whim, see "Self-Reliance," in *Essays: First Series*, 264; on not taking things too seriously, see "Heroism," in *Essays: First Series*, 378.

27 Kateb, *Emerson and Self-Reliance*, 31. The fact that Emerson's definition of self-reliance is not clear-cut makes for a rich echo of Nietzsche's conception of the "ambiguous character" of existence (GS, §373).

28 For "shadow," see Emerson, "Self-Reliance," in *Essays: First Series*, 270; for "soul of the whole," see the opening paragraphs of "The Over-Soul"; for "inextinguishable being," see the last sentence to "Heroism."

29 Emerson, "Heroism," in *Essays: First Series*, 373.

30 See Rawls, *Theory of Justice*, section 50, note 51.

31 In the early 1990s, moral perfectionism was taken up by Stanley Cavell under the label "Emersonian perfectionism" to name a non-deontological and non-utilitarian democratic morality calling onto the individual to develop the humanity which this individual carries (see Cavell, *Conditions*; and Goodman, "Moral Perfectionism"). North American commentators of Nietzsche who have read him from the point of view of perfectionism make up a long list: J. Conant, D. Conway, L. Hatab, V. Lemm, D. Owen, among others, to which we can add commentators who refer to him in the context of discussions of political and moral philosophy: K. Ansell-Pearson, R. Arneson, W. Brown, S. Cavell, A. Donagan, R. Gooding-Williams, B. Honig, T. Hurka, T. Strong, etc. For an informed analysis of both the perfectionist debates and Nietzsche's texts, see Lemm, "Perfectionist."

32 Strong, "Defense of Rhetoric," 523; the reference to Thoreau is to *Walden*. While Strong notes that "At times, for instance in the early text *The Greek State*, Nietzsche sounds like he shares this position [i.e., the first meaning]," it is clear from his remarks that Strong not only defends the second meaning of elitism, but also that he considers that other theorists — most notably those from the Frankfurt School — would benefit (as per their arguments, but also their rhetorical force) if they "could think to draw upon Nietzsche" (524).

33 *UO* 3 (*SE*), §1, in *CWN* 2, 174. For the previous quote, see *HAH* I, §300, in *CWN* 3, 198.
34 The question was raised, e.g., by Schacht, *Making Sense*, 157, and Conant, "Nietzsche's Perfectionism," 207.
35 *UO* 3 (*SE*), §1, in *CWN* 2, 173.
36 Ibid., 174.
37 *UO* 3 (*SE*), §8, in *CWN* 2, 241; see also §6, 215.
38 *UO* 3 (*SE*), §2, in *CWN* 2, 183.
39 The quotes in this paragraph are to *UO* 3 (*SE*), §2, in *CWN* 2, 177–9.
40 *UO* 3 (*SE*), §8, in *CWN* 2, 248.
41 See *EH*, "The Unfashionables," §3, in *CWN* 9, 266.
42 *UO* 3 (*SE*), §6, in *CWN* 2, 218–19.
43 Schopenhauer, "On University Philosophy," in, *Parerga*, vol. 1, 266. For the previous quote, see Nietzsche to Rohde, 15 December 1870, in *KSB* 3, 165.
44 *UO* 3 (*SE*), §3, in *CWN* 2, 183–4.
45 *UO* 3 (*SE*), §6, in *CWN* 2, 228.
46 NF 3[19], notes for "We Philologists," in *KSA* 8, 20.
47 *UO* 2 (*HL*), §7, in *CWN* 2, 136.
48 NF 3[69], notes for "We Philologists," in *KSA* 8, 34.
49 *UO* 3 (*SE*), §2, in *CWN* 2, 179.
50 *EH*, "The Unfashionables," §3, in *CWN* 9, 266.

CHAPTER FIVE

1 The draft for *We Philologists* is in Nietzsche's posthumous writings: see the notes in groups 2 and 3 for March 1875, in *KSA* 8.
2 NF 1[3] (Spring 1875), in *KSA* 8, 9.
3 Richard Wagner, "Open Letter," 59 (originally published in the *Norddeutsche allgemeine Zeitung* on 12 June 1872).
4 See, e.g., Cosima Wagner's diary, 9 April 1873: "In the evening we had intended to devote ourselves to Prof. N.'s work on the philosophers R. jokingly calls 'the sons of Thales,' i.e., Anaximander, Heraclitus, and Parmenides" (Wagner, *Diaries*, vol. 1, 621). Although Wagner preferred the term "drama," the use of the term Gesamtkunstwerk is now generalized to describe the Wagnerian artistic project. Gregor-Dellin points out, however, that this concept appears only twice "in Wagner's major essay" (*Richard Wagner*, 214). Wagner himself complained that his theoretical writings were little and poorly read, and that they

were remembered only as "those unfortunate formulas of *Sonderkunst* and *Gesamtkunst*" (letter to Franz Liszt, 16 August 1853, quoted in Westernhagen, *Wagner*, vol. 1, 146–7). In light of Wagner's 1849–51 theoretical writings (*Art and Revolution*, 1849; *The Artwork of the Future*, 1849, unfinished and posthumous; *Opera and Drama*, 1851; *A Communication to My Friends*, 1851), one can certainly interpret the expression as naming not only the ideal of collaboration of all the arts (poetry, music, dance, architecture, etc.) to produce a work of art, but also the ideal of a "new" art form and the participation of the people in the reception of the work and also in the creative process. For Wagner, a people reveals its natural creative capacities through its language and legends. The work of art can be total, collaborative, and popular in its construction, means, and impact, and can thus palliate the modern artistic and cultural decadence. For Nietzsche, the expression Gesamtkunstwerk is clearly relevant to name the Wagnerian project, since in his Wagner essay he constructs several expressions using that same root, "Gesamt —."

5 See Colli and Montinari, "Chronologie," 35; also see Nietzsche's account in *EH*, "Human, All Too Human, with two sequels," §2, in *CWN* 9, 268–9.

6 The second *Unfashionable Observation*, which is the most commented upon today, was the subject of three reviews in Nietzsche's time. The anonymous author of the first of these wrote: "Through more than a hundred Latin-font pages we find nothing more than quite obscure remarks that one ought to consider philosophical, which sound pretentious, pass for grandness, and are miscontent as to the present state of the world, and for all the examples that are provided not a single thought or a single quote is offered that could shed some new light onto — or simply an insight into — the present times" (Anonymous, *Literaturfreund*, 154).

7 See chapter 3, "An Imposing Project." I discuss Nietzsche's 1870s aborted projects in Béland, *Kulturkritik* (for a list, see, e.g., 282–3).

8 Meyer's review of the first *Unfashionable Observation*, published in the *Deutsche Warte* (which he edited) treated Nietzsche's essay as "the Wagnerians' new gospel" (Meyer, "Beiträge," 653). See, also, Leutsch, "Review." Otto Ribeck, who was a professor of philology in Kiel, considered *The Birth of Tragedy* as a "dithyramb of Schopenhauerian-Wagnerian aesthetic philosophy," but he did find it "penetrating and interesting" if "not particularly new" (letter to Wilhelm Dilthey, 29 April 1872, quoted in Dixsaut, *Querelle*, 75).

9 *EH*, "Human, All Too Human, with two sequels," §2, in *CWN* 9, 268–9. On Nietzsche's interest for French culture and critique of Germany, see Campioni, *Lectures françaises*; on Nietzsche's love of Bizet's 1875 opera *Carmen*, see Liébert, *Nietzsche and Music*.

10 Nietzsche to Rohde, 8 November 1868, in *KSB* 2.

11 See Janz, *Nietzsche*, vol. 1, 257.

12 On the idea of a Bayreuth journal, see C. Wagner's diary, 22 May 1871 (Wagner, *Diaries*, 368) and Nietzsche to Rohde, 20–21 November 1872, in *KSB* 4. In one of the first issues of what became the *Bayreuther Blätter*, in August 1878, Wagner criticized Nietzsche's book *Human, All Too Human* (see Wagner, "Publikum und Popularität," 1883, *GSD* 10, 116–17). Of Montaigne, Nietzsche has said that "The joy of living on this earth has truly been increased by the fact that such a person wrote" (*UO* 3 [*SE*], §2, in *CWN* 2, 181). Surprisingly, Nietzsche's affinities with Montaigne have not been the focus of much scholarly attention; see, e.g., Heitsch, "Nietzsche and Montaigne."

13 Nietzsche published his first three books with Fritzsch, and again in 1886–87 (see Schaberg, *Nietzsche Canon*, 19–46 and 126–40). Fritzsch also published the music magazine *Musikalisches Wochenblatt: Organ für Musiker und Musikfreunde*, which published five articles on Nietzsche's works between 1873 and 1889. Generally, these were quite critical: see, e.g., "Vom 'Bildungsphilister,'" published in August 1873 (Hauke Reich believes this critique was written by Fritzsch, but he does not give proofs to sustain this belief; see Reich, *Zeitgenossenlexikon*, 71–2).

14 Nietzsche to Rohde, 11 April 1872, in *KSB* 3.

15 Nietzsche to Rohde, 30 April 1872, in *KSB* 3. The Tribschen years (1866–72) were extremely important and productive for Wagner. It was at that time that he finished composing the *Ring* and *The Mastersingers of Nuremberg* (1867) and wrote his essay on *Beethoven* (1870), with which Nietzsche was enthralled, as well as other essays on Germany (*German Art and German Politics*, 1868). He married Cosima in 1870 and launched the Bayreuth project, the first traces of which appear in Cosima Wagner's diary during the spring of 1870 (see, e.g., 2 April 1870, in Wagner, *Diaries*, vol. 1, 205).

16 Nietzsche to Rohde, 25 October 1872, in *KSB* 4.

17 See the dedication to Cosima Wagner, in *KSA* 1. The 1872 prefaces were first published in 1956 in the Karl Schlechta edition of Nietzsche's works.

18 See Wagner to Nietzsche, 30 April 1873: "As for your Straussiana, only one thing bothers me: I absolutely cannot wait for it! Be done with it!" (Nietzsche, *Nietzsche und Wagner*, vol. 1, 224.) On the Wagner-Lachner-Strauss affair, see Gregor-Dellin, *Richard Wagner*, 665–6 (I refer to the German original, as the English translation omits this affair: about a hundred pages have been drastically shortened in the English version). Although many commentators, such as Gregor-Dellin, see in Wagner the main impetus to Nietzsche's decision to write against Strauss (see, e.g., Janz, *Nietzsche*, vol. 2, 9; and D'Iorio, "Philosophes préplatoniciens," 410), that position is simplistic. I have shown in chapter 3 how Strauss was a perfect aim for Nietzsche to concentrate his critique of the scholar; and I have shown elsewhere the many contexts within which Nietzsche's decision was made, most importantly, the common attack on liberal theology with his friend Franz Overbeck, and the fact that Wilamowitz-Möllendorff ended his second, very harsh critique of *BT* on a quote by Strauss. See Béland, *Kulturkritik*, 182–92 and Béland, "Nietzsche avant Brandes," 562–9.

19 Nietzsche, "Manruf an die Deutschen," *KSA* 1, 891–7. On Nietzsche's idea of a Swiss Wagner Society, see Nietzsche to Heckel, 27 November 1873, in *KSB* 4. In his "New Year" essay, Nietzsche criticized the essayist Alfred Dove who had recently wrote a favourable review of physician Theodor Puschmann's *Richard Wagner: Eine psychiatrische Studie* (1873) — but the same year, Dove had also published a negative review of the pamphlet against liberal theology by Nietzsche's close friend and Basel colleague Franz Overbeck (like Nietzsche's *Birth of Tragedy* and first *Unfashionable Observation*, Overbeck's book was printed by Wagner's publisher Fritzsch, on Nietzsche's suggestion). Nietzsche's article against Dove/Puschmann is his only publication in a *Zeitzschrift* (whether newspaper or magazine) in the 1870s, and his only contribution to a Zeitschrift other than his eight poems "Idyllen aus Messina" published in *Schmeitzner's internationale Monatsschrift* in the spring of 1882.

20 *UO* 3 (*SE*), §3, in *CWN* 2, 185. It is noteworthy that the second *Unfashionable Observation*, on history, is the only of Nietzsche's essays from the first half of the 1870s that makes no mention of Wagner. It is also the *Observation* that is the most read and commented upon today.

21 Nietzsche to Carl von Gersdorff, 26 September 1875, in *KSB* 5.

22 See *EH*, "The Unfashionables," beginning of §3, in *CWN* 9.

23 *Richard Wagner à Bayreuth*, translated by Marie Baumgartner and published in Schloss-Chemnitz by Ernst Schmeitzner, in 1877. The

fourth *Observation* had only two reviews in 1876: a short, anonymous one and a longer one in the *Musikalisches Wochenblatt*, by Richard Falckenberg.

24 Again, see *EH*, "The Unfashionables," §3, in *CWN* 9, 265. For "Mister Nietzsche," see *GS*, preface, §2, where Nietzsche talks about himself twice while using the moniker "Mister Nietzsche."

25 *UO* 4 (*RWB*), §1, in *CWN* 2, 259. The closing allusion to Burckhardt states that "power is evil": see *UO* 4 (*RWB*), §11, in *CWN* 2, 330.

26 Burckhardt's talk is in *Reflections on History*. Nietzsche attended his colleague's November 1870 talk: see Nietzsche to Gersdorff, 7 November 1870, in *KSB* 3. Burckhardt's manuscript from the talks was edited and published by his nephew after his death. The title of Burckhardt's book, *Weltgeschichtlichen Betrachtungen*, echoes that of Nietzsche's essays, *Unzeitgemäße Betrachtungen* — but the title was the nephew's; Burckhardt's title was more straightforward: "On the Study of History."

27 *UO* 4 (*RWB*), §4, in *CWN* 2, 273. Nietzsche also likens Wagner to Alexander, Aeschylus, or Demosthenes (see §4 and §9). The same isochronal view of history was behind Nietzsche's interest in the Pre-Socratic philosophers. See, e.g., his unfinished manuscript *Philosophy in the Tragic Age of the Greeks*. On Nietzsche's use of Burckhardt's conception of history, see Wotling, "Nietzsche et Burckhardt."

28 *UO* 4 (*RWB*), §1, in *CWN* 2, 259.

29 See *HAH* I, §33, in *CWN* 3.

30 *UO* 4 (*RWB*), §1, in *CWN* 2, 261.

31 *UO* 4 (*RWB*), §4, in *CWN* 2, 275–6.

32 *UO* 4 (*RWB*), §3, in *CWN* 2, 272.

33 *HAH* I, §2, in *CWN* 3, 17.

34 *UO* 4 (*RWB*), §11, in *CWN* 2, 327.

35 *UO* 3 (*SE*), §3, in *CWN* 2, 183–4.

36 Both French authors appear together in an 1876 note where Nietzsche lists authors whom he appreciates as he draws a plan for a book project: see 16[5] (1876), in *KSA* 8, 287. For Vauvenargues, see also *WS* (*HAH* II), §214, in *CWN* 3; for Chamfort, see *GS*, §95.

37 *UO* 4 (*RWB*), §5, in *CWN* 2, 281.

38 Ibid., 281–2.

39 *D*, §115, in *CWN* 5, 85.

40 *UO* 4 (*RWB*), §10, in *CWN* 2, 322.

41 *UO* 4 (*RWB*), §9, in *CWN* 2, 309–10.

42 See *UO* 4 (*RWB*), respectively §2, in *CWN* 2, 264; §3, in *CWN* 2, 267; and §8, in *CWN* 2, 297.

43 UO 4 (*RWB*), §2, in *CWN* 2, 264.
44 UO 4 (*RWB*), §10, in *CWN* 2, 324.
45 UO 4 (*RWB*), §8, in *CWN* 2, 298–9.
46 UO 4 (*RWB*), §3, in *CWN* 2, 267. On Wagner's masculine-feminine nature, see Nattiez, *Wagner Androgyne*. On gendered musicology, see McClary, *Feminine Endings*.
47 UO 4 (*RWB*), §7, in *CWN* 2, 296.
48 UO 4 (*RWB*), §4, in *CWN* 2, 280.
49 NF 37[8] (end of 1874), *KSA* 7, 834.
50 In UO 4 (*RWB*), §9, Nietzsche praises Wagner for his use of *Stabreim*. Wagner discusses the creative impact (poetically and mythically) of the alliterative form in his essay *Oper und Drama* (in GSD 4, 118–21). On *Stabreim*, see Borroff, "Challenge Episode."
51 For Nietzsche's (very Wagnerian) critique of Meyerbeer, see UO 4 (*RWB*), §8, in *CWN* 2, 298, e.g.
52 UO 4 (*RWB*), §4, in *CWN* 2, 274.
53 UO 4 (*RWB*), §7, in *CWN* 2, 295.
54 UO 4 (*RWB*), §9, in *CWN* 2, 311.

CHAPTER SIX

1 *The Birth of Tragedy*, his first opus, was quickly followed by the four *Unfashionable Observations*; the three books known under the title *Human, All Too Human* closed the 1870s; in the first half of the 1880s appeared *Dawn* and *The Gay Science*, as well as the first three *Zarathustra* books (which were published separately from one another over a nine-month period); and in the second half were published *Beyond Good and Evil*, *On the Genealogy of Morality*, and *The Case of Wagner*; in January 1889 Nietzsche's last book came out: *Twilight of the Idols*. To these publications one can add Nietzsche's reprint of *The Birth of Tragedy* (1878), his private printing of *Zarathustra*'s part IV (1885), and his many 1886 re-editions: that of his four *Unfashionable Observations* in one volume, his three *Zarathustras* in one volume, and his five major books (one, *The Gay Science*, in a much-expanded version). One can also add several short texts, poems, or excerpts that Nietzsche published in German magazines: the *Musikalisches Wochenblatt* (1873), *Schmeitzner's internationale Monatsschrift* (1882 and 1883), and *Die Gesellschaft* (twice in 1885). The publication history of Nietzsche's works is in Schaberg, *Nietzsche Canon*. See, at the end of this book, "A Very Short Chronology."

2 Nietzsche to Fritzsch, 16 August 1886, in KSB 7, 228.
3 Nietzsche to Overbeck, 14 November 1886, in KSB 7, 282.
4 Schacht, *Making Sense*, 243.
5 Nietzsche to von Salis, 14 September 1887, in KSB 8, 151.
6 See Andler, *Nietzsche*, 558; and Schaeffer, "Note sur la préface," 39. Schaeffer mostly examines the case of prefaces written by Spinoza, Hegel, Schopenhauer, Wittgenstein, and Derrida.
7 For "Herr Nietzsche," see GS, preface, §2.
8 See Schacht, *Making Sense*; Faustino, "Nietzsche and the Art"; Simson, "Typographie"; Tongeren, "Philosophische Experimente"; and Stegmaier, *Nietzsche zu Einführung*. For Nietzsche's 1886 prefaces published in German, see Nietzsche, *Ecce Auctor* (edited by C.-A. Scheier); in Italian, *Tentativo di autocritica* (edited by M. Brusotti); in French, *Six préfaces* (edited by M. Béland).
9 See "Preface" and "Foreword," in Merriam-Webster's Unabridged Dictionary. On the definition of a preface, see also Genette, *Paratexts*, 161.
10 See Mitterand, "Discours préfaciel," 4. See also BT, preface, §1, where Nietzsche notes that his "belated preface" is actually a "postscript" (17).
11 Derrida, "Outwork," 8.
12 Genette, *Paratexts*, 197.
13 Leiner, "Préface," 114 and 118.
14 See Schaeffer, "Note sur la préface," 37.
15 Hegel, *Phenomenology*, 9; Derrida, "Outwork," 9.
16 Derrida, "Outwork," 9.
17 Gervais-Zaninger, "Figure de l'auteur," 33.
18 Derrida, "Outwork," 20.
19 Ibid., 3.
20 For "enunciative event," see Maingueneau, "Énonciation philosophique," 40; for "act of communication," see Masson, "Marginalité," 14.
21 See Schaeffer, "Note sur la préface," 43.
22 Cossutta, "Analyse du discours," 19.
23 Tongeren counts about forty prefaces ("Philosophische Experimente," 6–7). This is because he counts unfinished prefaces from Nietzsche's notebooks and epigraphs, which he considers as prefatory texts. One could then go even further and add prefaces that Nietzsche wrote for his lectures (which he did not publish nor intend for publication), such as the one to his 1871 *Encyclopedia of Classical Philology* (on these lectures, see Porter, *Philology of the Future*, 167–224). Tongeren also distinguishes between Nietzsche's *Vorrede* and *Vorwörter*

by stating that the *Vorrede* are lengthier and thus more important — a distinction which does not seem justified (see, e.g., the *Vorwort* to *Ecce homo*).

24 Tongeren, "Philosophische Experimente," 7.

25 A literary theorist could say that these prefaces transgress literary categories, since they stand alone: that is, they do not accompany a main work.

26 Genette, *Paratexts*, 178.

27 Scheier, in Nietzsche, *Ecce Auctor*, x and viii; see also Janz, *Nietzsche*, 215.

28 On Nietzsche's contemporary reception, see Béland, "Nietzsche avant Brandes," 554 and 561. For the exact numbers of copies sold and unsold, see Schaberg, *Nietzsche Canon*.

29 Nietzsche to Förster-Nietzsche, mid-August 1885, in *KSB* 7, 80–2.

30 Nietzsche to Overbeck, early December 1885, in *KSB* 7, 117.

31 Nietzsche to Fritzsch, 16 August 1886, in *KSB* 7, 229–30.

32 On the lawsuit, see Schaberg, *Nietzsche Canon*, 109–19; on Nietzsche's self-publishing, see 122; on his repurchase transactions with Fritzsch, see 129. See also Nietzsche's 1886 letters to Fritzsch.

33 See Leiner, "Préface," 114 and 118, and Mitterand, "Discours préfaciel," 4.

34 One famous example is the title of book V in *GS*: "We Fearless Ones" (*Wir Furchtlosen*).

35 *HTH*'s subtitle is: *A Book for Free Spirits*.

36 *HTH* was among the least read of Nietzsche's books in the years following its original publication in 1878. See Béland, "Nietzsche avant Brandes," 557–9.

37 Tongeren, "Philosophische Experimente," 12.

38 Ibid., 14.

39 See *GS*, preface, §2, 5: "The unconscious disguise of physiological needs under the cloaks of the objective, ideal, purely spiritual goes frighteningly far, — and I have asked myself often enough whether, on the grand scale, philosophy has been no more than an interpretation of the body and a *misunderstanding of the body*."

40 For "hooks," see Nietzsche to Förster-Nietzsche, mid-August 1885, in *KSB* 7, 80–2.

41 *GS*, §110, 111.

42 See prefaces #16-§2 and #17-§4.

43 For immoralist and psychologist, see preface #13-§1. For solitary and pessimist, see prefaces #13, #15-§2, and #16-§1. For philosopher

and philologist, see prefaces #16-§2 and §5, and #17-§2 and §3. For poet and artist, see preface #17-§1 and §4. For Greek and German, see prefaces #17-§4 and #16-§3. For "good Europeans," see preface #15-§6. For free spirits, see prefaces #13-§7 and §8, #15-§1, and #13-§2.

44 On the notion of "open work," see Eco, *Open Work*. For prefaces as attempts to "finish" a work, see Duchet, "Fins," 12. For prefaces as a discursive act, see Maingueneau, "Énonciation philosophique," 40, and Masson, "Marginalité," 14.

45 Jauss, "Racine und Goethe," 383. For a parallel reading of Ingarden's philosophical aesthetics and Nietzsche's conception of interpretation, see Béland, "Expérience esthétique."

46 Jauss, "*Iphigénie*," 284. I refer to the translation in French, as Jauss changed his original paper in German for the sake of this translation (see the editors' note, in Jauss, "*Iphigénie*," 6): Jauss added about three pages, thereby deepening some of his arguments.

47 Iser, *Appellstruktur*, 16.

CHAPTER SEVEN

1 *HAH* I, §218, in *CWN* 3, 145–6.

2 Genette, *Épilogue*, 104. Genette (who died in 2018) did not take up this task, but a case study of Flaubert's use of the semicolon in one novel, *Bouvard et Pécuchet*, was undertaken by Herschberg Pierrot, "Ponctuation."

3 Turgeon, *Style de Genette*, 83.

4 Newmark, "Translation of Nietzsche," 327; Simson, "Typographie," 204, makes the same case.

5 Simson, "Typographie," 208; see Blondel, "Guillemets," and Roos, "Regeln."

6 See, e.g., *BGE*, §4, in *CWN* 8, 7; and *BT*, preface, §3, 20.

7 See Turgeon, *Style de Genette*, 83.

8 See Kofman, *Nietzsche and Metaphor*, 35–6. Nietzsche made this point throughout his career. One can read it early on, e.g., in his 1873 unfinished posthumous work *On Truth and Lie in the Unmoral Sense* and the *Unfashionable Observations*, but also in many later works, e.g., *TI*, "Reason in Philosophy," §5.

9 Roos, "Regeln," 23; emphasis added. See Bertram, *Attempt at a Mythology*, chapter 11.

10 Surprisingly, in his review of the rare literature on Nietzsche's dashes, Hanshe omits Bertram and, even more surprisingly, he omits Simson's

1995 paper on punctuation in Nietzsche's five 1886 prefaces, a paper in which Simson devotes two complete pages to the em-dash. See Hanshe, "Invisibly Revolving," 10n8.

11 See 35[8] (May–July 1885), 36[55] (June–July 1885), 40[70] (August–September 1885), 1[132] (Fall 1885–Early 1886), 2[43] (Fall 1885–Fall 1886), and 3[2] (Early 1886).

12 34[65], in *KSA* 11, 440, and 34[147], in *KSA* 11, 469. For the letter to his sister, 20 May 1885, see *KSB* 7, 53.

13 34[65], in *KSA* 11, 440.

14 For instance, the forty-four short aphorisms of the *Sayings and Arrows* — which open *TI* — almost all have at least one (and sometimes even two to three) em-dashes; thirty-one have at least one dash; and §4, §7, §14, §16, and §31 end on one. Since most of his texts are not composed of aphorisms per se, I use the term "textual unit" to refer to any section that is identifiable by a § number in Nietzsche's books, whether this § be a short aphorism (e.g., *D*, §85) or a long developmental paragraph (e.g., *BGE*, §208).

15 For *BGE*: 63 sections out of a total of 296 §, i.e., 21 per cent end on a dash; for book V of *GS*: 15 sections out of a total of 40, i.e., 38 per cent.

16 Within parentheses: see, e.g., *BGE*, §210 and §288, or *GM*, I, §3; ending a paragraph without a period: see, e.g., *BGE*, §51; separating a pronoun from its verb: see, e.g., *GM*, III, §20, or *CW*, §3; ensconcing a single word: see, e.g., *GS*, §364; and side by side with one or two other dashes or with other punctuation marks: see, e.g., *BGE*, §15.

17 On the dash as typographic sign, see Drillon, *Traité*, 338. The literature on the em-dash is scarce. In German, one can read Kammasch, "Der Gedankenstrich," or Sonnen, *Balancieren*.

18 See "Cadratin," in Lacroux, *Orthotypographie*.

19 See Pétillon and Petitjean, "Tiret de fin de phrase."

20 Drillon, *Traité*, 329. See also Tanguay, "Art de ponctuer," §176, and Crystal, *Making a Point*.

21 Strunk and White, *Elements of Style*, 16.

22 See Tanguay, "Art de ponctuer," §178, and Strunk and White, *Elements of Style*, 16.

23 Strunk and White, *Elements of Style*, 16. In his study of typography in Nietzsche's 1886 prefaces, Simson ("Typographie," 205) stresses that "the choice of a specific typographic means does not need to follow a criterium of syntax."

24 Although the treatises that I used examine mostly French and English works, they do also quote German ones, and the *Duden* lists the same general uses for the Gedankenstrich in German.

25 Gracq, *En lisant, en écrivant*, quoted by Drillon, *Traité*, 329–30; and Larousse 1876 quoted by Pétillon and Petitjean, "Tiret de fin de phrase." Pétillon and Petitjean note that while Goethe and Novalis were already using the Gedankenstrich in Germany, the cadratin was a new punctuation sign in nineteenth-century France. Barbey d'Aurevilly considered it a "modern invention" and the Larousse dictionary already judged in 1876 that French authors were "abusing" it, i.e., using it too much.

26 See Drillon, *Traité*, 332 and 234n36.

27 On interior dialogue, see Drillon, *Traité*, 331; on the voice, see Pétillon and Petitjean, "Tiret de fin de phrase."

28 See Drillon, *Traité*, 330 (on Heine) and 339 (on Mallarmé).

29 See, e.g., *BGE*, §99, §102, and §113.

30 For an example of two em-dashes aligned within an aphorism, see *BGE*, §296; for two dashes at the end of an aphorism, see, e.g., *BGE*, §29, §30, or §280.

31 Bertram does not give the complete reference to his quote from Goethe, only the year: 1809.

32 Hanshe, "Invisibly Revolving," 14.

33 For the publication history, see Schaberg, *Nietzsche Canon*.

34 It is worth noting, though, that Nietzsche does use — — more often in *Zarathustra* than in his other mid- to late-1880s books. In his texts published or authorized for publication between 1886 and 1888 (i.e., *BGE*, the 1886 prefaces, book V of *GS*, *GM*, *CW*, *TI*, *AC*, and *EH*) there are a total of thirty-eight printed double em-dashes, whereas there are thirty-nine in the *Zarathustra* alone: Hanshe certainly is justified in being enthralled by the double dash in the *Zarathustra*.

35 *HAH* I, preface, §8, in *CWN* 3, 13.

36 Hadot, "Symboles," 16.

37 Simson, "Typographie," 207. See Pétillon and Petitjean, "Tiret de fin de phrase": the authors study the "enunciation dash," which engages the talking subject within a text through the punctuative rhythm of speech.

38 See Simson, "Typographie," 206 and 215. Simson adds that the dash sometimes serves as a pause after which Nietzsche changes his discursive mode: he brings in a sudden level of abstraction, for instance, after a poetic enumeration of specific qualities. See, e.g., *HAH* I, preface, §3.

39 Simson, "Typographie," 214.

40 Roos, "Regeln," 23.

41 *BGE*, §246, in *CWN* 8, 153.

42 Blondel, *Body and Culture*, 35.

43 See Cytowic, *The Man* and *Synesthesia*. Hanshe ("Invisibly Revolving," 24) points to but does not discuss the presence of a "synesthetic epistemology" in Nietzsche's philosophy.
44 Hanshe, "Invisibly Revolving," 12.
45 Roos, "Regeln," 12–13.

EPILOGUE

1 Roos, "Regeln," 41.
2 Nietzsche to von Salomé, 8/24 August 1882, in *KSB* 6, 243.
3 A good example is the recent posthumous publication of the fourth part of Michel Foucault's *History of Sexuality*, although Foucault had specifically denied to his heirs the right to publish any posthumous writings. For a critique of the publication of Foucault's unfinished manuscript and the ethical questions it raises, see Pouradier, "Enjeux éthiques."
4 In French, the etymological root of "curator" is also present in the word meaning guardianship: *curatelle*.
5 See the mission statement of the Leonard and Bina Ellen Gallery (Concordia University, Montreal): "The Gallery's programme of exhibitions, events, activities and publications focuses on artmaking today and on its recent history as it interfaces with various curatorial strategies." http://ellengallery.concordia.ca/information/about/programming-and-history/?lang=en (accessed 9 August 2023).
6 Whether the context be historical, sociological, biographical, technical, or aesthetic: possible relevant criteria according to which one can assemble works together are numerous.
7 See, respectively, Ingarden, *Literary Work of Art*; Eco, *Limits of Interpretation*; Ricoeur, *From Text to Action*; and Le Blanc, *Hermes Complex*.
8 See, e.g., Genette, *Paratexts*, and Roos, "Regeln."
9 For a short definition of the wide and not always well-defined field of "digital humanities," see McCarty, "*Studia Digitalia*." One can consult the website of the Department of Digital Humanities (founded in 1992) at King's College London, which specifies that studying digital humanities "brings together theory and practical approaches from the humanities, cultural and media studies, sociology, computing, and information sciences." https://www.kcl.ac.uk/ddh/undergraduate/undergraduate (accessed 9 August 2023).

10 Ingarden, "Phenomenological Aesthetics," 260. Ingarden delivered his talk at the University of Amsterdam's Institut for Aesthetics on 17 March 1969. It was translated into English in 1975 in the *Journal of Aesthetics and Art Criticism*, and then in French in 2011. I developed some of these ideas in more detail in Béland, "Expérience esthétique."

11 Ingarden, "Phenomenological Aesthetics," 260.

12 Ingarden, *Esthétique et ontologie*, 53. Ingarden limited the field of aesthetics to written works of literature. On Ingarden's poetics, see Falk, *Poetics*; for an expansion of Ingarden's aesthetics to works of philosophy, in conjunction with Nietzsche's notion of writing and reading, see Béland, "Experience esthétique."

13 On Lefort's *Wirkungsgeschichte*, see Simard, "Heurs et malheurs," 148–51.

14 It is worth comparing Lefort, *Travail de l'oeuvre* (French edition) to Lefort, *Machiavelli* (American edition).

15 Roos, "Regeln," 16.

16 On the falsity of *The Will to Power* as a book, see Montinari, "Volontà di potenza." It is worth recalling the immense reception of this fake book of Nietzsche's, not only in Germany in the twentieth century (Heidegger, for instance, based most of his interpretation of Nietzsche on *The Will to Power*: see Heidegger, *Nietzsche*), but also in France and in the English-speaking countries in its French and English translations (a good example is Nehamas, who feels he must justify his use of *The Will to Power* although those notes do not constitute a work: see Nehamas, *Life as Literature*, 9). It goes without saying that the simple act of reissuing this text unfortunately adds to its varnish of "respectability."

17 Zavatta, "Historical Sense," 375.

18 Roos, "Regeln," 17–18; emphasis added.

19 Ibid., 41.

20 The *HyperNietzsche* project is digitizing and giving free online access to Nietzsche's manuscripts and notebooks. www.nietzschesource.org/DFGA (accessed 9 August 2023).

21 Schleiermacher, "Methods of Translating," 230 ("*zu einem lebendigen Festhalten des Zusammenhanges gedeiht*") and 228; on translation's two goals regarding understanding and pleasure, see 237. The Romantic conception of language is revived today by philosophers of translation such as Le Blanc, *Hermes Complex*.

22 Specific examples in the case of Nietzsche could be the evolving senses in which he used the terms "will" or "Dionysian."

23 See Derrida, *Oreille de l'autre*, 27: "There are no more shadows and all statements, before and after, to the left and to the right, are both possible (Nietzsche said almost everything) and necessarily contradictory (he said things that are wholly incompatible, and he said that he was saying them)." My translation.

24 It is also in this perspective that one can situate Iser's notion of an "implicit reader," i.e., the idea that the reading structure inscribed within the text functions as a constraint on the reader but also permits the text's effect (see Iser, *Implizite Leser*). See Derrida, *Oreille de l'autre*, 27; on this issue, see Béland, "Herméneutique et perspectivisme."

25 See the 1899 French translation of the preface to the first volume of *HTH* by Alexandre-Marie Desrousseaux (1861–1955), whose alias was Bracke.

26 McCarty, "Digital Humanities," 4 (where he quotes Wittig, "Computer") and 14. McCarty suggests drawing new analogies for texts from the field of biological evolution, which evokes images of organic co-evolution and openness (see McCarty, "Digital Humanities," 14, and McCarty, "*Studia Digitalia*," 6). See also Humboldt, *Essai sur les langues*, 313, and Gadamer, *Truth and Method*, 436.

27 On this issue, see Vandendorpe, *From Papyrus to Hypertext*.

28 McCarty, "*Studia Digitalia*," 6. McCarty is loosely referring to Gooding, *Experiment*.

29 Whereas linearity describes "a series of elements that follow each other in an inviolable or pre-established order" (Vandendorpe, *From Papyrus to Hypertext*, 22).

30 See Vandendorpe, *From Papyrus to Hypertext*, 25: "In reading highly tabular texts, and aphorisms or fragments in general, the automatic reflexes of reading may become less effective and play a lesser role, because of the fact that the context for understanding has to be recreated by the reader for every new block of text."

Bibliography

WORKS BY NIETZSCHE

The Complete Works of Friedrich Nietzsche. Edited by E. Behler, B. Magnus, A.D. Schrift, D. Large, and A. Del Caro. 19 vols. Redwood City, CA: Stanford University Press, 1995–. [CWN] Volumes published:

Vol. 2: *Unfashionable Observations*. Translated by R.T. Gray. 1995.

Vol. 3: *Human, All Too Human (I)*. Translated by G. Handwerk. 1997.

Vol. 4: *Human, All Too Human (II)*. Translated by G. Handwerk. 2012.

Vol. 5: *Dawn. Thoughts on the Presumptions of Morality*. Translated by K. Ansell-Pearson. 2011.

Vol. 8: *Beyond Good and Evil / On the Genealogy of Morality*. Translated by A. Del Caro. 2014.

Vol. 9: *The Case of Wagner / Twilight of the Idols / The Antichrist / Ecce Homo / Dionysus Dithyrambs / Nietzsche contra Wagner*. Translated by A. Del Caro, C. Diethe, D. Large, G.H. Leiner, P.S. Loeb, A.D. Schrift, D.F. Tinsley, and M. Wittwar. 2021.

Vol. 11: *Unpublished Writings from the Period of* Unfashionable Observations. Translated by R.T. Gray. 1999.

Vol. 12: *Unpublished Fragments from the Period of* Human, All Too Human I *(Winter 1874/75–Winter 1877/78)*. Translated by G. Handwerk. 2021.

Vol. 14: *Unpublished Fragments from the Period of* Thus Spoke Zarathustra *(Summer 1882–Winter 1883/84)*. Translated by P.S. Loeb and D.F. Tinsley. 2019.

Vol. 16: *Unpublished Fragments (Spring 1885–Spring 1886)*. Translated by A. Del Caro. 2019.

OTHER EDITIONS OF NIETZSCHE'S WORKS

The Birth of Tragedy and The Case of Wagner. Translated by W. Kaufmann. New York: Vintage Books, 1967.

Ecce Auctor: Die Vorreden von 1886. Edited by C.-A. Scheier. Hamburg: Felix Meiner, 1990.

The Gay Science. Translated by J. Nauckhoff and A. Del Caro, edited by B. Williams. Cambridge: Cambridge University Press, 2001.

Introduction aux études de philologie classique. Translated by F. Dastur and M. Haar. Paris: Encre marine, 1994.

Nietzsche und Wagner: Stationen einer epochalen Begegnung. Edited by D. Borch-Meyer and J. Salaquarda. 2 vols. Frankfurt/Leipzig: Insel, 1994.

On the Future of Our Educational Institutions. Translated and with an introduction by M.W. Grenke. South Bend, IN: St Augustine's Press, 2004.

The Portable Nietzsche. Translated and edited by W. Kaufmann. New York: Viking, 1976.

Sämtliche Briefe: Kritische Studienausgabe. Edited by G. Colli and M. Montinari. 8 vols. Berlin: de Gruyter/DTV, 2003. [*KSB*]

Six préfaces, 1886–1887. Edited by M. Béland. Montreal: Bleu du ciel, 2019.

Tentativo di autocritica 1886–1887. Edited and translated by M. Brusotti. Genoa: Il Melangolo, 1992.

Werke: Kritische Gesamtausgabe. Edited by G. Colli and M. Montinari. Vol. 1, part 2: *Philologica: Philologische Schriften (1867–1873)*, edited by F. Bornmann and M. Carpitella. Berlin/New York: de Gruyter, 1982. [*KGW*]

Werke: Kritische Studienausgabe. Edited by G. Colli and M. Montinari. 15 vols. Berlin: de Gruyter/DTV, 1999. [*KSA*]

OTHER WORKS CITED

Abert, Anna Amalie, and Thomas Baumann. "Hiller, Johann Adam." In *The New Grove Dictionary of Music and Musicians*, edited by S. Sadie. London: Macmillan, 2001.

Accaoui, Christian. *Éléments d'esthétique musicale*. Arles: Actes Sud, 2011.

Andler, Charles. *Nietzsche, sa vie et sa pensée*, vol. 2: *Le pessimisme esthétique de Nietzsche, La maturité de Nietzsche*. Paris: Gallimard, 1958.

Anonymous. [No title]. *Literaturfreund* 2, no. 9 (1874): 154.

— "Die Vertreter der Philosophie an der Universität Basel." *Philosophische Monatshefte* 8 (1872): 93–5.

Ansell-Pearson, Keith. "Nietzsche on the Knowledge of the Sufferer: A Contribution to the Philosophy of Emotions." *Agonist* 13, nos. 1–2 (2019–20): 12–22.

Ansell-Pearson, Keith, and Rebecca Bamford. *Nietzsche's* Dawn*: Philosophy, Ethics, and the Passion of Knowledge*. Hoboken, NJ: Wiley-Blackwell, 2020.

Aschheim, Steven E. *The Nietzsche Legacy in Germany 1890–1990*. Oakland, CA: University of California Press, 1992.

Babich, Babette. *Words in Blood, Like Flowers: Philosophy and Poetry, Music and Eros in Hölderlin, Nietzsche, and Heidegger*. New York: State University of New York Press, 2006.

Barthes, Roland. "The Old Rhetoric: An Aide-Mémoire." In *The Semiotic Challenge*, translated by R. Howard, 11–93. Oxford: Basil Blackwell, 1988.

Bazzano, Manu. *Nietzsche and Psychotherapy*. London/New York: Routledge, 2019.

Beiser, Frederick C. *David Friedrich Strauß, Father of Unbelief: An Intellectual Biography*. Oxford: Oxford University Press, 2020.

Béland, Martine. *Kulturkritik et philosophie thérapeutique chez le jeune Nietzsche*. Montreal: Presses de l'Université de Montréal, 2012.

— "Nietzsche avant Brandes: une étude de réception germanophone (1872–1889)." *Nietzsche-Studien* 39 (2010): 551–72.

— "La réception comme expérience esthétique: Nietzsche face aux limites de l'esthétique phénoménologique de Roman Ingarden." In *Nietzsche et la phénoménologie*, edited by C. Bertot and J. Leclercq, 327–53. Paris: Garnier, 2019.

— "Tout n'est pas possible: herméneutique et perspectivisme." *L'art du comprendre* 24 (2015): 83–98.

Berry, Mark. "Nietzsche and Wagner." In *The New Cambridge Companion to Nietzsche*, edited by T. Stern, 97–120. Cambridge: Cambridge University Press, 2019.

Bertram, Ernst. *Nietzsche: Attempt at a Mythology*. Translated and with an introduction by R.E. Norton. Urbana/Chicago, IL: University of Illinois Press, 2009.

Blackbourn, David. *The Long Nineteenth Century: A History of Germany, 1780–1918*. New York/Oxford: Oxford University Press, 1998.

Blondel, Éric. "Les guillemets de Nietzsche: philologie et généalogie." In *Nietzsche aujourd'hui?*, edited by Centre Culturel International de Cerisy-la-Salle, vol. 2, 153–78. Paris: 10/18, 1973.

— *Nietzsche: The Body and Culture, Philosophy as a Philological Genealogy*. Translated by S. Hand. Stanford: Stanford University Press, 1991.

Blue, Daniel. "What was Nietzsche's Nationality?" *Journal of Nietzsche Studies* 33 (2007): 73–82.

Böhm, C., ed. *Johann Adam Hiller: Kapellmeister und Kantor, Komponist und Kritiker*. Altenburg: Kamprad, 2005.

Borroff, Marie. "The Challenge Episode: A Stylistic Interpretation." In *Sir Gawain and the Green Knight: An Authoritative Translation, Contexts, Criticism*, edited by M. Borroff and L.L. Howes, translated by M. Borroff, vii–xiii. New York: W.W. Norton, 2009.

Brobjer, Thomaş. *Nietzsche's Philosophical Context: An Intellectual Biography*. Urbana/Chicago, IL: University of Illinois Press, 2008.

Burckhardt, Jacob. *Reflections on History*. Translated by M.D. Hottinger. London: George Allen & Unwin, 1943.

Caccini, Giulio. *Le nuove musiche*. Translated by H.W. Hitchcock. Middleton, WI: AR Editor, 2009.

Campioni, Giuliano. *Les lectures françaises de Nietzsche*. Translated by C. Lavigne-Mouilleron. Paris: PUF, 2001.

Cancik, Hubert. "Der Nietzsche-Kult in Weimar: Ein Beitrag zur Religionsgeschichte der wilhelminischen Ära." *Nietzsche-Studien* 16 (1987): 405–29.

— *Nietzsches Antike: Vorlesungen*. Stuttgart: J.B. Metzler, 1995.

Cannone, Belinda. *Philosophie de la musique, 1752–1780*. Paris: Klincksieck, 1990.

Cavell, Stanley. *Conditions Handsome and Unhandsome: The Constitution of Emersonian Perfectionism*. Chicago: University of Chicago Press, 1990.

Chapin Massey, Marilyn. "The Literature of Young Germany and D.F. Strauss's 'Life of Jesus.'" *Journal of Religion* 59, no. 3 (1979): 298–323.

Charlton, David. "L'orchestre et la métaphore du temps de Mozart." In *Mozart: les chemins de l'Europe*, edited by B. Massin, 105–12. Strasburg: Conseil de l'Europe, 1997.

Clark, William. *Academic Charisma and the Origins of the Research University*. Chicago: University of Chicago Press, 2006.

Colli, Giorgio, and Mazzino Montinari. "Chronologie der Absendeorte." In *Nachträge (Stand Ende 1986) und Register zu Nietzsches Sämtlichen Briefen*, 35–6. Berlin/New York: de Gruyter, 1987.

Compagnon, Antoine. *Literature, Theory, and Common Sense*. Translated by C. Cosman. Princeton: Princeton University Press, 2004.

Conant, James. "Nietzsche's Perfectionism: A Reading of Schopenhauer as Educator." In *Nietzsche's Postmoralism: Essays on Nietzsche's Prelude to Philosophy's Future*, edited by R. Schacht, 181–257. Cambridge: Cambridge University Press, 2001.

Cossutta, Frédéric. "Pour une analyse du discours philosophique." *Langages* 29, no. 119 (1995): 12–39.

Crystal, David. *Making a Point: The Persnickety Story of English Punctuation*. New York: St Martin's Press, 2015.

Cytowic, Richard. *The Man Who Tasted Shapes*. Boston: MIT Press, 2003.

— *Synesthesia: A Union of the Senses*. Boston: MIT Press, 2002.

Dahlhaus, Carl. *Esthetics of Music*. Translated by W. Austin. Cambridge: Cambridge University Press, 1995.

Daston, Lorraine. "The Academies and the Unity of Knowledge: The Disciplining of the Disciplines." *Differences* 10, no. 2 (1998): 67–86.

Davidson, Donald. "What Metaphors Mean." In *Inquiries into Truth and Interpretation*. Oxford: Oxford University Press, 1984.

Denat, Céline, and Patrick Wotling. *Dictionnaire Nietzsche*. Paris: Ellipses, 2013.

Derrida, Jacques. *L'oreille de l'autre: Otobiographies, transferts, traductions*. Montreal: VLB, 1982.

— "Outwork, Prefacing." In *Dissemination*, translated and with an introduction by B. Johnson, 1–59. London: The Athlone Press, 1981.

— "Y a-t-il une langue philosophique?" *Autrement* 102 (1988).

D'Iorio, Paolo. "L'image des philosophes préplatoniciens chez le jeune Nietzsche." In *Centauren-Geburten: Wissenschaft, Kunst und Philosophie beim jungen Nietzsche*, edited by T. Borsche et al., 383–417. Berlin: de Gruyter, 2011.

— "La naissance de la philosophie enfantée par l'esprit scientifique." In F. Nietzsche, *Les philosophes préplatoniciens*, edited by P. D'Iorio, translated by N. Ferrand, 11–49. Combas: L'Éclat, 1994.

Dixsaut, Monique, ed. *Querelle autour de* La naissance de la tragédie, *écrits et lettres de F. Nietzsche, F. Ritschl, E. Rohde, U. von Wilamowitz-Möllendorff et R. et C. Wagner (1871–1873)*. Translated by M. Cohen-Halimi. Paris: Vrin, 1995.

Drillon, Jacques. *Traité de la ponctuation française*. Paris: Gallimard, 1991.

Du Bois-Reymond, Emil. "Über die wissenschaftlichen Zustande der Gegenwart." In *Reden*, vol. 2, 448–64. Leipzig: Veit, 1886.

Duboc, Julius. *Jenseits vom Wirklichen: Eine Studie aus der Gegenwart*. Dresden: Hellmuth Heukler, 1896.

Duchet, Claude. "Fins, finition, finalité, infinitude." In *Genèse des fins: de Balzac à Beckett, de Michelet à Ponge*, edited by C. Duchet and I. Tournier, 5–27. St-Denis: Presses universitaires de Vincennes, 1996.

Duden. "*Gedankenstrich*." Accessed 22 August 2023. www.duden.de/sprachwissen/rechtschreibregeln/gedankenstrich.

Eco, Umberto. *The Limits of Interpretation*. Bloomington: Indiana University Press, 1994.

— *The Open Work*. Translated by A. Cancogni, with an introduction by D. Robey. Cambridge, MA: Harvard University Press, 1962.

Emden, Christian J. "The Invention of Antiquity: Nietzsche on Classicism, Classicality, and the Classical Tradition." In *Nietzsche and Antiquity: His Reaction and Response to the Classical Tradition*, edited by P. Bishop, 372–90. Rochester: Camden House, 2004.

Emerson, Ralph Waldo. "Essays: First Series." In *Essays and Lectures*, edited by J. Porte, 231–440. New York: Library of America, 1983.

— "Essays: Second Series." In *Essays and Lectures*, edited by J. Porte, 441–587. New York: Library of America, 1983.

Fabre, Florence. *Nietzsche musicien: la musique et son ombre*. Rennes: Presses universitaires de Rennes, 2006.

Falk, Eugene H. *The Poetics of Roman Ingarden*. Chapel Hill: University of North Carolina Press, 1981.

Faustino, Marta. "Nietzsche and the Art of Forming his Readers: The 1886 Prefaces." In *Nietzsche on Making Sense of Nietzsche*, edited by M. Béland, C. Denat, C. Piazzesi, and P. Wotling, 249–64. Reims: Éditions et presses de l'Université de Reims, 2021.

Fischer, Ole W. "The Birth of Modernity out of the Spirit of Music? Henry van de Velde and the Nietzsche Archive." In *The Humanities in Architectural Design: A Contemporary and Historical Perspective*, edited by S. Bandyopadhyay, J. Lomholt, N. Temple, and R. Tobe, 237–46. London and New York: Routledge, 2010.

Franck, Thomas. "De l'anti-moralisme pacifiste au matérialisme nihiliste: sur quelques influences contradictoires de Nietzsche dans l'œuvre rollandienne." In *Romain Rolland, der Erste Weltkrieg und die deutschsprachigen Länder*, edited by M. Ortrud and M. Hertrampf. Berlin: Frank und Timme, 2018.

Gadamer, Hans-Georg. *Truth and Method*. Translated by J. Weinsheimer and D.G. Marshall. London and New York: Continuum, 1989.

Gerhardt, Volker. "Die Perspektive des Perspektivismus." *Nietzsche-Studien* 18 (1989): 260–82.

Gerlach, Hans-Martin and Volker Caysa, ed. *Nietzsche und die Linke*. Leipzig: Rosa-Luxemburg-Stiftung, 2006.

Genette, Gérard. *Épilogue*. Paris: Seuil, 2014.

— *Paratexts: Thresholds of Interpretation*. Translated by J.E. Lewin. Cambridge: Cambridge University Press, 1997.

Gervais-Zaninger, Marie-Annick. "La figure de l'auteur dans le texte préfaciel: un jeu de masques." In *Le texte préfaciel*, edited by L. Kohn-Pireaux, 23–34. Nancy: Presses universitaires de Nancy, 2000.

Golomb, Jacob, Weaver Santaniello, and Ronald Lehrer, eds. *Nietzsche and Depth Psychology*. Albany: State University of New York Press, 1999.

Gooding, David. *Experiment and the Making of Meaning: Human Agency in Scientific Observation and Experiment*. Dordrecht: Kluwer, 1990.

Goodman, Russell B. "Moral Perfectionism and Democracy: Emerson, Nietzsche, Cavell." In *Emerson/Nietzsche*, edited by M. Lopez, 159–80. Pullman: Washington State University Press, 1985.

Gould, Glenn. *The Glenn Gould Reader*. Edited by T. Page. Toronto: Lester & Orpen Dennys, 1984.

Gregor-Dellin, Martin. *Richard Wagner: Sein Leben, sein Werk, sein Jahrhundert*. Munich: Goldmann Verlag, 1983.

Gründer, Karlfried, ed. *Der Streit um Nietzsches* Geburt der Tragödie. Hildesheim, Zurich, and New York: Olms, 1989.

Guertin, Ghyslaine. "L'universel et le singulier: l'esthétique de Michel-Paul-Guy de Chabanon." *Horizons philosophiques* 13, no. 2 (2003): 43–50.

Hadot, Pierre. "Symboles." In Ernst Bertram, *Nietzsche: Essai de mythologie*, translated by R. Pitrou, 5–44. Paris: Félin, 2007.

Hanshe, Rainer J. "Invisibly Revolving — — Inaudibly Revolving: The Riddle of the Double *Gedankenstrich*." *Agonist* 3, no. 1 (2010): 7–26.

Hanslick, Eduard. *On the Musically Beautiful: A New Translation*. Translated by L. Rothfarb and C. Landerer. Oxford: Oxford University Press, 2018.

Haskell, Harry. *The Early Music Revival: A History*. London: Thames & Hudson, 1988.

Heidegger, Martin. *Nietzsche*. Translated by D. Farrell Krell. New York: Harper, 1991.

Hegel, Georg Wilhelm Friedrich. *Phenomenology of Spirit*. Translated by T. Pinkard. Cambridge: Cambridge University Press, 2018.

Heitsch, Dorothea B. "Nietzsche and Montaigne: Concepts of Style." *Rhetorica* 16, no. 4 (1999): 411–31.

Herrig, Hans. "Ein moderner 'Freigeist.'" *Die Gegenwart* 18, no. 32 (1880): 85–7.

Herschberg Pierrot, Anne. "Ponctuation, édition, interprétation: l'exemple du point-virgule dans *Bouvard et Pécuchet*." *Flaubert: Revue critique et génétique* 8 (2012). https://journals.openedition.org/flaubert/1865.

Hoffmann, David Marc. *Zur Geschichte des Nietzsche-Archivs*. Berlin and New York: de Gruyter, 1991.

Hoffmann, E.T.A. "Rezension der 5. Symphonie von Ludwig van Beethoven." *Allgemeine musikalische Zeitung* 12, no. 40 (1810): 630–42; and no. 41 (1810): 652–9 https://web.archive.org/web/20140223002959/http://85.214.96.74:8080/zbk/zbk-html/A1094.html.

Hollis, Richard. *Henry van de Velde: The Artist as Designer*. London: Occasional Papers, 2019.

Humboldt, Wilhelm von. *Essai sur les langues du nouveau continent*. Archive in Tegel, Berlin. Manuscript (68 half-written folio pages) from *Complete Works*, vol. 3 (1812), 300–27. Retrieved from Centre de recherches en histoire et épistémologie comparée de la linguistique d'Europe centrale et orientale at Université de Lausanne. Accessed 9 August 2023. https://crecleco.seriot.ch/textes/Humboldt1812.html#a1.

Ingarden, Roman. *Esthétique et ontologie de l'œuvre d'art: choix de textes 1937–1969*. Translated by P. Limido-Heulot. Paris: Vrin, 2011.

— *The Literary Work of Art: An Investigation on the Borderlines of Ontology, Logic, and Theory of Literature*. Translated by G. Grabowicz. Evanston, IL: Northwestern University Press, 1973.

— "Phenomenological Aesthetics: An Attempt at Defining Its Range." Translated by A. Czerniawski. *Journal of Aesthetics and Art Criticism* 33, no. 3 (1975): 257–69.

Iser, Wolfgang. *Die Appellstruktur der Texte: Unbestimmtheit als Wirkungsbedingung literarischer Prosa*. Konstanz: Universitätsverlag, 1971.

— *Der implizite Leser: Kommunikationsformen des Romans von Bunyan bis Beckett*. Munich: Fink, 1972.

Janz, Curt Paul. *Friedrich Nietzsche Biographie*. Munich: Carl Hanser, 1978.

Jauss, Hans Robert. "De l'*Iphigénie* de Racine à celle de Goethe (avec une postface)." In *Pour une esthétique de la réception*, translated by C. Maillard, 230–87. Paris: Gallimard, 2015.

— "Racines und Goethes *Iphigenie*. Mit einem Nachwort über die Partialität der rezeptionsästhetischen Methode." In *Rezeptionsästhetik: Theorie und Praxis*, edited by R. Warning, 353–400. Munich: Wilhelm Fink, 1979.

Kammasch, Tim. "Der Gedankenstrich: 'still Ekstase.'" In *Punkt, Punkt, Komma, Strich? Geste, Gestalt und Bedetung philosophischer Zeichensetzung*, edited by C. Abbt and T. Kammasch, 119–38. Bielefeld: Transcript, 2009.

Kateb, George. *Emerson and Self-Reliance*. Lanham: Rowman & Littlefield, 2002.

Kofman, Sarah. *Nietzsche and Metaphor*. Translated and with an introduction by D. Large. Stanford: Stanford University Press, 1993.

Koßler, Matthias, ed. *Musik als Wille und Welt: Schopenhauers Philosophie der Musik*. Würzburg: Königshausen & Neumann, 2011.

Kowalsky, Borys M., and Joseph Phelan. "Nietzsche and Modernist Art, a Review Essay." *Interpretation: A Journal of Political Philosophy* 47, nos. 2/3 (2021).

Lacroux, Jean-Pierre. *Orthotypographie*. 2 vols. Paris: Quintette, 2007. www.orthotypographie.fr.

Large, Duncan. "'Der Bauernaufstand des Geistes': Nietzsche, Luther and the Reformation." In *Nietzsche and the German Tradition*, edited by N. Martin, 111–37. Bern: Peter Lang, 2003.

Le Blanc, Charles. *The Hermes Complex: Philosophical Reflections on Translation*. Translated by B. Folkart. Ottawa: University of Ottawa Press, 2012.

Le Rider, Jacques. *L'Allemagne au temps du réalisme: de l'espoir au désenchantement, 1848–1890*. Paris: Albin Michel, 2009.

— *Nietzsche en France: de la fin du 19e siècle au temps présent*. Paris: PUF, 1999.

Lebeau-Henry, Charles. "'Apprendre à bien écrire': le style comme voie vers l'Europe dans le §87 du *Voyageur et son ombre*." In *Nietzsche et l'Europe*, edited by C. Bertot, P. De Corte, and P. Wotling, 195–213. Louvain: Presses universitaires de Louvain, 2023.

Lefort, Claude. *Machiavelli in the Making*. Translated by M.B. Smith. Evanston, IL: Northwestern University Press, 2012.

— *Le travail de l'œuvre Machiavel*. Paris: Gallimard, 1972.

Leiner, Wolfgang. "Préface à la journée des préfaces." *Cahiers de l'Association internationale des études françaises* 42 (1990): 111–19.

Lemm, Vanessa. "Is Nietzsche a Perfectionist? Rawls, Cavell, and the Politics of Culture in Nietzsche's *Schopenhauer as Educator*." *Journal of Nietzsche Studies* 34 (2007): 5–27.

Leutsch, Ernst von. Review of *Die Geburt der Tragödie* by F. Nietzsche. *Philologischer Anzeiger* 5, no. 3 (1873): 134–8.

Liébert, Georges. *Nietzsche and Music*. Translated by D. Pellauer and G. Parkes. Chicago: University of Chicago Press, 2004.

Lippman, E.A., ed. *Musical Aesthetics: A Historical Reader*. New York: Pendragon Press, 1986.

Lloyd-Jones, Hugh. "Introduction." In Ulrich von Wilamowitz-Möllendorff, *History of Classical Scholarship*, translated by A. Harris, xxviii–xxix. Baltimore: Johns Hopkins University Press, 1982.

Lussy, M. "Chabanon, précurseur de Hanslick." *Gazette musicale de la Suisse romande*, 7 May 1896.

Lyall, H.R. *A French Music Aesthetic of the Eighteenth Century: A Translation and Commentary on Michel Paul Gui de Chabanon's* Musique considérée en elle-même et dans ses rapports avec la parole, les langues, la poésie et le théâtre. Denton: North Texas State University, 1975.

Maingueneau, Dominique. "L'énonciation philosophique comme institution discursive." *Langages* 29, no. 119 (1995): 40–62.

Marcuse, Ludwig. "Nietzsche in America." *South Atlantic Quarterly* 50 (1951): 330–9.

Mash, Roy. "How Important for Philosophers is the History of Philosophy?" *History and Theory* 26, no. 3 (1987): 287–99.

Masson, Pierre. "Marginalité de la préface auctoriale." In *L'art de la préface*, edited by P. Forest. Nantes: Cécile Defau, 2006.

McCarty, Willard. "The Future of the Digital Humanities are a Matter of Words." In *Companion to New Media Dynamics*, edited by J. Hartley, J. Burgess, and A. Bruns, 33–52. Oxford: Blackwell, 2013.

— "What are *Studia Digitalia*?" *Studia Digitalia* 62, no. 1 (2017): 5–6.

McClary, Susan. *Feminine Endings: Music, Gender and Sexuality*. Minneapolis: University of Minnesota Press, 1991.

McClellan, M.E. *Colonialism and Science: Saint-Domingue in the Old Regime*. Baltimore: Johns Hopkins University Press, 1992.

Merriam-Webster's Unabridged Dictionary. "Foreword." Accessed 22 August 2023. https://unabridged.merriam-webster.com/unabridged/foreword.

— "Preface." Accessed 22 August 2023. https://unabridged.merriam-webster.com/unabridged/preface.

Meyer, Bruno. "Beiträge zur Wagner-Frage: In eigener Sache." *Deutsche Warte* 5, no. 11 (1873): 641–67.

Mitterand, Henri. "Le discours préfaciel." In *La lecture sociocritique du texte romanesque*, edited by G. Falconer and H. Mitterand. Toronto: Samuel Stevens Hakkerte & Co., 1975.

Mommsen, Theodor. "Ansprache am Leibnizschen Gedächtnistage." In *Reden und Aufsätze*. Berlin: Weidmannsche Buchhandlung, 1905.

Montinari, Mazzino. "Volontà di potenza e critica del testo." In *Su Nietzsche*, edited by M. Montinari, 47–65. Roma: Editori Riuniti, 1981.

Müller-Lauter, Wolfgang. *Nietzsche: His Philosophy of Contradictions and the Contradictions of His Philosophy*. Translated by D.J. Parent, with a foreword by R. Schacht. Urbana, IL: University of Illinois Press, 1999.

Naake, Erhard. *Nietzsche und Weimar: Werk und Wirkung im 20. Jahrhundert*. Köln and Weimar: Böhlau Verlag, 2000.

Nattiez, Jean-Jacques. "Introduction à l'esthétique de Hanslick." In E. Hanslick, *Du beau dans la musique: essai de réforme de l'esthétique musicale*, translated by C. Bannelier. Paris: Christian Bourgois, 1986.

— *Wagner Androgyne*. Translated by S. Spencer. Princeton: Princeton University Press, 2016.

Nehamas, Alexander. *Nietzsche: Life as Literature*. Cambridge, MA: Harvard University Press, 1985.

Newmark, Peter. "Paragraphs on the Translation of Nietzsche." *German Life and Letters* 43, no. 4 (1990): 325–42.

Neymeyr, Barbara. "Sprache als Medium für die 'verwegensten Kunststücke': Nietzsches Experimental-Metaphorik." In *Nietzsche zwischen Philosophie und Literatur: Von der* Fröhlichen Wissenschaft *zu* Also sprach Zarathustra, edited by K. Grätz and S. Kaufmann, 323–54. Heidelberg: Universitätsverlag Winter, 2016.

Norton, Robert E. "Attempt at a Demythologization." In E. Bertram, *Nietzsche: Attempt at a Mythology*, translated by R.E. Norton, xi–xxxv. Evanston, IL: University of Illinois Press, 2009.

Obenaus, Sibylle. *Literarische und politische Zeitschriften 1848–1880*. Stuttgart: Metzler, 1987.

Oliver, Kelly, and Marilyn Pearsall, eds. *Feminist Interpretations of Friedrich Nietzsche*. University Park: Pennsylvania State University Press, 1998.

Otabe, Tanehisa. "Chabanon et Hiller, les *Observations sur la musique* en Allemagne." *Musicorum* 6 (2007–8).

Ottmann, Henning, ed. *Nietzsche Handbuch: Leben, Werk, Wirkung*. Stuttgart: Metzler, 2011.

Ottomeyer, Hans, Klaus Albrecht Schröder, and Laurie Winters. *Biedermeier: The Invention of Simplicity*. Milwaukee: Milwaukee Art Museum, 2006.

Plato. *The Republic of Plato*. Translated by A. Bloom. New York: Basic Books, 1968.

Pétillon, Sabine, and André Petitjean. "Le tiret de fin de phrase dans *Un coeur simple* — un stylème flaubertien?" *Flaubert: Revue critique et génétique* 8 (2012). https://journals.openedition.org/flaubert/1867?gathStatIcon=true.

Porter, James I. "'Don't Quote Me on That!' Wilamowitz contra Nietzsche in 1872 and 1873." *Journal of Nietzsche Studies* 42 (2011): 73–99.

— *Nietzsche and the Philology of the Future*. Stanford: Stanford University Press, 2000.

— "Nietzsche, Homer, and the Classical Tradition." In *Nietzsche and Antiquity*, edited by P. Bishop, 7–26. Rochester, NY: Camden House, 2004.

— "'Rare Impressions.' Nietzsche's Philologica: A Review of the Colli-Montinari Critical Edition." *International Journal of the Classical Tradition* (2000): 409–31.

Pouradier, Maud. "*Les aveux de la chair* de Michel Foucault: Réflexions sur les enjeux éthiques et scientifiques d'une édition posthume." *Archives de Philosophie* 82, no. 4 (2019): 808–12.

Ratner-Rosenhagen, Jennifer. *American Nietzsche*. Chicago: Chicago University Press, 2012.

Rawls, John. *A Theory of Justice*. Cambridge: Harvard University Press, 1971.

Reich, Hauke. *Nietzsche-Zeitgenossenlexikon: Verwandete und Vorfahren, Freunde und Feinde, Verehrer und Kritiker von Friedrich Nietzsche*. Basel: Schwabe, 2004.

Reinhardt, Karl. "Die klassische Philologie und das Klassische." In *Vermächtnis der Antike: Gesammelte Essays zur Philosophie und Geschichtsschreibung*, 334–60. Goettingen: Vandenhoeck & Ruprecht, 1989.

Ricoeur, Paul. *Le conflit des interprétations: Essais d'herméneutique*. Paris: Seuil, 1969.

— *From Text to Action: Essays in Hermeneutics II*. Translated by K. Blamey and J.B. Thompson. Evanston, IL: Northwestern University Press, 1991.

— *The Rule of Metaphor: The Creation of Meaning in Language*. Translated by R. Czerny. London and New York: Routledge, 2004.

Roos, Richard. "Regeln zu einer philologischen Lesung Nietzsches." In *Nietzsche, Kontrovers VI*, edited by R. Berlinger and W. Schrader, 7–42. Würzburg: Koenigshausen und Neumann, 1987.

Rousseau, Jean-Jacques. *Dictionary of Music*. Translated by W. Waring. London: J. French, No. 47, opposite Hatton-Garden, Holborn, 1775[?].

Roy, Pascal. *From Naturalism to Expressionism: German Literature and Society, 1880–1918*. London: Weidenfeld & Nicolson, 1973.

Rüegg, Walter. *A History of the University in Europe*, vol. 3: *Universities in the Nineteenth and Early Twentieth Centuries (1800–1945)*. Cambridge: Cambridge University Press, 2004.

Ruin, Hans. "Nietzsche and the Aesthetics of Philosophy." *Nietzsche-Studien* 50 (2021): 320–8.

Salomon, O.F. "Chabanon and Chastellux on Music and Language, 1764–1773." *International Review of the Aesthetics and Sociology of Music* 20, no. 2 (1992).

Schaberg, William H. *The Nietzsche Canon: A Publication History and Bibliography*. Chicago: University of Chicago Press, 1995.

Schacht, Richard. *Making Sense of Nietzsche: Reflections Timely and Untimely*. Urbana, IL: University of Illinois Press, 1995.

Schaeffer, Jean-Marie. "Note sur la préface philosophique." *Poétique* 69 (1987): 35–44.

Schelling, F.W.J. von. *On University Studies*. Translated by E.S. Morgan, with an introduction by N. Guterman. Athens: Ohio University Press, 1966.

Schleiermacher, Friedrich. "On the Different Methods of Translating." In *Western Translation Theory: From Herodotus to Nietzsche*, translated and edited by D. Robinson, 225–38. Manchester: St Jerome Publishing, 2002.

Schopenhauer, Arthur. *The Art of Always Being Right*. Edited and with an introduction by A.C. Grayling. Translated by T. Bailey Saunders. London: Gibson Square, 2011.

— *Der handschriftliche Nachlass*. 5 vols. Berlin: DTV, 1985.

— *Parerga and Paralipomena: Short Philosophical Essays*. Edited by A. Del Caro and C. Janaway. Translated by A. Del Caro. 2 vols. Cambridge: Cambridge University Press, 2015.

— *The World as Will and as Representation*. Translated by J. Norman, A. Welchman, and C. Janaway. 2 vols. Cambridge: Cambridge University Press, 2010/2018.

Schütze, Sebastian, ed. *Friedrich Nietzsche and the Artists of the New Weimar*. Milan and Ottawa: Five Continents Editions and National Gallery of Canada, 2019.

Simard, Augustin. "Heurs et malheurs de la réception en idées politiques." In *Ceci n'est pas une idée politique*, edited by D. Giroux and D. Karmis, 133–53. Quebec: Presses de l'Université Laval, 2013.

Simson, Wojciech. "Beobachtungen zur Typographie in Nietzsches Vorreden von 86/87." *Nietzsche-Studien* 24 (1995): 204–22.

Sonnen, Irmgard. *Balancieren auf dem Gendankenstrich: Zwischen Schweigen und Reden*. Düsseldorf: Queredo, 2009.

Spitzer, Leo. *Stilstudien*. Munich: Hüber, 1928.

Stegmaier, Werner. *Friedrich Nietzsche zur Einführung*. Hamburg: Junius, 2011.

Strauss, David Friedrich. *The Life of Jesus, Critically Examined*. Translated by G. Eliot. 3 vols. Cambridge: Cambridge University Press, 2010.

Strong, Tracy B. "In Defense of Rhetoric, Or How Hard It Is to Take a Writer Seriously: The Case of Nietzsche." *Political Theory* 41, no. 4 (2013): 507–32.

Strunk, William, Jr, and E.B. White. *The Elements of Style*. Illustrated by M. Kalman. New York: Penguin Books, 2000.

Stump, Doris. "'Nietzsche sprach von seinen geistigen Interessen …' Meta von Salis' Begegnung mit Friedrich Nietzsche." In *Nietzsche und die Schweiz*, edited by D.M. Hoffmann, 99–101. Zurich: Offizin Zürich and Strauhof Zürich, 1994.

Sweet, Dennis. "The Birth of *The Birth of Tragedy*." *Journal of the History of Ideas* 60, no. 2 (1999): 345–59.

Tanguay, Bernard. *L'art de ponctuer*. Montreal: Québec-Amérique, 2006.

Tönnies, Ferdinand. *Der Nietzsche Kultus*. Leipzig: Reisland, 1897.

Tongeren, Paul van. "Nietzsches philosophische Experimente mit der literarischen Form der Vorrede." *Nietzsche-Studien* 41 (2012): 1–16.

Trebilcock, Clive. *The Industrialization of the Continental Powers: 1780–1914*. London and New York: Routledge, 1981.

Turgeon, David. *À propos du style de Genette*. Montreal: Quartanier, 2018.

Turner, R. Steven. "Historicism, Kritik, and the Prussian Professoriate, 1790 to 1840." In *Philologie et herméneutique au 19e siècle*, edited by M. Bollack and H. Wismann, 450–77. Goettingen: Vandenhoeck & Ruprecht, 1983.

Vandendorpe, Christian. *From Papyrus to Hypertext: Toward the Universal Digital Library*. Translated by P. Aronoff and H. Scott. Urbana, IL: University of Illinois Press, 2009.

Wagner, Cosima. *Cosima Wagner's Diaries*. Edited by M. Gregor-Dellin and D. Mack. Translated and with an introduction by G. Skelton. 2 vols. New York and London: Harcourt Brace Jovanovich, 1978–80.

Wagner, Richard. *Gesammelte Schriften und Dichtungen*. 10 vols. Leipzig: E.W. Fritzsch, 1871–83. [*GSD*] Works cited: "Beethoven," 1873 (in *GSD* 9, 75–151), "Das Kunstwerk der Zukunft," 1872 (in *GSD* 3, 51–210), "Oper und Drama," 1851 (in *GSD* 4), "Publikum und Popularität," 1883 (in *GSD* 10, 85–122).

— "An Open Letter to Friedrich Nietzsche, Ordinary Professor of Classical Philology at the University of Basel." In *Der Streit um Nietzsches* Geburt der Tragödie, edited by K. Gründer, 57–64. Hildesheim, Zurich, and New York: Olms, 1989.

Wartenweiler, Rahel. "Charles Andler et la politisation de Nietzsche: Une analyse de la dimension politique d'un transfert culturel (1890–1933)." Master's diss., École des hautes études en sciences sociales, Paris, 2009.

Weber, Max. *The Protestant Ethic and the Spirit of Capitalism*. Translated by T. Parsons. Introduction by A. Giddens. London and New York: Routledge, 2001.

— "Science as Vocation." In *The Vocation Lectures*, edited by D. Owen and T. Strong, translated by R. Livingstone, 1–31. Indianapolis: Hackett Books, 2004.

Westernhagen, C. von. *Wagner: A Biography*. 2 vols. Cambridge: Cambridge University Press, 1978.

Whitman, James Q. "Nietzsche in the Magisterial Tradition of German Classical Philology." *Journal of the History of Ideas* 47, no. 3 (1986): 453–68.

Wilamowitz-Möllendorff, Ulrich von. "Zukunftsphilologie!" In *Der Streit um Nietzsches* Geburt der Tragödie, edited by K. Gründer, 27–55. Hildesheim, Zurich, and New York: Olms, 1989.

Wilkerson, Dale. *Nietzsche and the Greeks*. London and New York: Continuum Press, 2006.

Wittig, Susan. "The Computer and the Concept of Text." *Computers and the Humanities* 11, no. 4 (1978): 211–15.

Wotling, Patrick. "L'utilisation de l'histoire chez Nietzsche et Burckhardt." In *Lectures nietzschéennes: sources et réceptions*, edited by M. Béland, 201–16. Montreal: Presses de l'Université de Montréal, 2015.

— "What Languages Do Drives Speak?" In *Nietzsche on Instinct and Language*, edited by J. Constancio and M.J. Mayer Branco, 63–79. Berlin: de Gruyter, 2011.

Wundt, Wilhelm. "Mission de la philosophie dans le temps présent." *Revue philosophique de la France et de l'étranger* 1 (1876): 113–24.

Zavatta, Benedetta. "Historical Sense as Vice and Virtue in Nietzsche's Reading of Emerson." *Journal of Nietzsche Studies* 44, no. 3 (2013): 372–97.

— *Individuality and Beyond: Nietzsche Reads Emerson*. Oxford: Oxford University Press, 2019.

Zittel, Claus. "Der Dialog als philosophische Form bei Nietzsche." *Nietzsche-Studien* 45 (2016): 81–112.

Index

Page numbers in italics denote illustrative material